FARNHAM IN WAR AND PEACE

Much of Farnham shows to advantage at back and sides: a drawing by Harold Falkner.

FARNHAM
In War and Peace

W. Ewbank-Smith

PHILLIMORE

1983

Published by
PHILLIMORE & CO. LTD.

Head Office: Shopwyke Hall,
Chichester, Sussex, England

ISBN 0 85033 522 1

Printed and bound in Great Britain by
THE CAMELOT PRESS LTD.
Southampton, Hants

CONTENTS

LIST OF PLATES
(between pages 116–117)

LIST OF TEXT ILLUSTRATIONS

Frontispiece: Much of Farnham shows to advantage at back and sides

FOREWORD

'It is good, in Discourse . . . to vary and entermingle . . . Jest with
Earnest. For it a dull Thing to tire and, as we say now, to Jade, any
Thing too farre.'

Francis Bacon: *Of Discourse*

This volume, which discourses upon the local scene during the years between the
First and Second World Wars, with an epitome fore and aft, ends my series of
essays depicting life in Farnham in times more recent than the periods normally
covered by works of local history. *Victorian Farnham, Edwardian Farnham,* and
this latest offering were prompted by more than one factor.

Whilst the various contemporary records from which they have been compiled
are in fairly safe custody, the local copy of at least one source is exposed to risk.
Already an arduous undertaking, research could at any time become more
complex. It has been widely agreed that, whilst it remains possible, a useful
purpose is served in passing on the contents of these records, however summarily,
in an easily accessible form in bookshop or library. The events related in the three
books now rank as history, in that they were conceived by a past, or now passing,
generation. There is, additionally, a personal reason for writing them. Farnham
has put up with me for half a century, observing my weaknesses, yet withholding
nothing of its abundant charm. Therefore, I owe the town a debt of gratitude.
This I have attempted to repay, in the way I know best, before following my
characters to, reputedly, an even nicer place.

My own arrival in Farnham midway through the period which this latest
volume covers introduces a new dimension to the narrative. For I witnessed at
first hand many of the events that took place from 1929 onwards. At the expense
of discovering that I am now old enough to feature in a history book, I have had
the pleasure of reviving long-forgotten memories. Once again, I am able to view
the town through the questing eyes of youth. Visually, apart from Woolmead
and, here and there, some replaced shop-front, there has been little change. The
fantasies of the architecturally freakish '20s and '30s were so controlled and
channelled by certain benefactors as to render the townscape not only acceptable
to, but wholeheartedly approved by, later generations. The Farnham that was
then fashioned out of earlier neglect established the local pattern for all time.

Man adapts to his environment. There are more people about these days, some
doing things undreamed of 50 years ago, but otherwise distinguishable from their

predecessors only by the clothes they wear—except for one thing. Being in the main newcomers to Farnham, they have to adapt; 50 years ago this was not necessary, for by and large the inhabitants were to the manner born.

Some day, perhaps, another writer may decide to carry on where I have left off. He will miss the 'human interest' element—for individualism has given place to anonymity. Also, a few years into his plot, he will find that the Farnham Urban District Council is wound up. With these two important ingredients withdrawn, history on a localised scale will have come to an end.

ACKNOWLEDGEMENTS

I am indebted to the Waverley District Council and to Castle Newspapers, Ltd., for my two main sources, namely the minute books of the late Farnham Urban District Council, and contemporary copies of the *Farnham Herald*.

My quest for illustrations was rendered an easy task by the enthusiastic response of a number of ladies and gentlemen.

The publishers join me in expressing gratitude to the Farnham Society for their generous loan towards the cost of publication. Also for similar loans by two anonymous benefactors, one of whom shares with Francis Bacon the belief that money is like muck—no good except it be spread.

I should like to thank the following persons and organisations for providing illustrations: Farnham Museum for Plate 1; the executors of Miss Winifred Borelli for Plates, 3, 10, 12, 16, 18, 21, 22; E. C. Griffith of Farnham (photographers) for Plates 7, 19 and 26; the Farnham branch of Surrey County Libraries for Plates 8, 9, 28 and 29; Miss Ealand for Plate 11; Mr. R. N. Sargent for Plates 30 and 36; John Chitty for Plate 25. All other illustrations are my own property.

W.E-S.

1

PRELUDE TO PEACE

1914 - 1918

WASTED YEARS

Keep the home fires burning while your hearts are yearning,
Though your lads are far away, they dream of home,
There's a silver lining through the dark clouds shining;
Turn the dark clouds inside out, till the boys come home.

Lena Ford, War Chant, 1914

THROUGHOUT THE SUMMER MONTHS of 1914 the people went about their lawful peaceful occasions. That is to say, cricketers, tennis players, swimmers and bowlers were locked in battle. Mr. Langham published, in his *Farnham Herald* of 1 August, the opening chapters of a new Mrs. L. T. Meade serial entitled 'The Mystery of Patricia' (in which, promised the blurb, Patricia Hampton, a beautiful girl, burdened by a great secret, would be blackmailed by Henry Fortescue, a rogue who would threaten to reveal that secret. Pat, however, would be saved from a fate worse than death by Arthur Clovelly, the squire). And the Farnham Council, having earlier that year annexed the Hale Ward of their neighbours, the Farnham Rural District Council, under the pretext of introducing drainage to that primitive quarter, were toying with the idea of grabbing the Bourne and Wrecclesham Wards as well.

Meanwhile, Kaiser William was toying with the idea of grabbing the rest of the world outside Germany. This he set out to do on 1 August and, three days later, Farnham went to war. The upheaval had to come; many of the lesser breeds had been heaving up ever since the myth of British supremacy had begun to wane with the passing of Victoria. The Germans had developed territorial ambitions, just like Britain had had once. But, never mind, it would all be over by Christmas. Not all peacetime pursuits were dropped. The cricket and other contests continued unabated, and the Patricia Hampton serial ran its course; but the Council's own territorial ambitions in the Bourne and Wrecclesham, like other civic schemes, were put in mothballs. For in wartime the Council had other things to think about.

Most ordinary practices are set aside for the duration. Its manpower depleted, the town limps on as best it can, struggling against restrictions imposed by Westminster to keep the fires burning on rationed coal; to maintain a watered-down service to ratepayers; to foster committees of townspeople for this, that and the other purpose; to sponsor flag-days for deserving causes; to promote canteens for khakied strangers. Above all, the local authority, though a mere puppet of central government, is, for the duration, master in the town it serves.

When domestic affairs—the chief contributory feature of a local history— are in abeyance, little that happens in the town is of consequence. It is not, however, necessarily without interest; for a war can be counted on to provide events of rare vintage even in the smallest of provincial towns. And when, like Farnham, that town happens to be so close to army concentration centres such as Aldershot and Bordon as to be deemed an integral part of one huge military complex, anything can happen—as, indeed, it did, within hours of the declaration of war on Tuesday, 4 August 1914.

For troop mobility purposes, the railway between Aldershot and Bordon had been commandeered immediately by the War Office and manned by some 50 men of the 4th City of London Territorial Regiment. Sentries were posted at strategic points up and down the line, and the station platforms bristled with musketry. Colonel H. Torkington, J.P., of Willey Park, a man whose word was above suspicion, pieced together the following story for a *Herald* reporter. At 12.45 a.m. on Wednesday, 5 August, he was awakened by the sound of gunfire. On investigating, he discovered that four Germans had approached the railway line and struck a sentry over the head with a revolver. The sentry was able to summon his colleagues, and the attackers ran off into some woods, pursued by bullets. Three of the Germans were captured and taken to Bordon; the fourth, though wounded, made good his escape. In another incident, at nearby Alice Holt, two men of foreign appearance rushed a sentry and hit him on the head, breaking his glasses. They were thought to be from a party of campers who had lately been using the *Railway Arms* public house.

On Thursday, 6 August, a suspected German spy was arrested at Farnham station. A tall, fair-moustached, mysterious-looking stranger was seen making notes and taking photographs. He gave his name as 'Kali', but failed to give satisfactory answers when questioned further. He was locked in a waiting-room and later marched through the town to Hales in The Borough, where the photographs in his camera were examined. He was later released. It seemed that he was some sort of practical joker. A Guildford man, he was writing a letter whilst waiting for his train. At the moment of his arrest, he had written the words 'I suppose they are taking me for a German spy'. Thus Farnham got away to an action-packed start. The locals had seen the whites of the enemy's eyes.

*　　*　　*　　*　　*

It was not long before the town felt the first grievous impact of war: the departure of the first of its young men—those who go voluntarily at the outbreak of all wars, without waiting for enforced conscription. The *Herald* of 15 August reported that the exodus had already begun. Names were mentioned. Father

Etienne Robo, the Roman Catholic priest, had left for France to seek enlistment in the French Army (rejected as unfit, he returned to Farnham a few weeks later). H. C. Patrick, called up in the Surrey Yeomanry, put his business in the hands of his brother, Mr. Sidney Patrick. Frank Swain of Swain and Jones, the motor people, had gone; also Tom Mitchell's son, Lionel. Solicitor E. F. Crundwell had been given a commission. Of the Bishop of Winchester's sons, the Rev. Neville Talbot and the Rev. Edward Talbot had volunteered as army chaplains, and Gilbert, the youngest, had applied for a commission in the Rifle Brigade. E (Farnham) Company, 5th (later, the 3rd) Battalion, The Queen's Royal West Surrey Regiment (Territorial Force), with a strength of about 130 men, had been recalled from summer camp to mobilise at their battalion H.Q. in Guildford.

Forty-three men had already signed on at the recruiting office in the Corn Exchange when Lord Kitchener's heart-rending appeal for an army of 1,400,000 volunteers accelerated enlistment. Within a month some 328 men between 18 and 30 had registered. One was G. R. R. Combe, only son of Richard Combe of Pierrepont, Frensham, who enlisted as a trooper in Lovat's Scouts. Another was Tommy Simmonds, son of the police superintendent. The call to the colours was difficult to resist. Mr. Langham went to lengths each week to mention the volunteers by name, under the heading 'Roll of Honour', displaying notices of the YOUR KING AND COUNTRY NEED YOU variety, and hinting vaguely at white feathers. His own name appeared in the Roll dated 24 October. Architect Harold Falkner joined the R.E.s as a sapper. He wrote from camp at Gillingham, finding fault with conditions there. The bread, he said, tasted of paraffin; 'Tell Kempson', he added, 'that I smoke B.D.V. cigarettes'.

Then, in September, came the first news of casualties. Lieutenant-Commander Bartellot was killed on the *Liberty* in action off Heligoland, a son-in-law of T. B. Burnham, formerly of Moor Park. Lieutenant Soames (20 Hussars), killed on 3 September, was the brother of Mr. Soames, currently of Moor Park. Captain H. H. Short (The Berkshires) of Bourne Place, was reported missing. The list lengthened: Petty-Officer William Parsons, 65 Castle Street, lost in a naval disaster; Charles Parratt, Fairthorne Terrace, whilst serving on *The Cressy*; Major Chrystie, son of Colonel George Chrystie of Shortheath Lodge; Able Seamen R. S. Jackson and A. E. Robinson, both of Babbs Mead, on the *Bulwark*, blown up in Sheerness Harbour.

The government's grip on the civilian population tightened. The people were told that anyone buying more than his or her immediate needs was either thoughtlessly or wickedly robbing the poor, and that tradesmen overcharging were thieves and traitors. Bishop Talbot offered Farnham Castle as a hospital if required, and the park as a grazing area for ill-conditioned horses. Mrs. Lewin gave up 'The Hill', Gong Hill, for a hospital. Waverley Abbey House was accepted by the War Office as an annexe to the Cambridge Hospital, Aldershot—the first batch of 17 wounded officers was moved in on 24 September, after Robins and Sons had converted the gound floor of the house.

Meanwhile recruits for Kitchener's Army arrived at the camps on Frensham Common, their marshalling ground and training depot before shipment overseas. 'Farnham', wrote Mr. Langham on 26 September, 'the quiet little residential town, is rapidly changing its character. For it has been invaded and captured by a section of Kitchener's Army. The movement which led to the fall of the town commenced on Friday of last week when, throughout the day, troop trains ran into the siding, discharged their loads and went off for more. The troops lined up in the yard and marched out of the town centre to their camps on Frensham Common'. The town itself took the overspill from Aldershot in the shape of some 3,000 men of the King's Liverpool Regiment, who arrived early in December and were billeted in private houses and suitable empty properties. Soldiers' canteens were opened at the Corn Exchange and in the church halls. A number of Belgian refugees were also in the town.

Major J. Higgins of Farnham, a Squadron Commander in the Royal Flying Corps, won the French Legion of Honour. One of the war's first Victoria Crosses went to Sergeant-Major George Thomas Dorrell of the Royal Horse Artillery. He was known in Farnham as, on several occasions, an official at the Bank Holiday Military Tournaments. He received the honour of 1 September for bravery at Nery in continuing to man a gun after all his officers had been killed or wounded. He finished up as a lieutenant-colonel.

In November it was learnt that the local Territorials had arrived safely in India, thus allaying rumours that they had come to grief at sea. But the news of casualties continued to depress. Major Bacon of 'The Lodge', Upper Hale, was reported killed; also a Private T. Cuff of that village. Christmas was low-key. 'Let us', voiced the *Herald,* 'try to spend a happy Christmas, sparing more than one thought for our countrymen in France or on the high seas, and for those women and children to whom great sorrow has come because of the empty chair'.

The townspeople did their best. They gave the Liverpudlians a right royal time. The Rev. Neville Talbot, on leave from the 3rd Rifle Brigade, looked in at the canteen in the Corn Exchange and held soldiers spellbound. There was news of a further 630 men to be billeted in private houses. Dippenhall Grange was adapted for the Belgian refugees. Kitchener inspected the troops on Frensham Common. A partial black-out was imposed between 5.30 and 7.30 p.m.; the sound of foreign aircraft had been reported; some said they had seen a Zeppelin over the Bourne.

On the home front, William Robert Worsam, the Downing Street baker, died from a heart attack on 3 March, aged forty-nine. William Willett, M.P., the London builder, also died that spring. It was he who masterminded the Daylight Saving Bill, which became law in 1916. He was understood to have been born, on 18 August 1836, the son of William and Maria Willett of Waggon Yard, Farnham, alongside Beavers House, 79 West Street, prior to the building of that house on the site of a hop-kiln in the early 1870s. Opinions on this point, however, vary: an earlier *Herald* gives the parents' place of abode as the Bourne (*vide Edwardian Farnham*).

And so passed the first winter of the Great War—a winter spent in coming to terms with the bizarre conditions into which Farnham had been plunged in August 1914.

*   *   *   *   *

As far as the Farnham Urban District Council were concerned, the winter had been what some writers might describe as a traumatic experience. With most normal administrative functions curtailed, they were now virtually a caretaker government. They wielded authority over the town's war effort, but this, because of the unstinted co-operation of the ratepayers, was fast settling down to a routine pattern which required little effort from the councillors.

This enviable respite from the more usual cares of a local authority was, however, marred by one big worry—the Hale Ward. At the time of its acquisition on 1 April 1914, it had been stipulated at the enquiry before the Local Government Board that, immediately upon transfer, the Urban Council should take steps to sewer the Ward, a condition that was wholeheartedly endorsed by the inhabitants. Hale Ward comprised the areas of Lower and Upper Hale, Heath End, Weybourne, and Badshot Lea—together roughly twice the acreage of the absorbing urban district. These villages had no sewers; they did not, however, lack sewer smells. With a prevailing south-west wind, these were imported from the town's sewage farm at Monkton Lane nearby. The town thus had the drains but no smells, whilst Hale had the smells but no drains. It all seemed a little unfair.

It wasn't only the drains; the area in those days lacked refinements of any kind. The *casbah* at Upper Hale, for instance, which had sprouted into being following the arrival of Aldershot Camp in the 1850s, resembled, say, the Alfama district in Lisbon. The tortuous alleyways were neither paved nor lit, their fronting cottages were unnumbered, and in many cases unidentified by name. Strangers were advised not to enter the region after dark without police protection.

Committed at least to sewering the place, the Council at once engaged a civil engineer, a Mr. Midgeley Taylor, to mastermind the undertaking. In view of the international situation, he and the Council's surveyor expedited the preliminary work, but it was not until early in 1915 that the specifications could be finalised and application made to the Local Government Board for sanction to borrow £15,240 for the drainage works.

When it came to roads, the Council set a high standard. Back in 1903, Mr. Cass, the surveyor, had been instrumental in pioneering the use of tarred flints on road surfaces. Such treatment in the Hale Ward was estimated to cost £3,580. With regard to street-lighting, the Council had freely elected to linger in the gas age rather than go electric; this would add £437 to the bill. They also assigned £350 for public improvements generally. Nobody could accuse them of not doing the decent thing by their new parishioners; the days of the linkboy in Hale were numbered, even if the houses were not. They bought another horse, four scavengers' trucks, six wheelbarrows, two tarring machines, one tar-boiler, two night-soil carts, and two street-sweeping machines. They hired a motor car at 6d. a mile to hurry Mr. Cass around his enlarged area, and installed their first lady typist, a Miss Jessup. It was clear to all, in the winter of 1914, that the Council and their staff had much in common with Hercules, the son of Zeus. The task which faced them was daunting. Norman Raffin of the surveyor's staff accompanied Tommy Simmonds of Clerk's into the 1st Surrey Rifles. The remaining staff, including two chief officers, could be counted on the fingers of both hands, with one or two fingers to spare.

*   *   *   *   *

There was, on the other hand, no manpower shortage across the bamboo-curtain which segregates the professional local government officer from his masters, the councillors. Now joined by six from the Hale Ward, these numbered eighteen. They were:

> Edgar Kempson, 'Wickham House', West Street, Chairman.
> Arthur James Barnard, 'Burlington House', South Street, Vice-Chairman.
> George Ethelbert Aldridge, 'Mossdale', Beaufort Road.
> George Baigent, 1 Havelock Villas, Tilford Road.
> Hamilton Kendall Bentall, 'Rozel', Tilford Road.
> Charles Ernest Borelli, 35 The Borough.
> Arthur James Figg, builder, Long Garden Walk.
> Thomas Mitchell, 'The Lindens', Tilford Road.
> George Murrell, High Park Corner.
> John Robert Nash, 'Thorncroft', Hale Road.
> Thomas Patterson, 'Woodville', Frensham Road.
> Richard Preston, 'Lancaster Lodge', Great Austins.
> Percy Joseph Caesar, 'The Gables', Upper Hale.
> Alfred Leonard de Mornay, 'Wellesley', Upper Hale.
> John Edwards, 'The Rest', Upper Hale.
> Maurice Arthur Rice, 'Ravenswood', Hale.
> Arthur Rose Robins, Park Farm, Badshot Lea.
> John William Swansborough, High View, Hale.

In this all-male society, the transition from a peacetime to a wartime economy was rapid. There remained certain ends to tie up—such as safety warning notices at dangerous street crossings (the fatal traffic accidents had begun), vetting plans for new houses in the then-developing Ridgway Road area, and a new parsonage at Badshot Lea for the Rev. H. Durrant; the Co-op were expanding in Union Road, and the Capital and Counties were planning alterations at their bank in Castle Street. As a welcoming gesture, they placed three new seats in the Hale Recreation Ground, and persuaded the postmaster to install a public telephone at Badshot Lea sub-post office, on the understanding that receipts therefrom would not fall below £14 10s. 0d. annually. Then, of course, there was the ceaseless vigilance necessary as the sanitary authority, on potential sources of disease, for if unchecked the people would soon revert to malpractices.

The war had first intruded in the Council Chamber with a spate of precepts from Whitehall, and a warning that the Liverpool Regiment was on its way. Committees for the Farnham and District War Relief and the County War Distress were the first of many fund-raising bodies. Measures were taken to protect the reservoir at St Thomas' Hill from possible enemy action. Friday, 21 August 1914 was declared a Day of National Intercession, and the councillors attended a service at the parish church. A food economy campaign, under the chairmanship of Councillor Nash, was launched to arrange lectures on wartime cooking, cheap foods, and likely rationing prospects. Allotment holders were encouraged to dig for victory.

A deputation from the Women's Co-operative Guild and the National Union of Women's Suffrage Society, led by Mrs. A. A. Russell, saw fit to choose this difficult time to demand that the Council should establish a maternity centre in Farnham. The County Council considered the scheme to be currently inappropriate, but agreed to one of the school nurses acting part-time as a health visitor. Mrs. Russell was not satisfied with this because the nurse, a Miss Beatrice Batchelder, was not maternity-qualified.

In November, everyone was glad to hear that Major Higgins, R.F.C., was recovering satisfactorily from wounds . . . A fire at Hale got out of hand because a policeman had failed to break the glass properly on the alarm at the fire station in South Street . . . Councillor Borelli proposed that the fire station doors should be painted green instead of red, but was defeated by six votes to eight . . . Powers were sought to extend the existing speed limit; it was heard, in stunned silence, that the Traction Company's buses sometimes exceeded the statutory 12 miles per hour.

Accommodation for the Liverpudlians was found in St James' School, the British School, the Church House, the old Picture Palace in Bear Lane, and the Castle Street Institute. The Regiment's Commanding Officer, Lieutenant-Colonel Bayley, was informed that, if required, Gostrey Meadow could be used as somewhere 'where the soldiers might rehearse their war games'. Relations with the occupying troops proved to be amicable. A Minute in March 1915, recorded that the Regiment was warmly thanked by the Council for voluntarily improving the road near the *Shepherd and Flock*. Then, on 24 March, the soldiers left Farnham for France. Their going was regretted. Colonel Bayley, in a polite exchange of letters, thanked Edgar Kempson, Chairman of the Farnham Soldiers' Entertainment Committee, for the town's splendid efforts to make his unit's stay in Farnham a really happy one. Throughout the ensuing months of war, ties between Farnham people and their temporary guests were maintained with enthusiasm, and continued in a modified way after the war.

The Council's workforce was sadly depleted when the Royal Aircraft factory at Farnborough siphoned off 11 of them for munition work. This meant paring services like scavenging and watering roads. When the county asked later if Farnham could spare any labour for the harvest, they were told an emphatic 'no'.

There was a poor turn-out for the local elections on 29 March 1915; these no longer seemed important. There were no strange faces in the Chamber: Councillor Aldridge became the new chairman, with J. R. Nash as vice-chairman.

Nurse Batchelder had entered a military hospital; she was replaced by a Miss MacRae, whose qualifications were acceptable to Mrs. Russell. Clinics for expectant 'mums' were opened one afternoon a week in Farnham and Hale.

There was news in March of Sergeant H. C. Patrick (Surrey Yeomanry), seriously ill in a Camberwell hospital. He had at first been reported wounded, but it transpired that he had been brought out of the front line with appendicitis. Captain Mervyn Lloyd (Northumberland Fusiliers), son of R. B. Lloyd of 'Firgrove House', died from wounds. Private J. Fitzpatrick, lately employed by Lewis Ferguson of West Street, was killed in the trenches.

The sinking of the *Lusitania* by a German submarine on 7 May 1915 brought a tidal wave of revulsion. Among those drowned was an entire family from Churt —parents, their six children, and the nanny. Maitland Kempson, brother of Farnham's Edgar Kempson, was among the survivors.

The *Herald* of 3 April referred nostalgically to the one-time custom of the farmers of making their men work on Good Fridays until 10 a.m.; then each man would be given a bun and half-a-pint of beer, and paid for a full day's work, on condition that he attended church. It was a fine sight to see the men in church in their white smocks.

In May, that inventive genius, John Henry Knight of Barfield, demonstrated in a meadow adjoining Heath and Wiltshires his 'trench bomb thrower', a wood-constructed engine on the lines of a Roman ballista, which lobbed a 2½lb. bomb over a distance of up to 130 yards.

In June, the Local Government Board informed the Council that, as the Hale drainage scheme was not a wartime necessity, sanction to borrow £15,240 was just not on. With the roadworks and street-lighting package also in jeopardy, it seemed that the Council had been let off the hook for the duration. They could, like local authorities everywhere, now put their feet up and watch the war go by. They took them down temporarily in July to act as local agents under the Government's National Registration Act 1915, which foreshadowed the compulsory conscription which might be introduced should voluntary enlistment drag its heels. A team of some 70 enumerators distributed census forms at 1,750 dwellings in Farnham, and 800 in the Hale Ward. These questionnaires demanded information on all persons between the ages of 15 and 65 not already in the forces.

On 8 June, a particularly nasty accident happened in East Street. The Gas Company were laying a new main across the street opposite Trimmers Hospital, and had barriered an open trench. Alfred Masters, a drayman employed by Watney Combe Reid and Co., returning from a late round, failed to see this barrier and horse, van and driver fell into the trench. A 40ft. flame shot up, and Masters became a human torch.

Farnham was able to claim an indirect association with one of the starred events of the war, in which Flight-Lieutenant R. A. J. Warneford of the Royal Naval Air Service destroyed a Zeppelin over Belgium in the early hours of 7 June 1915. Climbing 6,000ft. in his Morane monoplane, he dropped six bombs on top of the Zeppelin from close range, the last of which set fire to the airship. The blast turned his plane upside-down and he was forced to land in enemy territory, but he was able to take off again and return to base. For this feat Warneford was awarded the Victoria Cross. His mother, now the wife of Lieutenant-Colonel M. P. Corkery, was staying at the time at 'The White Lodge', Runfold. Interviewed by a *Herald* reporter, she remarked that her son was an ordinary, quiet sort of lad, but he had been heard, when last on leave, to declare, 'I must do something for my country'. Ten days later, he was killed when making a trial flight in a new Henri Farman aircraft near Paris. His passenger was also killed— he was H. B. Needham, known on both sides of the Atlantic as a writer of magazine articles.

Corporal Harold Falkner was in the Connaught Hospital, Aldershot, following an injury to a leg in a collision with a cart whilst motor-cycling near Newbury. Blood poisoning had set in, and he was seriously ill. He was to limp for the rest of his life.

In June, the new extension to the Farnham School of Art (the brick-built part on the corner of Victoria Road and South Street) was *Heralded* with glee. It was said at the time to be to the design of Mr. Storey, the County Architect, though it has been more generally attributed to Harold Falkner. Farnham, said the paper, was indeed fortunate in being the smallest town in the country to maintain a School of Art all these years since its formation in the 1870s.

*   *   *   *   *

The *Farnham Herald* kept up a remarkably detailed liaison with local men in their various theatres of war. There was a two-way traffic of letters written home and copies of the paper sent to the front. One of the correspondents, H. R. Robins, for instance, vividly described a narrow shave when hit in the leg by an enemy bullet. The German trenches at that time were barely 40 yards distant and the snipers on each side were kept busy. There were full accounts, too, of the casualties. By July, when the war was scarcely one year old, these had become a depressing weekly feature of the paper—dismal enough when reading its columns some 60 years later. One day, perhaps, a detailed history exclusive to Farnham's role in the Great War years will be written, for there is enough of it to fill a book. In a brief synopsis such as this short section of a longer record, only certain isolated instances can be cited. The death of Gilbert Talbot on 31 July 1915 must be one, in that his parents lived at Farnham Castle and, further, that its happening was to acquire a wider significance, in post-war years, throughout the English-speaking world.

Gilbert Walter Lyttleton Talbot, youngest son of the Bishop of Winchester, was 23 years old. Educated at Winchester and Christ Church (where he became President of the Oxford Union), he displayed a remarkable aptitude for debate and an outstanding ability in everything he undertook. In local circles, he played for the Farnham Cricket Club. As a lieutenant in charge of a platoon of the 7th Rifle Brigade, he was ordered to take and hold a shell crater in Flanders, and the platoon was virtually wiped out.

One of the more emotive tributes paid to Gilbert Talbot was that of Canon Scott Holland in *The Commonwealth* in September, in which the author claimed an acquaintanceship with 'this young man of great promise'. The Rev. Neville Talbot, Gilbert's brother, also in the Rifle Brigade, could not bear the thought of the body rotting out there in no-man's land, uncoffined and without a grave, and resolved to recover his brother's remains. He was advised not to venture out in such a dangerous sector. 'He heard a voice within him, bidding him risk it, and the call of blood drove him on. Creeping out of the far end of the trench as dusk fell, he crawled through the grass on hands and knees in spite of shells and snipers, dropping flat on the ground as the flares shot up from the German trenches. And at last, 30 yards away in the open, he felt he was touching young Woodruffe's body, another subaltern, and knew he was close to what he sought. Two yards further he found it. He could stroke with his hand the fair young head he knew so well . . .'.

A week later, Neville Talbot had arranged with three volunteers to form a stretcher party to recover the body. This he buried in a quiet cemetery under a wooden cross. The sequel is widely known—how, later in 1915, he founded a soldiers' institute in Poperinghe and named it Talbot House in memory of his dead brother. How this was abbreviated by the signallers to 'Toc H'. And so, Gilbert Talbot of Farnham Castle became the 'Known Soldier' who spoke for those who died, of whom Binyon wrote 'they shall grow not old, as we that are left grow old; age shall not weary them, nor the years condemn'.

The ground floor of the tall house in the squalid village of Poperinghe was given over to creature comforts; the first-floor boasted a library and chaplain's room. The lumber room, reached by a ladder, extended over the whole area of the house; here services were held, with an old carpenter's bench as altar. On the walls of the house were notices which read 'All rank abandon, ye who enter here', and 'If you are in the habit of spitting on the carpet at home, please spit here'. An annexe in Ypres was called Little Talbot House. *Punch* commented at the time that the canteen 'brought a corner of Heaven into the Hell of men's and officers' lives'.

The first anniversary of the outbreak of war was recognised in Farnham by a united service of prayer in Castle Street, presided over by the Bishop of Winchester . . . The King, passing through the town on 19 August on his way to visit military camps was halted for several minutes at the level-crossing gates . . . Sergeant Patrick was granted a commission in the Army Ordnance Corps at Stirling . . . Stanley Mitchell, one of Tom Mitchell's sons, became a midshipman on H.M.S. *Excellent* at Portsmouth . . . Farnham's hop crop for 1915 was written off as a failure; but then the town's once great industry was in decline.

The Council expressed to their fellow townsman, Corporal William James Kimber of the 2nd Queen's Royal West Surreys, their hearty congratulations on being awarded the Distinguished Conduct Medal. Kimber, on seeing a wounded man trying to crawl to his trench, went out in broad daylight to help him. He wrote on 15 August from Lewisham Military Hospital:

> I wish to thank you very much for your kind vote of congratulations to me on being awarded the D.C.M. I can assure you I was quite surprised to see my name on the list of honours as I only did what I thought my duty. I am pleased to say my wounds are progressing well and I hope soon to be in Farnham on sick furlough before rejoining my regiment.

Corporal Kimber was more at home on the football field. He was persuaded against his natural shyness to be the hero of the hour at a public meeting at which Mr. Aldridge, the Council Chairman, presented him with a gold watch and chain.

In September the Council expressed sympathy with the family of Private James Austin, a local postman who had been killed in the Dardanelles. At their meeting on 7 September, Mr. Kempson proposed that a Roll of Honour should be kept, listing the names of all Farnham men serving in the forces, in the form of a handsome book in which the names could be inscribed on vellum. In days to come, he said, people would treasure such a record. If the auditor refused permission to spend public money on it then he would pay for it himself.

On 2 October, a Grand Recruiting Rally was held in the town, with parades of uniformed men, the Fire Brigade and the Boy Scouts. There were public meetings, and films at the Picture Palace; and, doubtless, the handing out of white feathers by those secure in the knowledge that they themselves would not be called upon to face death in the mud and blood of Flanders. In spite of all the drum-beating and flag-waving, the response was disappointing. Lord Derby's scheme to 'invite' men between the ages of 18 and 41 to enlist, which worked on the principle of peaceful though potent persuasion, accounted that autumn for little more than half the number of civilians still unattested. Compulsory conscription was introduced early in 1916.

In October, Joseph King, M.P., voiced his opinion that, after the present war, Germany would quickly revive and at some future date would inflict another bloodbath on humanity. 'This', said the *Herald,* 'say in 60, 100 or even 200 years' time, must be prevented at all costs. The terms imposed by the Allies at the end of the present conflict must be framed to ensure that such a disaster could not arise. Germany, it was said, was a highly organised race and the people were used to doing what they were told by their ambitious masters. A very real danger existed'.

The town heard in November that the 5th Queen's, who had been in Lucknow, India, for almost a year, had been put on active service posting and were about to go to war.

A well-known local figure, Samuel Bide of Alma Nursery, Runfold, died on 25 November. A son of Richard Bide, Sam had lived all his life in the district. The *Herald* added that the nursery got its name because it was started on the day, 20 September 1854, when the Battle of Alma in the Crimean War was fought.

Christmas 1915 was subdued, wet and windy, with excessive rain on the day and a gale on Boxing Day. People were war-weary and numb. The war had reached a stage where it would go either way; whilst the halting of the pre-trained and powerful German army by a scratch, hastily improvised expeditionary force had done much to raise the Allies' spirits, it required a further boosting of the war effort to sway the balance. This came with the Military Service Act, which introduced compulsory conscription. In a public notice dated 1 January 1916, the Council gave eligible men one last chance to join up of their own free will. Farnham, said the notice, had done well in the initial Kitchener's drive, but latterly, in Lord Derby's round-up, enlistment had been disappointing. Farnham's name was at stake!

The town's War Service Tribunal under the Act consisted of Messrs. Soames, Aldridge, Kempson, Nash, Howard, and Tomlin. One of the first cases before them was that of Mr. L. H. Starling, whose work in the Council's surveyor's office was of importance. But, before the case could be considered, Mr. Starling had signed on. Applications for exemption from military service which came before the Tribunal tended to follow certain patterns, the chief being the applicant's indispensibility. Evidence usually came from aged parents dependent on their sons' earnings, or from employers whose businesses would be at risk. In March, the first conscientious objector appeared. Asked what his reaction would be if he saw his mother shot or his sister raped, he replied that he would take the guilty party on one side, and talk to him of God.

The Rev. Neville Talbot was awarded the Military Cross . . . Women conductresses appeared on the buses . . . Pubs were restricted to 5½ hours opening time a day, and treating was prohibited . . . The Headmaster of the Grammar School published a list of 200 old boys currently in the forces. One, Louis Renault, a boarder from 1911 to 1912, had joined the French army and been killed in the hotly-contested Hartmannsweilerkopf region. Lloyds Bank opened their first branch in Farnham, in The Borough, on 14 February 1916, under the managership of Horace Scott Evans. It was later moved to Norman Shaw's bank at 75 Castle Street . . . Mrs. Elias Morgan organised a fund for the relief of prisoners-of-war from the local Queen's Regiment . . . The police were given powers to visit houses in order to check on conscription dodgers. Later in the year, the names of truants were published in the local press, together with an appeal for information as to their whereabouts.

On Wednesday, 10 May, the gloom was lifted partially with a revival of the old Farnham Fair. An idea of the local farmers, it was opened by Rupert Anderson of Waverley and raised over £1,600 for Red Cross funds. Old-timers recalled the days when livestock was pounded all the way up Castle Street and booths pitched up the rise almost as far as the gates of the residence of My Lord of Winchester. Now stalls loaded with local produce lined the street, and there was a wide variety of side-shows. One of these displayed captured German war equipment, such as trench mortars, grenades, and part of a Zeppelin destroyed over Revigney.

A Staffordshire paper praised Crosby and Co. of Farnham for carrying out a contract in rapid time and in adverse weather conditions at Dudley. This was the erection of 98 temporary timber cottages and 10 larger hostel buildings. The Great War was not the only war to blow a fair wind into Crosbys' workshops.

Lord Kitchener's death on the *Hampshire*, which struck a mine on 5 June 1916 whilst on the way to Russia, was acknowledged with shocked feelings in the Council Chamber. Of the Council's pre-war workforce of 55 men, 21 were of military age. Of these, 14 were already in the forces, the remainder, except for one, being unfit for service.

*   *   *   *   *

Sister Reeves, head staff nurse at the Waverley Abbey Military Hospital, was awarded the Royal Red Cross in the King's Birthday Honours. The King and Queen, on their way to visit the Canadian troops on Hankley Common, looked in at Waverley and were much pleased with what they saw. The King was particularly interested in Bogey, a black Pomeranian regarded by staff and patients as the 'mascot of Waverley'.

At their July meeting, the councillors sympathised with John Edwards of Hale, who had received news of his son's death in the Baltic whilst serving as a wireless operator in a submarine.

A D.S.M. was awarded posthumously to Able Seaman Bruce Beagley, ex-postman of 12 Abbey Street, who had been killed on 25 September 1915 whilst serving on the New Zealand ship, H.M.S. *Philomel*. He had taken part in a land force operation against the Turks in the desert some 10 miles north of Aden, and had died of heat exhaustion, having earlier surrendered his camel to an exhausted comrade. Sergeant Doulton, R.A.M.C., in peace-time employed by the International Meat Co., won the Military Medal for bravery in tending the wounded under heavy shell fire. Mr. J. E. Spencer of The Borough had a letter from his son, Sidney, serving in the Bankers Battalion of the Royal Fusiliers, who was recovering from wounds in a hospital at Brighton. The letter was a great relief, for Sidney had been reported missing. Later, on the Somme on 28 February 1917, the Germans tried again; this time they killed him.

The main road through Hale had taken a battering from army traffic and was in urgent need of resurfacing. The War Office agreed to contribute £1,500 of the £2,500 cost . . . The Council accepted an engraving by Stephen Elmer, the

18th-century local artist, of 'John Cartwright of Farnham, Surrey, gardener and florist, 1748' . . . A closing order was clamped on a public well near The White City in Upper Hale . . . The 29 riparians along the River Wey were rounded up to share the cost of clearing out the river bed . . . The town was in darkness at night, except for seven street-lamps, because of the likelihood of air-raids.

Private P. Smith, whose parents lived in Lower Church Lane, was awarded the Military Medal for saving his unit's gun, and attending to wounded men under shell fire. He was not quite 18 years old, having joined up when he was sixteen. 'I wish I could get home', he wrote, 'I've had enough; fifteen months of this is too long'. Corporal Harold Falkner did get home, his leg injury having incapacitated him for further army service. He was soon back in his true role. An article by him was published in the September copy of *The Architectural Review*—on 'Farnham: its history and hop industry'.

Chief Petty Officer R. C. Smith of High Park Road won a D.S.M. at Jutland. An M.M. went to Sapper John Hewitt of 'Fern Villa', Hale Road, for bravery at the Hohenzollern Redoubt on 4 October 1915; he had been a carpenter at Goddards. A D.C.M. was awarded to Sergeant H. Radford of Upper Hale for coolly repairing barbed-wire defences in daylight and under machine-gun fire in the Battle of the Somme; he had worked for Mardon and Mills. And a posthumous D.C.M. went to Sergeant Baker of the Queen's, once a gardener at Thumblands, Runfold, who single-handedly captured an enemy machine gun, killing its German crew. Farnham, remarked the *Herald* in October, seemed to be getting a fair share of the medals. But side-by-side with these press accounts were the Area Recruiting Commandant's lists of wanted men who had gone into hiding to avoid call-up.

An October *Daily Mirror* featured the Waverley Abbey Hospital, with photographs of Mrs. Rupert Anderson and her four daughters, all nurses—Amy, Nancy, and Betty at Waverley, and Millie in France . . . Mr. R. Courtenay Welch, who ran a prep school for Sandhurst at Heath End, was granted permission to erect a war shrine on the Hale Recreation Ground. Six months later, a £1 reward was offered for information leading to the arrest of the persons who had vandalised it . . . With an apparent belief in the future, the Local Government Board requested particulars of the Council's schemes lined up for after the war. An equally optimistic reply was £19,615's worth already on the drawing-board, plus a probable 60 council houses.

Indeed, Winston Churchill's words at the Guildhall on 9 November 1914— 'The maxim of the British people is business as usual'—had not fallen on deaf ears. With the big schemes suspended, the surveyor was able to give more time to less urgent matters. In the Hoghatch area of the Hale Ward, he and the Medical Officer of Health found that, out of 73 cottages inspected, no less than 52 were unfit for human habitation. This was so bad that the Council called in the L.G.B. Controller of Housing. His advice was that, for the remaining period of the war, the Council would have to lower their sights from Housing Act standards unless conditions became detrimental to health.

In November, the police called on householders, asking how many soldiers they could take in on a 'sleeping only' basis, at 6d. a night for the first man, and 4d. thereafter, because more soldiers were expected to arrive in Farnham at any time. This provoked mixed feelings, which prompted the *Herald* to remind house-holders that soldiers also had mums and sisters somewhere, and were fully house-trained.

At their meeting on 4 December 1916, the councillors mourned the death of William Thomas Coleman, for 25 years a farmer and hop-planter and forage merchant in Waggon Yard. Coming from Wiltshire, Mr. Coleman had taken Farnham to his bosom; contrary to normal custom, Farnham had taken Coleman to their's. He had become a pillar of the Church, the Council (of which he was Chairman in 1898/9), the Bench of Magistrates, the Conservative stronghold, and other right circles. Miss Hazell presented the Council Chamber with a portrait of her late uncle, William H. Hazell, one of the first members of the old Farnham Local Board, and Chairman, 1871-1880. He once made ladies' stays at the factory in Ivy Lane.

The observant Mr. Cass had noticed gravel differs in the government pits north of the Farnham–Odiham road at Upper Hale making occasional sorties across the road into an area of land used as a gathering ground by the Farnham Water Company. His supicions were justified when he found a large quantity of fresh human excrement in close proximity to the very spot at which the town's drinking water began its flow downhill. The Council threw the book at the Company, whose secretary, Mr. D. Graham, replied that he was aware of some slight trespass by the gravel diggers, but that the situation was not bad enough to cause alarm.

The German attempt to starve Britain out of the war by means of submarine attacks on merchant shipping was beginning to bite by the end of 1916. In a panic, the government passed the Cultivation of Lands Order 1916 by which local authorities were to requisition all vacant land and induce their subjects into growing vegetables. Farnham was rather smug about its earlier 'Dig for Victory' campaigns, but these were not enough. Allotments, declared the government, were of vital importance to the successful issue of the war; no stone should be left unturned to increase home-grown produce. The local soil contain-ing more than the average number of stones, the Council had to use pressure to persuade volunteers to rent the 10-rod plots, even with the lure of cheap seed potatoes and manure.

*   *   *   *   *

1917 dawned, cold and windy. But the ill wind from Flanders which blew death into the homes of luckless soldiers continued to bring nothing but prosperity into the overworked breweries and establishments like that of

Messrs. Crosby and Co., Ltd. That firm's riverside workshops in South Street proved inadequate for fulfilling wartime contracts, and they hit upon the expedient of erecting a platform across the river from their bank to the Gostrey Meadow side. This would, they claimed, provide a surface area on which to assemble, among other urgent war equipment, the cases required for shipping aeroplanes over to France. The Council were nervous on security grounds; they also deplored the use by Crosbys' 64 employees of sawdust in the privies instead of dry earth. They did a deal—the firm put in water-closets in return for sanction for their raft.

William Aldwin Soames of Moor Park died suddenly at the age of 66 and was buried at Tilford. Unassuming by nature, he had contributed nothing to the history of his estate; his involvement in local affairs was limited to the chairmanship of the Farnham War Service Tribunal. His will was proved at £288,833 gross, a considerable fortune in 1917.

The *Herald* recalled that remarkable British stand against superior odds in the Zulu wars of 1879, when 80 men of the 24th Regiment faced 4,000 Zulu warriors at Rorkes Drift. The few survivors still living included Henry Parker, now aged 73, who had covered himself with glory by saving the regimental colours. Still working, as a mess steward at Aldershot, Parker lived at 'Beech Villa', Park Road, Farnham.

C.S.M. Arthur Hole (West Yorkshire Regiment), of 3 Coopers Terrace, East Street, won the D.C.M. for rescuing five wounded men. Trooper C. Bradford (The Queen's), son of Mr. Bradford, who kept the corner shop in Alfred Road, was reported killed.

The Chancellor of the Exchequer's launching of the Victory War Loan, at a conference at the Central Hall, Westminster, and attended by Councillor Nash, met with enthusiastic support in Farnham. Half-page notices in the *Herald* pressed people to invest £4 14s. 0d. to get five pounds. The Council themselves borrowed £3,000 to invest in the 5 per cent. inscribed stock of the Loan, as well as other available money—they decided to sell fir trees at Black Lake at about 2s. 6d. each, and invest that, too. By the time the list closed, some £186,896 had been subscribed in the Farnham area. Of this, £12,921 had been taken in the post office—£1,081 in lovely golden sovereigns (the pound had changed to paper in 1914).

Nine pigs were installed at the sewage farm, probably adding to the smell therefrom . . . Mr. H. K. Bentall presented a portrait of his grandfather, Josiah Bentall (Chairman, 1868–1872). Sixty years later, these portraits lie discarded in a damp-infested store, unwanted and unloved . . . Dr. G. (Paddy) Miles, 19 East Street, Farnham's favourite medicine man, farmed out his practice and joined the R.A.M.C. He was next heard of at Salonika. The *Herald* met the new restrictions on newsprint by cutting down their issues from eight pages to four. The serial story and other regular features were cut . . . A film at the Picture Palace in April gave people their first fascinating glimpse of Britain's latest weapon, the tank, which was now striking fear into the Germans.

Charles Borelli died on 18 April from an attack of bronchitis. Born in 1843 at Germasino, near Lake Como, he had come to England as a boy to live with an uncle in Farnham, at the jeweller's shop in The Borough started in 1828 by another uncle, Donato Borelli. In due course, he took over the business from Uncle Clemente. Now, in 1917, it was in the hands of Mr. C. E. Borelli and his brother, Leo. Harry Loe, 'Silwood', West End Grove, died, too; he was eighty-one. He had come in 1878 from Bishop's Sutton as manager to the Farnham United Breweries. His son, Willie, stepped into his shoes.

May's dispatches from Whitehall included, unexpectedly, some stuff on a National Baby Week, which was given the full treatment in Farnham. It was held in July under the auspices of the Maternity and Child Welfare Advisory Committee (President, Mrs. Clare Crum, wife of the rector). Festivities were opened at the Church House by Lady Napier and the Hon. Mrs. Talbot. The judges who had the unenviable task of picking the winners, in a field of 291 exhibits, were Dr. Marion Archibald of Guildford, Dr. Lindsay of Aldershot, Dr. Travers of the Bourne, and Mrs. Walters of Crooksbury. Bishop Talbot and his wife presented the prizes. Afterwards, a cavalcade of prams and pushchairs processed through the town to the Castle, where 600 people sat down to a free tea of bread substitute and fruit, accompanied by music from a military band, and, doubtless, a vocal rendering from 291 candidates for the next war.

Mrs. Caldwell Crofton of Heathyfield, Tilford, President of the Economy Campaign Committee, ran cooking demonstrations in the area, using wartime rations. To help with the preservation of fruits, the Council bought 200 dozen Kilner jars and distributed them at 5s. a dozen. Sugar was, of course, in short supply. When issuing ration cards in August to some 3,000 households, it was calculated that each had an average of 3.17 persons. In total, this revealed a deficiency in the normal peacetime population of Farnham of about 2,200 persons, and this was adopted as a number of local people currently away in the Services.

John Henry Knight of Barfield, Runfold, died on 8 September, aged seventy. Son of John Knight of Weybourne House—the residence of the Knight family for upwards of 100 years—J. H. was trained as an engineer. Having no need to earn a living, he was able to please himself how he put his knowledge into practice. This he had done in no uncertain way. In 1868, he constructed a steam carriage, which was a familiar sight on the local roads for two or three years. In 1887, he patented the 'Trusty Oil Engine', one of the earliest oil-driven engines in the country. He was among the first to anticipate the motoring age when, in 1896, he designed the first two-seater petrol-driven car made in England. It was built by George Elliot and was on the roads until the police served two summonses on Knight for not having a man with a red flag walking in front. He was fined 2s. 6d. on each count. He also invented a bricklaying machine and wooden sprung tyres for motor vehicles. Later he became interested in flying machines. He was a founder member of the Automobile Club, the

Self-propelled Traffic Association, and the Camera Club. In addition to frequent lecture engagements, he published books under the following titles: *Electric Lighting for Country Houses*; *Notes on Motor Carriages, Light Motor Cars and Voiturettes*;*A Catechism of the Motor Car*; and *Reminiscences of a Country Town.*

A workman repairing a surface water drain at the Darvills Lane junction in South Street found a human skeleton in a shallow grave. It was known that the nearby Fairfield was the site of a Roman cemetery—two cremation vessels had been found there in 1902—but otherwise the area was unexcavated, and the discovery created much interest in archaeological circles.

The Rev. F. J. Layton arrived from Lytham, Lancs., and gave his first service in the Congregational church on 7 October. Before his appointment, said Mr. Layton, two Farnham gentlemen had gone up to Lytham to vet him. They had looked rather suspicious to his landlady, who reported them to the police as possible German spies.

Air-raids were now a regular nightly feature over London. George Sturt recorded in his diary seeing strangers in Farnham, presumably refugees from the capital. Mrs. Hoptroff (specialist tea merchant and tobacconist in Downing Street) called the Council's attention to 'the large influx of persons owing to the air-raids' and the need to provide accommodation for them.

Councillor de Mornay of Hale left on military service and wondered whether he should resign from the Council. His departure, and that of Mr. A. R. Robins, created two vacancies in the ranks of the Food Control Committee. The Aldershot, Farnham and Farnborough Trades and Labour Council, quick to seize their opportunity, nominated W. G. Day, C. Reed, and W. Culver. The Council, equally quick to avert trouble, voted in Miss K. Sloman and John Edwards. The English Labour Party were emerging as a force to be reckoned with.

Heath and Wiltshires sought permission to take flexible pipes across and above the pavement fronting their garages in Union Road and West Street for the purpose of filling the petrol containers on motor cars . . . The West Surrey War Museum invited information on the exploits of local serving men and other wartime memorabilia. Mr. Baigent thought it might be nice to mount a German gun in Gostrey Meadow, preferably one captured by the lads in the Queen's Regiment . . . Dr. Brown complained about the town's water supply; so had everyone else since the Water Company's formation in 1836. The Council should take over . . . The brewery agreed to round off the corner of the *Royal Deer* pub to provide a nice sweep round from East Street into South Street . . . There was talk of getting German P.o.W.s to clean out the river bed. Sir Julian Byng's victory over the Germans at Cambrai in November 1917 was celebrated in Farnham with a peal from the long silent parish church bells. But the war was not over yet. Christmas, remarked the *Herald,* was a more sober and quiet festival than any in the past—no seasonal luxuries, no entertainments. just war weariness, and the killings.

*   *   *   *   *

That quaint practice at the commencement of the year of wishing each other 'A Happy and Prosperous New Year' was duly observed at the January meeting in the Council Chamber. The councillors' immediate concern was the establishment of a civic restaurant in Farnham. This gastronomic venture had been conceived in December with the object of providing the public with *ersatz* food at minimal cost. Overheads would be trifling, for the hall and kitchen at the Church House were at a nominal rent, donations had been promised for meeting the estimated £150 for equipment, and the Ministry of Food was willing to bear 25 per cent. of expenses. With 'an excellent cook', an experienced buyer (Willie Loe), and volunteers to do the washing-up, the restaurant was opened with a flourish on 26 February by Mr. J. R. Nash. Weekly takings soon reached an average of £24, from some 250 customers daily. These came from all ranks of society, from working girls to people of means. War was a great leveller.

The British Workers League convened a public meeting at the Corn Exchange in January with a view to drumming up support among the local downtrodden for the formation of a branch of the League in Farnham. The Workers of the World's keynote was 'Uniting'. The Tories diluted the poison somewhat by themselves attending the meeting (if you can't beat 'em, join 'em) and warmly congratulating the speakers on their worthy objects. Certainly the lower orders were asserting themselves. Still smarting over their recent defeat in the Food Control Committee topping-up, they demanded the expansion of that committee by three additional members to be chosen from the following: Harry Sanders (Co-op), Mrs. A. A. Russell (Co-op Women's Guild), W. G. Day (Branch secretary, N.U.R.), Mr. H. Meddows Taylor (N.U.T.), Mr. Splatt (Carpenters and Joiners). The Workers Union, the Postmen's Federation, and the Tailors Union also fielded candidates. Strong tactics which paid off—Mrs. Russell, Mr. Day and Mr. Meddows Taylor were duly elected.

Father Robo left again on 3 January, this time to join the auxiliary forces of the French army. Writing later to thank the Board of Guardians for keeping his place on that Board open, pending his return, he expressed his belief that the end of the war was a very long way off. In his absence, a Father Hemans acted as *locum* in the Farnham Catholic church.

John F. Cobbett, grandson of William, died at Brighton on 27 January, aged 65, and was buried in the family vault in Farnham churchyard . . . Mr. Aldridge remonstrated with the Aldershot Traction Co. over drivers exceeding the 12 m.p.h. (10 m.p.h. in towns) speed limit, and stipulated that journeys between Farnham and Aldershot should in future take not less than 30 minutes . . . The Council argued with the Timber Controller about the drastic felling of trees in the Crooksbury and Black Lake areas. Some modifications were won, but the trees were urgently required for war purposes. After a Canadian Forestry Unit had been at work, Farnham's famous landmark at Crooksbury never looked the same. 'The trees', deplored George Sturt in his *The Wheelwright's Shop,* 'cut into lengths, stripped of their bark and stacked in piles, gave to many an erstwhile secluded hillside a staring publicity. This or that quiet place, the home of peace, was turned into a ghastly battlefield, with the naked and maimed corpses of trees lying about'.

About this time, No. 10 The Borough, that less notable though equally eye-catching west gatepost to Castle Street, came in for 'the Treatment'—an unexpected oasis in the barren wastes of war. The Treatment, a term implicitly understood by first-half 20th-century Farnhamians, meant simply Mr. Borelli and Mr. Falkner, two men of sharply contrasting character who formed an abiding relationship through one common interest, namely an Italianate flair for restoring ancient buildings, coupled with Falkner's genius for halting further destruction of the town's ancient buildings. With their deaths, their combined skills have passed into legend, though their monuments remain.

No. 10 The Borough, on the corner of Castle Street, had been well botched up by generations of vandals. Originally it formed part of the *Coach and Horses* pub at 2 Castle Street, and that pub's licence still officially covered the whole block, though the two parts had long since gone their separate ways. The Mangles had opened their West Surrey bank in the corner premises, and latterly Hearns' 'Borough Stores' was lettered largely over the front. Then the Borelli–Falkner partnership moved in. One of the latter's maxims was 'act first and argue after-wards'—his *fait accompli,* usually sublime, was in most cases, though not always, nine points of the law, and Farnham owes much to his boldness. In this instance, being officially part of a building subject to a pub licence, even though no longer used as such, the licensing authorities, sensitive to structural alterations, huffed and puffed, but in the end had to concede that the licence should rightly be deemed to cover the *Coach and Horses* part only. Both Borelli and Falkner joined the Royal Air Force (its new name as from April 1918) that summer, though there is nothing to suggest that they were run out of town by the infuriated licensing justices, or by critics of their architectural policies—for many people were slow-witted and needed time to appreciate that beautiful things were being done to their town.

Mrs. Rupert Anderson was awarded an O.B.E. for services at the Waverley Hospital. On her return from Buckingham Palace, she was met at Farnham station by nurses and several of 'her boys' from the hospital. Nurse Reeves presented her with a bouquet of flowers.

In an attempt to boost morale, the government released war supplements to weekly provincial newspapers which contained reassuring accounts of the fighting and hopeful prophesies for the successful outcome. But the deaths went on—among them that of Captain Alan Crundwell, son of Ernest Crundwell of Gorsehanger.

The Rev. Samuel Priestley, Headmaster of the Grammar School, died on 22 October. He had come to Farnham from Maidstone Grammar School in 1897, in succession to Charles Stroud.

With an eye to post-war housing, the Council provisionally negotiated for six acres of land (Sheephouse) off Firgrove Hill, at a price of £1,200, and six and three-quarters acres (Stoke Hills) off East Street. The housing of the working classes, as local authorities' schemes were called, loomed largely upon the horizon. Their own workmen were granted one week's leave of absence a year, deferred until after the war—in the words of one councillor, this was 'a wise principle'.

The government, too, were arming themselves against a possible Russian-style war which might break out once peace was declared with Germany. The Western Division of Surrey, comprising Chertsey, Farnham and Guildford was Conservative; it would be a wanton waste of good Tory votes to keep it that way. So the government hived Farnham off and teamed it up with Woking, which was marginal, and as a result created two safe Tory seats instead of one, and another that could be expected to swing to Labour.

Woking considered themselves to be senior partner and suggested that the new Division should be named the Woking Division. That would never do; there were countermoves and, in November, the Farnham Council came up with the following resolution:

> That in view of the fact that, after hearing all parties interested, the Boundary Commission is decided that the new Western Division of the County should be named the Farnham Division, this Council is of the opinion that as a natural sequence the place for the receipt of nomination papers, for the counting of votes and for the declaration of results of the polls of elections for that Division should be the ancient town of Farnham from which the Division is named, and that the Clerk be directed to forward copies of this Resolution to the High Sheriff and to the Acting Returning Officer for the County . . .

The Farnham and District Allied Trades Council—who seem to have become separated from their Aldershot brothers—asked for the use of Gostrey Meadow on Whit Monday in order to hold a meeting. To which the Tory-dominated Council replied:

> Whilst the Council have every sympathy with the proposed Labour demonstration and service, they regret they cannot give permission for the holding of a public meeting in the South Street pleasure grounds as they have consistently declined to permit other bodies or associations to hold public meetings in these grounds as it appears to the Council as to do so would be to divert the grounds from the purpose for which they were provided, *viz.* for public walks and pleasure grounds for the use of the inhabitants generally.

Then the Allied Trades Council stormed the citadel itself with a demand that the two vacancies once filled by Councillors Coleman and Kempson, and since kept unfilled pending the first election after the war, should immediately be filled by 'representatives of Organised Labour'. By July there was a field of no less than 17 candidates for the two vacancies: they were:

> Mrs. A. A. Russell; Mrs. Faires; W. G. Day; A. H. Lunn; Mrs. Tanner; Mrs. J. Price; A. G. Ransom; C. Bradford; – Giles; H. Sanders; E. C. Kerley; W. Culver; G. W. Ballard; John Codman; A. G. Mardon; Henry Clist; and Richard Preston.

From a cursory glance, this list of runners included at least four who were non-union members, being, indeed, employers of the downtrodden working classes, and therefore doubtless of sound Tory principles; which suggests that they had been nominated by an agency other than the Allied Trades Council. One from each camp was picked out, Arthur George Ransom of The Borough, and Henry Clist of Tilford Road being sworn in as co-opted councillors. Their votes on any motion could be expected to cancel each other out, thus leaving the Council where they were before the whole wretched business erupted.

Following protracted negotiations with the charitable trust in which it was vested, the swimming bath was handed over into the care of the Council in June, together with the petty cash, various club trophies and other treasures. The bath was enjoying a wartime boom. It was the only one within miles, and requests for the use of it came from as far afield as the Aircraft Establishment at Farnborough.

Dr. Ealand offered as a gift a model of the old market house in Castle Street, demolished in 1865—the work of a disabled soldier at the Hill Hospital. . . . The Food Committee were considering rabbits as a source of meat . . . Mr. Aldridge called for volunteers to help with the harvest . . . Local allotment holders held an exhibition at Broomleaf on August Bank Holiday and sent the London General Hospital a gift of 30 sacks of potatoes and other produce.

George Murrell proposed that General Sir Archibald Murray should be asked to spare two captured enemy guns for Gostrey Meadow. Mr. Swansborough wanted two as well for the Hale Rec. . . . The Chairman thought that, as the war was nearing its end, they could have a little more street-lighting . . . Mr. Borelli wrote telling of his life in the R.A.F.

At a special meeting on 11 November 1918, Mr. A. J. Barnard stated:

> That it had fallen to his lot as Chairman of the Council to receive the news of the Armistice, which was signed at 5 o'clock that morning and under which hostilities ceased at 11 o'clock.

He moved:

> That this Council desires with all reverence and humility to express thanks to Almighty God for the mercies vouchsafed to our Nation and its Allies in the cessation of hostilities and the triumph of our cause, it also desires to place on record its debt of gratitude to all those brave men and women who have steadfastly served their Country during the war, it also desires respectfully to extend its sincere sympathy to the families of those in the District who have laid down their lives for their King and Country and to whose sacrifices the triumph of our Navies and Armies is due.

2

THE PIPING TIMES OF PEACE

1918-1919

RESIDUUM

The troops at Aldershot, it is said, have knocked off for the day
and are already painting the town red.
Rumour circulating early on 11 November 1918

AT FIRST, ONE COULDN'T BE SURE—not absolutely certain, that is. Hopes ran high, only to be dashed—and rise again. The staff of a locally-based government department, it was said, had been heard singing the National Anthem. Here and there, flags flew uncertainly at windows. Presently a flag was hoisted on the tower of the parish church. A Press Association telegram, delivered to the offices of the local paper, brought the information that Reuters Agency were unable to confirm rumours of peace. Later, the cheering began, a veritable groundswell of rejoicing which brought people from their doors to mingle in the street in wild surmise, asking unanswered questions of each other. More and more, flags and streamers coloured the town and hopes stayed high. With the dawning of certainty, the burden of war that had, for four years and a quarter, lain so heavily upon one's shoulders, rolled away and a light-hearted abandon filled its place.

The shops closed that day at 3 o'clock. An hour later, crowds pressed closely to a platform hurriedly erected outside Watney's Brewery in Castle Street; on the platform were the town's worthies. A solemn though joyous speech from Chairman Barnard was followed by prayers from the rector and the Rev. F. J. Layton. Then the Doxology and the National Anthem, and the people dispersed, to celebrate the victory each in his own way.

A Farnham man could claim to be the initiator of that Armistice Day ritual, the evocative two-minutes silence. Mr. J. Alfred Eggar told George Sturt that the idea had originated in his office during the mock-up Farnham Fair on 10 May 1916. Bishop Talbot and Archbishop Davidson had both refused their support, and finally it was Canon Cunningham who helped to make it a success. Sturt wondered—had the gentry really resented the move because the lead had not come from themselves? Government ultimately adopted the idea as a mark of respect, and Eggar received a letter of thanks from the Home Secretary.

The Armistice had brought about merely the cessation of hostilities. The precise termination of the state of war with Germany was not officially recognised until 31 August 1921, when respective governments had ratified the treaties. The end of war with Turkey came even later, on 6 August 1924. So really, down at local government level, little criticism was justified of those councils which failed to restore the peacetime *status quo* by one minute past 11 o'clock on Armistice Day. After all, there had to be a decent interval for refreshments, especially in a country which, on paper, found itself to be on the winning side.

So congratulations to the Farnham Council for being quickly off the mark with their post-war manifesto. Certainly, while resting with their feet up during the war years, they had been working on it intermittently in a desultory sort of way. They also had the benefit of inspired advice from ratepayers who wrote letters to the *Herald*. Their catalogue of intentions was impressive—possibly here and there a trifle over-optimistic. There was something in it for everybody.

1. Housing schemes
2. Maternity and child welfare centres
3. Hale Ward drainage
4. Hale Ward lighting
5. Private street works
6. Sanitary inspection in the Hale Ward
7. Minor highway improvements
8. Roll of Honour
9. War trophies
10. War memorial
11. Completion of Gostrey Recreation Ground
12. Extension of the Council Offices
13. Provision of additional allotments
14. Purchase of market rights and provision of a public market
15. Provision of a public slaughterhouse
16. War museum and public reading-room
17. Incorporation of the town.

Works in the Hale Ward were arrears brought forward from 1914. More houses for the working classes was the resumption of a pre-war practice: (2) was a sop to Mrs. Russell and her amazons; (5) and (7) were routine duties, now urgent because of interruptions; Gostrey Meadow needed the finishing touches; (14) was a cry from the heart in the long-standing deadlock between the Council and the Market House and Town Hall Co., Ltd., which concerned the cobbled area in Castle Street, over which the Company exercised full sovereignty (and, presumably, derived much pleasure from twisting the Council's tail by letting in undesirable hucksters and the like). The slaughterhouse project was designed to eradicate the suspect conditions under which some butchers still processed their wares.

Last, but not least, on the agenda was the seeking of borough status. The inclusion of the Hale Ward, and, it was to be hoped, perhaps Bourne and Wrecclesham Wards, certainly merited a renewed application for incorporation. In the field of local government, becoming a borough could be likened to what, in feline circles, growing a second tail means to an ambitious cat. It allows more say at local levels in the town's affairs, and cuts more ice with the superior beings at County Hall. But, more importantly, the enhanced status tends to keep at bay predatory, two-pip neighbours with territorial gains in mind.

The further boundary of the Hale Ward now formed Farnham's north-east frontier; it followed the line of the River Blackwater, and was also the county border. The River Blackwater, which started its journey on the London clay at Heath End, had never quite made it. Robbed of its headwaters, geologists think in the early Upper Palaeolithic times, it continued on its course as a mere trickle and, in places, it was difficult to see with the naked eye. On the further bank of this non-stream, lay the Urban District of Aldershot. Covered with glory from two victorious wars, not to mention minor skirmishes in various parts of the world, Aldershot was obviously looking for municipal honours. It was conceivable, therefore, that the Home of the British Army, once it had dried out its drink problem, would take steps to swallow up its neighbours. Now, when a grateful government could refuse no demand from Aldershot, things across the Blackwater looked black indeed. Promotion in the league tables would at least give Farnham a weapon with which to defend herself.

The ink was hardly dry on the Council's manifesto when the general election scheduled for April 1919 was precipitated by the abrupt dissolution of parliament on 25 November 1918. All the hurly-burly of the hustings swept through the town. Fussing the babies in the Farnham Division were Arthur Michael Samuel (Tory)—W. E. Horne, local member since 1910, had chosen to remain with the now separate Guildford Division—Corporal John Hayes, R.A.M.C. (Labour), and a Woking barrister, John Henry Harris (Independent). Polling day, 14 December, was wet. Described by the *Herald* as the 'dullest election on record', not more than 50 per cent. of the electorate bothered to turn out. Labour won 59 seats in the Commons—Hayes was not one of these. Samuel took 7,558 votes, 4,024 more than Hayes; the Independent did well, with 3,289. In Guildford, Mr. Horne had a majority of 8,071. Afterwards, there was some nastiness about 'very serious defects' found in the voters lists. It was even suggested that certain residents had been deliberately left off because of their suspected political leanings.

That Christmas, the parish church bells rang out, and there was a dusting of snow. In the parlours, the yule-logs brightly burnt, though the empty chairs beckoned a silent message.

*   *   *   *   *

With the onset of 1919, it was found that the already substandard conditions in the Hale Ward had been further impaired by over four years' close involvement in the Aldershot Camp overspill. The people of Hale were less than happy about the situation, and leant on an embarrassed Council for improvements. A catalogue of grievances was sent to the Local Government Board, with an appeal for urgent attention. It was a dismal list. The better hovels sported pail-closets, the night-soil being removed by scavengers to the sewage farm at Monkton Lane. Some even had cesspits. The villagers drew their water from shallow, often polluted wells. Water from this source had been used during the war in about 30 cottage laundries, each having some hundred soldiers on its books. The dirty suds from 3,000 soldiers' washing each week had been thrown out on to the gardens. Military traffic had torn the primitive roads to shreds. Overcrowding was rife, and a real danger to health existed. The Local Government Board had been established in 1871; it was in the process of becoming the Ministry of Health. It was also currently on the receiving end of a flood of appeals from local authorities throughout the country seeking to restore their towns to peacetime. Patience, was the keynote of their replies—all in good time.

There was considerable disturbance over item (9) on the manifesto. Captured German guns had become status symbols; all the other towns wanted them, too. Mounted in recreation grounds or school playgrounds, they could wield an illusory effect of personal involvement. One gun had been delivered in December, and exhibited for a time in Castle Street, but there were many sites in the district calling out for weaponry. The War Office recommended the Council to try the War Trophies Committee, who suggested that they applied direct to military units. In due course, the local Queen's Regiment produced half-a-dozen German machine-guns, complete with ammunition. They had been hoping for something heavier, like a field gun; machine-guns lacked visual impact.

No. 10 on their list was also proving to be a worry. There was more to erecting a permanent memorial to the town's dead than, say, attaching a plaque to a wall in the church. Not everyone went to church these days; it would have to be in some more prominent place where all would see it. The committee set up to consider ways and means, and held public meetings in the Corn Exchange.

Those still alive of the town's 2,000-odd amateur servicemen came marching home. Ideally, it would have been nice to have them all marching back together and met, say, by the *Albion,* by the townspeople, led by the Council's Chairman and with bands playing. But they didn't—they came, unfussily, in dribs and drabs. Rankine of Badshot Lea, Chuter of East Street School, S. R. Secret, Ross Smither, Major H. C. Patrick, Lieutenant-Colonel J. Atkinson of Park Road (four mentions in despatches and five medals), Charles Borelli, H. C. Kingcome of the Grammar School, the German brothers—Sydney, William and Percy, and many others.

Peacetime things came back, too. The *Herald* restored their format of eight pages . . . The Chamber of Commerce promoted the first post-war public dinner in Farnham . . . The railway drivers went on strike over hours of duty . . . The laundry asked for more street-lighting in Darvills Lane, 'where immorality takes place nightly and people blunder into pools of rainwater'.

There were 220 applications for the post of headmaster at the Grammar School to fill the vacancy caused by the early death of Mr. Priestley. Mr. John Reynolds Strickland, M.A., of Blackheath, was selected from a short-list of six. At present serving as a captain in the army, he was a son of J. H. Strickland, Chief Adviser to the Board of Spirit Control. Prior to army service, J. R. had been Senior

Maths master at St Paul's School, West Kensington. Soon after his arrival in May, Mr. Strickland was concerned that the Grammar School, which had been built to take 150 pupils in seven classrooms, now had 200 in eight forms. Extensions, it was said, were in the air. Mr. J. W. Withinshaw, the French master, was demobbed, and a new member of the staff, Mr. W. R. Osborn, M.A., appointed.

No. 1 on the list of good intentions—council houses—was quick to arouse public clamour. To keep them quiet, the Council announced the initial building of 30 houses in the town—on a seven-acre site belonging to Mr. A. G. Mardon, the builder—and 30 more in the Hale Ward. Then Mr. Mardon opted out because he had decided to develop the site off Firgrove Hill himself. The Council were a bit huffy at first, but Mr. Mardon was a man of strong character, and, fortunately, another offer of a seven-acre site (Sheephouse) came from the Trustees of the Ward family, owners of the old Firgrove Estate. It was cheaper than Mr. Mardon's land, anyway.

There was, then, no shortage of building land in the district, for private or speculative development did not reach its peak until the 1930s. Several offers of Council house sites came in—from Bides (of land at Chantreys), Major Naderson (Bridge Field), 10 acres in Crondall Lane, and others. But the L.G.B. forbade wholesale housing projects, and sanctioned only the two schemes now in the pipeline, and these only with strings attached. Government called for detailed information concerning one of the sites, together with lay-out plans of both. Each house should have a parlour, three bedrooms, and, ideally, a bathroom; then, and not before, loan sanction might be considered.

The War Memorial Committee, whose fumbling deliberations had not yet borne fruit, also came in for criticism from the public. Other bodies in the town had already erected memorials to their dead. The decision was finally reached in November 1919 to instruct Mr. Watson to design a monument which would be placed inside the South Street entrance to Gostrey Meadow.

The Waverley Abbey Hospital closed on 19 March in a blaze of limelight. It had opened, on 23 September 1914, with 70 beds. In the autumn of 1915, two huts, named 'Kenilworth' and 'Rob Roy', after Scott's *Waverley Novels,* brought the number to one hundred. By 1918, tented accommodation had increased this to two hundred and forty-six. Some 5,019 patients had received treatment. This wartime hospital, one of the first to be opened, had attracted wide publicity. Royalty had been frequent visitors. At a farewell dinner on 28 March, Mrs. Rupert Anderson was presented by Sister Reeves with a water-colour depicting the last service held in the hut in the grounds used as a church. Two other temporary hospitals in Farnham—one was Charrington's, Frensham Hill— were also shut down about this time, in comparative obscurity.

Farnham has produced international figures, at some time or other, in most spheres of human activity, but none so unexpectedly as in prize-fighting. In March and April 1919, the papers were excited about 'Boy' McCormick, a locally-based

Irishman risen to be Britain's youngest middle-weight boxer. By defeating his Canadian opponent at the National Sporting Club in April, he became the new official champion in his class, and the first person ever to bring a Lonsdale belt back to Farnham. He was made much of at an At Home in the Church House.

Lady Baden-Powell, sister of B.P. of nearby Bentley, visited the Castle in April, throwing out hints that Farnham should start a group of the newly-formed Girl Guides movement. A follow-up meeting at the Church House, chaired by the Hon. Mrs. Pleydell-Bouverie, succeeded in getting one going.

Father Robo was now back with his flock in Bear Lane. Mostly, demobbed men were returning to their old jobs, which had been kept open for them; others found that 'Blighty' was not the land fit for heroes that they had been led to expect. All sorts of imaginative jobs were dreamed up—the building of a light railway between Farnham and Basingstoke, for instance, or restoring the Basingstoke canal—but funds to pay for them were non-existent.

A Ministry of Food inspector paid a visit to Farnham's wartime National Kitchen in the Church House on 28 February, and was full of praise for the Council and staff. He hoped that it would be kept open, but receipts had fallen, and the restaurant was closed on 6 June. During its 54 weeks in business, takings had amounted to £1,408 17s. 2d., against expenses of £1,273.

Mr. Barnard was warmly thanked for his term in office as Chairman. The first post-war election took place on 7 April, with 13 candidates standing for six seats. The result was as follows:

Harry Clist, 'Cranbourne', Alfred Road	432 (elected)
William George Day, 1 St Mary's Villas, St Georges Road	199
Arthur James Figg, Long Garden Walk	572 (elected)
Arthur George Mardon, 'Hawarden', Firgrove Hill	501 (elected)
Annie Miller, 'Corrymeela', Old Farnham Lane	331 (elected)
Thomas Patterson, Firgrove Hill	273
Agnes Alice Russell, 'Manor Cottage', Hale Road	151
Henry Sanders, 'Sanfield', Lancaster Avenue	204
Gertrude Annie Stroud, The Grammar School	194
John Edwards, 'The Rest', Upper Hale	135
Henry William Grace, 'The Oaks', Hale	70
William Norris, 'Perseverence Cottage', Upper Hale	166 (elected)
John William Swansborough, 'High View', Hale	185 (elected)

Farnham Council thus acquired a lady member for the first time in history. George Baigent became the new Chairman, with Mr. Barnard as Vice-Chairman. Later that year, Councillor P. J. Caesar of the Hale Ward retired for business reasons, and Mr. de Mornay left the district. Fortunately there were only two nominations, thus avoiding a by-election, and, on 21 August, Charles Edward Atkins of 4 Vale Cottages, Heath End, and William James Baker, 'The Cricketers', Upper Hale, were sworn in as councillors.

The Council renewed contact with Mr. Midgeley Taylor, the engineer engaged in 1914 to superintend the Hale drainage scheme, and he advised that the work should be done by stages, with separate tenders from contractors . . . The building firm of Mardon and Mills in Longbridge was dissolved and the partners went their separate ways . . . Major Rupert Anderson of Waverley was awarded the O.B.E. (Military Division) for war services.

The signing of the Treaty of Versailles on 28 June 1919 was the excuse for a second round of refreshments. The Council made peace with the Chamber of Commerce and other bodies in the town and arranged a Peace Day on 19 July. Bishop Talbot put the park at their disposal; there would be a 'real, old-fashioned country fair', with swings and roundabouts, sporting events and entertainments for the young, and dancing in the evening for the not-so-young. An illuminated address would, at a later function, be presented to every man who had served in the forces. The public contributed £622, and the Council found the balance. Whitsun that June was also a carefree time. People threw off the yoke of war and revelled in the sunshine. Farnham filled with visitors from London. Cricket was in full swing, with Rupert Thorp and W. Tanner Farnham's opening pair, Archie Harrison half way down, and Willie Loe last man in.

As a sign of women's growing importance, the Council provided them with a public lavatory. This was sandwiched in between the existing gentlemen's convenience in South Street and the Council office building. W. J. Wilkinson built it for £62 11s. 0d., but the ladies had to wait until November because a strike of railwaymen, from 26 September to 5 October, delayed delivery of the cisterns.

Mr. G. E. Alexander, manager of the old Capital and Counties Bank at 75 Castle Street, retired on 30 June, whereupon Lloyds Bank gave up their premises at 5-7 The Borough and moved to Castle Street. Their manager, Horace Scott Evans, became the Council's Treasurer in place of Alexander. Nos. 5-7 The Borough were bought by Mr. Borelli, and in due course received 'the Treatment'.

The post office announced three deliveries daily, of letters sent the day before, or in some instances the same day . . . The Council's pigs were sold, at 55s. each, to allotment holders.

Mr. A. J. Stedman produced his plans and specifications for 34 houses in Sheephouse, arranged, some would say, in the shape of a tennis racket with a play area where the ball bounces. Harold Falkner was having cost problems with the scheme at Hale. The price of the site, £1,400, plus the cost of the house-type stipulated would bring the total above the permitted ceiling. There were also objections from nearby residents. As time was pressing, Councillor Figg suggested putting up temporary timber dwellings.

The Farnham Rural Council were said to be considering a drainage scheme for the Bourne and Wrecclesham Wards. This would never do, for it would undermine the Town Council's argument for takeover, and the scheme was abandoned.

The six German machine guns were on display in the little garden next to the public lavatories in South Street (later named the Haren Gardens). One night in September, vandals climbed the railings, dragged the guns across to the river and threw four of them into the water. It was generally agreed that that was the best place for them.

The Venison Dinner was revived on 6 November, the first since 1913. The event was kept an all-male function, because space in the Corn Exchange was limited. Bishop Talbot renewed the ancient gift of a fat buck, and presided at the table.

Broomleaf Farm came on the market in August. Though aware of its potential value for public purposes—the field fronting the Waverley Lane had been used for some years, by permission of the owner, for fairs and gymkhanas—the Council did not attend the auction, for a more important property claimed their attention. This was 'Brightwells', off East Street. A curious feature about 'Lowlands'—as it was once known—is why this small gentleman's residence should have been built (by Thomas Turner in the 1790s), right in the midst of hopkilns, workshops, piggeries, pub, cattle market, and a river which served as the town's sewer; within a few years, the gasworks had been added to the environment. In 1816, the house was occupied by William Lowndes Stone from Brightwell Baldwin, Oxfordshire, who later (1824) purchased it for £900. He married Elizabeth, daughter of Richard Garth, lord of the manor of Morden. The estate passed to three daughters and, on their deaths, to Richard, second son of William and Elizabeth, who changed his name to Richard Stone Garth. It was he who enlarged the house by the addition of a wing on adjacent land to the west. A daughter, Frances, married Lieutenant-Colonel Patrick Paget of the Scots Guards. It is known that Arthur Sullivan was a guest of the Pagets for a week in July 1865; he composed a piece of music which he called *Idyll for violincello* in honour of his visit, the original of which is in an American museum. Another notable visitor from time to time was Florence Nightingale, when staying with her aunt, Mrs. Nicholson, at Waverley Abbey. It has been said that she spent her last night in England at 'Brightwells' before leaving for Scutari. She was godmother to the Pagets' daughter, Florence, who was named after her.

Colonel Paget died in 1879 and his widow in 1912. Miss Florence Paget had an antique business at 17 East Street, which she later moved to the Spinning Wheel, 40 The Borough. Brightwells House was let, in 1919, to a Mrs. Jupp. Now the house and grounds were offered to the Council for £4,000. The Council digested this most attractive offer. The house might prove a solution to their accommodation problem; the grounds would provide space for tennis courts, an additional bowling-green perhaps, and enable an extension of the swimming bath. They could expect revenue which would offset loan interest. At a special meeting on 25 September, they resolved to bid £3,500. They finally settled at £3,750: they got a bargain, even at 1919 prices.

Those very active monitors, the Chamber of Commerce, had been nudging the councillors' elbows over the proposed petition for the incorporation of Farnham. On 24 October, the following resolution was passed:

> That in the opinion of this Council it is in the interests of the future
> welfare of this District that an application should be made for a Charter of
> Incorporation for the Farnham Urban District and that this Council pledges
> itself to support such application if made by all means in their power.

The incipient Ministry of Health launched a countrywide campaign against
rats, creatures which, up to then, seemed to have enjoyed the freedom of the
city. Farnham appointed a rat-catcher in November and urged people to take
steps to reduce the rodent population in their homes. Councillor Barnard
represented the Council at the Royal Sanitary Institute Congress held in
July; his report is worthy of repetition if only because of its rare absence of
gobbledigok.

> *Saturday, July 26.* Left Farnham 10.16; left King's Cross 1.20; reached New-
> castle 7.45; partook of tea etc. at the *Douglas* Hotel. Walked to the Town
> Moor and saw the last of the Peace Pageant, which had been going on all that
> week. Proceeded to St. Dunstan's Hospital; it was a very elaborate presenta-
> tion, performed mainly by ladies assisted by the R.F.A. and Infantry who
> made use of their guns and rifles, making the show very realistic.
>
> *Sunday, July 27.* Attended a special service in St. Nicholas Cathedral,
> which was attended by the Lord Mayor and all his retinue in full regalia. The
> service was splendidly rendered, the Sermon very appropriate, and everything
> done for the comfortable seating of all the Delegates, a very large number of
> whom attended. Everyone enjoyed a delightful service; Sermon by Rev.
> Canon Newsome. In the afternoon, I explored various parts of the Town.

Following an inaugural address on Monday by the Duke of Northumberland,
Congress got down to business. There were lectures on Housing and Maternity and
Child Welfare, papers were read on Rats and Mice, and Fleas found on rats.
Labour-saving devices for the kitchen were on display at the School of Cookery.
Up-to-date housing designs, incorporating central heating and hot water supplies
were eagerly studied by the ladies in the party. It was a full programme, inter-
spersed with receptions and social occasions. Mr. Barnard returned to Farnham a
better man; his first action was to take it out on the local rats—and his expenses,
doubtless, out of the local rates.

The War Service Tribunal had wound up their affairs and published their
report. They had dealt with 1,333 applications for exemption from military
service; there had been 131 appeals against the Tribunal's decisions, most of
which had failed. Their unpleasant duty had been carried out with no regrettable
incidents, and they held a letter from the Prime Minister personally thanking
them.

The Chamber of Commerce was represented by Mr. J. E. Spencer, the draper
in The Borough, on the local committee formed under the Profiteering Act
(19 August 1919) to halt the post-war tide of inflation . . . Mr. Figg had reason
to believe that some of the demobbed men were disappointed with the town's
welcome on their return . . . The Council toyed briefly with the idea of turning
to mechanical transport. Horses were on their way out. The surveyor was voted

an allowance of £50 a year and told to get a motorcycle . . . Gifts of strips of frontage in Weybourne Road, from Mrs. Hewitt at the Duke of York and Major-General Higgins of the Elm Tree (was he the wartime air-ace?), enabled improvements to be carried out in that road.

People in Hale complained that sewage matter was being dumped on certain land in Alma Lane, but were told that this was standard practice until such time as drainage was introduced. Moves had already been made in that direction, for approximately two-thirds of the scheme had been costed, at £19,738, and the Council were awaiting loan sanction for this.

Miss E. M. Clarke, Head of the Girls' Grammar School, retired on 1 November after 16 years. Her successor, chosen in December, was Miss C. N. Williams, second in command of the Colston's Girls School at Bristol. There had been 98 applications—opportunities for women were few. It has been said that Miss Williams, during her six-year stay in Farnham, lifted the school out of its Victorian austerity into the 20th-century.

The observance of Remembrance Day on 11 November was a solemn occasion which was reported in the *Herald* under the heading 'The Great Silence'. Many people had gathered in Castle Street, others were in churches, but most were going about their ordinary activities. At 11 o'clock, however, hooters at the brewery and the waterworks sounded; all traffic stopped and people halted where they were. A deep silence descended. The silence, commented the *Herald,* had been the King's suggestion, probably that of his advisers. Strangely—for Mr. Langham usually had his ear to the ground—no mention was made of James Alfred Eggar.

The Council were still reluctant to lower their sights from the uneconomic five-roomed houses planned on the Farnham Gravel Company's seven-acre plot of land in Hale, and wondering whether to convert the abandoned army huts in Hungry Hill as a temporary measure. Mr. Parker, a government inspector, came down on 8 December to sort things out. He advised the Council to forget the whole thing, and, instead, buy four small sites that he had nosed out—one at Lawday House (for 10 houses); Lamport's land (six); Major-General Higgins's land at the Elm Tree (eight); and Knight's land at Badshot Lea (eight)—32 houses altogether. Furthermore, he, Parker, was prepared to sanction two-bedroomed dwellings as a means of keeping the cost down. He didn't fancy the huts, but the Council could submit a scheme if they wished. And so, Farnham passed into the 'Roaring 'Twenties'.

1920

We have no intention of letting Farnham Castle pass either to the
Jesuits or to an an American millionaire.
Lord Selborne: Diocesan Conference, 11 October 1920

IN JANUARY, the Happy New Year wishers had on paper a fairly strong case.
Peace had taken root; already the politicians were promising that, just round
the corner, a New Age was approaching which would bring nothing but good to
all mankind. Just round the corner was the Farnham Council's 17-point
manifesto. The Council picked one out of the hat: it was No. 1—housing of the
working classes. It was true to say that some progress had already been made in
this field. They had bought Sheephouse for £1,161 5s. 6d., and accepted
Goddard and Sons' estimate of £28,443, for the building of the 34 houses.
Roadworks and sewers (tender of E. S. Crow) would cost £1,759 0s. 6d.; fences,
£124 10s. 0d.; fees, £1,271; legal costs and contingencies, £292 4s. 0d. A total
of £33,051, or £972 per house. At a little ceremony on 16 March 1920,
Councillor Miss Miller cut the first sod. Then Goddards asked for a 12 per cent.
increase in their contract price.

1920 was to prove a bumper year for inflation, making nonsense of the
£100,000's worth of schemes already on the surveyor's drawingboard. In
January, labourers' wages shot up from 11d. to 1s. 1d. an hour, and bricklayers'
from 1s. 2d. to 1s. 4d., while carters' weekly wages rose from 45s. to 50s. In
Hale, Caesar Bros. were asking £2,555 for converting seven discarded army huts
into 14 dwellings, and W. J. Wilkinsons £1,655 for turning the old cookhouse
into three tenements, and the N.C.O.s mess into four. The War Office wanted a
rent of £180 yearly for the site. The file was sent to the Government's Housing
Commissioner for his reluctant approval.

Farnham's M.P., Arthur Samuel, was gaining a reputation as a 'very live wire',
setting the Thames on fire with what *The Times* described as 'powerful speeches'.
In boxing circles, Farnham's 'Boy' McCormick was gaining an even bigger
reputation. Cancelling an Australian tour, the 'Boy' was now knocking them for
six in America. He had beaten 'Gunboat' Smith in four rounds, a feat which had
labelled him as the future hope of British boxing, and had gone on to vanquish
Frank Farmer of Tacoma. In 14 fights, he had not lost a decision. It was said
that he had challenged Joe Beckett, who was none too willing to accept.

Tom Mitchell of 'The Lindens' promised sand for the baseworks of the war memorial in Gostrey, and George Murrell said he would give plants. Harold Falkner took a keen interest, for his drawings for the Southport memorial (at a cost of £14,000, reputedly the largest in the country) had won him second prize in the architects' competition. The two flags which had adorned the entrance to the Waverley Abbey Hospital were presented to the Tilford parish church and placed, one on each side, at the west window of the north aisle. The town learnt that Nurse L. Reeves had been appointed a health visitor by the Borough of Yeovil.

Dr. George (Badger) Brown, science master at the Grammar School, retired. He had become a legend in his lifetime. 'Dear Old Badger! I can see him now', reminisces one Old Boy, a pupil in 1904–1909, 'sailing round the lab. armed with a metre-rule, striking out wildly at some impudent youngster who had baited him into a state of impotent fury. I was terrified of him at first, but later on I grew to admire him tremendously; a brilliant man, who was absolutely wasted trying to teach young ruffians like us.' Dr. Brown was one of those who personified the Farnham Grammar School. In those days the story of an anciently endowed grammar school was in effect the story of the town it served. This was particularly so in Farnham, where an intruder from a rival, though no less distinguished school, was never completely admitted to the exclusive circle. Mr. H. S. Shelton, B.Sc., became the new science master; he came from Hastings Grammar School.

With effect from midnight on Friday, 16 January, prohibition was enforced in America. Over here, this caused consternation in drinking circles and a flutter of hope amongst the temperance societies, total abstinence advocates, and the stricter churches. What the States did usually spread to Britain; we teetered on the brink for long anxious months before common sense prevailed; it was a near thing. The Farnham Licensing Justices were not, in the main, entirely opposed to public drinking; they just thought that too much of it went on. They had caused a nation-wide sensation during Edward VII's reign by ruthlessly thinning out the town's admittedly over-generous quota of pubs, and were ever on the lookout for further closures. In February, F. W. Hook, landlord of *The Feathers* in Lower Church Lane, died, and his widow sought to have the licence transferred to her. At about the same time, J. W. Coute of the *Red Lion* inn, which formed part of Farnham United Breweries' premises in Red Lion Lane, applied for the renewal of his licence. The magistrates refused both applications, and referred the files to the Compensation Authority.

Major-General E. M. Perceval was refused permission to erect a hut in Brightwells for the 3rd Farnham Troop of Boy Scouts. This was later built in Guildford Road and opened by Baden-Powell in person . . . Councillor Baker retired from the Council as a member for Hale . . . They entered the New Age with the purchase of a Ford one-ton truck chassis, with pneumatic front tyres and solid back ones, for £350. Sturt and Goatcher fitted the body for £64. George Sturt, now out of the business and writing, lamented the passing of the horse and cart. The *Herald* of 14 February reviewed his latest book—*William Smith, Potter and Farmer* (Chatto and Windus, 6s.). 'Playing at authorship', Sturt understated his abundant talent. He possessed the three essentials—an urge to write, something to write about, and a discerning publisher.

On 30 March, a third of the electorate went to the polls. Results in the two wards were as follows:

Town Ward

Arthur James Barnard, 'Burlington House', South Street .. .. 573 (re-elected)
William George Day, 1 St Mary's Villas, St George's Road 140
George Murrell, 'Albany House', West End Grove .. .. .. 769 (re-elected)
Arthur George Ransom, 'Highwick', Fairfield .. .. 614 (re-elected)
Henry Sanders, 'Sanfield', Lancester Avenue 338
Gertrude Anne Stroud, 'Elmsleigh', Station Hill .. .. 383 (elected)

Hale Ward

Charles Edward Atkins, 4 Vale Cottages, Heath End .. .. .. 238 (re-elected)
Herbert Edward Bide, Alma Nurseries 105
John Hawkes, 'Mayfield Cottage', Upper Hale .. .. 139 (elected)
George Langrish, Badshot Farm 60
Ernest James Varney, Upper Hale .. .. 110 (elected)

In Mrs. Stroud, Councillor Miss Miller thus gained female support. To have been the sole lady member must have been a daunting experience. Mrs. Stroud was the wife of William Stroud, the Grammar School master.

With the summer looming up, the Aldershot and District Traction Company, formed in 1912 for the purpose of jolting passengers from A to B., advertised 'char-a-banc' excursions to seaside towns and inland places of interest, such as Hampton Court or Windsor. There was, enthused the *Herald,* no more delightful way of seeing the countryside than in one of the company's 'new and luxurious vehicles'. For those unable to afford holidays, a day's outing to Southsea or Bognor, at a return fare of 10s., often brought a first glimpse of the sea. In the company of about two dozen fellow adventurers, one could rattle uncertainly and noisily along the narrow Sussex roads in open-topped, hard-seated boneshakers. The Traction Co. had by now more or less staked their claim within a wide radius of Aldershot, elbowing smaller operators off the road, and the bus was the accepted means of travel between neighbouring towns and villages. Perhaps it had made its debut too impatiently, before noise could be eliminated and passenger comfort introduced—prompting writers like A. D. Godley to remark:

> What is this that roareth thus?
> Can it be a Motor Bus?
> Yes, the smell and hideous hum
> Indicat Motorem bum.

Loan sanction was duly received for the purchase of Brightwells, and possession was fixed for 24 June. Mrs. Jupp, the tenant, was given notice to quit and the councillors began making plans for the conversion of the house and grounds to public use.

Mr. J. H. Wilcox died in April, aged sixty-three. He had come from Portsmouth 35 years earlier, and joined Abrahams's outfitters business in South Street, taking it over two years later. His son, Arthur, succeeded him.

A Miss Seawell, deceased, of 'Marelands', Bentley, willed a gift of a water-colour by Samuel Seawell, dated 1849, entitled 'Grindstone Oak', together with a screen and other articles, for safe keeping until they could be placed in a museum. The painting depicted a mere skeleton of the tree, which had once stood in Alice Holt. It was reputed, in Gilbert White's *Selborne,* to have been the largest oak in the country, measuring 34ft. round the trunk at a height of seven feet.

A senior assistant in the Clerk's department was appointed in April. He was Arthur Albert Minns, and he came from the Malden and Coombe Council offices. He was to stay in Farnham, as so many others have, for the rest of his life.

Farnham's Petition for Incorporation had reached the Lords of His Majesty's Most Honourable Privy Council and was listed for consideration on 23 June. The relevant points were discussed by the General Purposes Committee of the Surrey County Council—i.e., that the townspeople wanted it despite the apparent certainty of a rise in the rates: that Farnham at one time was a borough; that a higher status would give added protection against 'invasion' from across the border (especially important since Aldershot was on the brink of becoming a borough); and the current likelihood of a further extension of the Urban District. All, one would have thought, weighty factors in Farnham's favour. Yet the General Purposes Committee saw fit to withhold their support. The Privy Councillors did like to feel that, in matters referred to them, the locals were in one accord. They now postponed consideration to allow time for the two local authorities to see eye to eye.

At a special service at St Paul's Cathedral on 24 June, the Rev. Neville Talbot was inducted as Bishop of Pretoria. He said goodbye to Farnham from the pulpit of the parish church on 25 July before departing for the Transvaal, and spoke of the racial differences he expected to encounter.

Mr. R. M. Sargent was appointed as sanitary inspector, and commenced duties on 22 June. His duties had been severed from those of the surveyor, because of Mr. Cass's now heavy commitments. Owners of land at Weybourne and Badshot Lea, earmarked for council houses, were unco-operative, and the Council considered compulsory purchase. To raise funds for local authorities' housing programmes, the government inaugurated a Housing Bond Campaign. On 8 June, a local meeting at the Corn Exchange, chaired by Dr. Hussey, was addressed by Sir Kingsley Wood, M.P., Parliamentary Secretary to the Ministry of Health. Arthur Samuel, M.P., was also present. Meanwhile sanction for the Hale drainage loan had come through, enabling the main contract with Hardy and Co. to be signed, but not soon enough to avoid an increase in the amount because of a threatened strike by that company's workforce. A Mr. J. D. Chassereau was adopted as Clerk of Works.

The Bishop and Mrs. Talbot were presented by the councillors on 29 June with an illuminated address on the occasion of their golden wedding . . . In Gostrey Meadow, people were walking the grass thin, for paths still had to be laid down and ashphalted.

F. W. Charley, the postmaster, retired. The Post-Master General announced his intention not to replace him, but to make Farnham's post office a sub-office of Aldershot's. Farnham saw red; without wasting time, they went straight to the top with the request that Arthur Samuel, M.P., should lodge a protest. The P.M.G. gave way. The *Herald* was jubilant—'Although Aldershot and Farnham are but three miles apart, they are as far asunder as the poles in all things that count in local life'. Mr. C. A. Hall of Birkenhead came in August as the new postmaster.

Workmen digging a manhole near Coxbridge discovered an old road six feet down, built of flints embedded in one-foot thick cement, which was identified as part of the Roman road from London to Winchester.

'Boy' McCormick, meanwhile, was commuting to and fro across the Atlantic, gathering laurels on each trip. On a recent arrival in the States, he was greeted by hundreds of fans eager to grasp his 'mighty mitt', whilst a Canadian pipe band played a 'bally blow'. He had outboxed all opponents America could put up, including Willie Meehan, the 'roly-poly San Franciscan', and was aspiring to challenge the winner of the coming Levinsky–Carpentier fight. He was not sure about being free to put in an appearance at the August Bank Holiday revels at Broomleaf, though he was keeping December open for his coming-of-age celebrations in the old home-town.

But a matter of real concern gripped the minds of the people during the summer of 1920—it concerned the future of Farnham Castle. Rumours had leaked for some time from the closed fastnesses of the Winchester Diocesan Board that its huge geographical area might be split and a new Diocese created. Now this was a foregone conclusion which needed only the approval of the Diocesan Conference, due in October 1920, to make it a *fait accompli*. The Bishop of Winchester had always lived in Farnham, so as to be central to his district; he did so traditionally, but with reluctance, for the castle was an ancient building with no mod-cons to speak of, and cripplingly expensive to maintain. Bishop Talbot had been heard to remark that he lived there 'by generosity', 'that his successor would prefer something more modern and economic and preferably within walking distance of the Cathedral'. In the words of the Rev. E. H. Firth, giving tongue in Aldershot, Farnham Castle looked like becoming a white elephant; the 'pile of brick and rubble' would be better out of the way; it would be an act of providence if it could be removed by an earthquake. This incensed Farnham. An elephant had a long memory; this one, for instance, could remember a long line of bishops in residence since the 12th century—700 years before Aldershot had first donned army-issue nappies. In the proposed new diocese, Farnham would find itself on the western fringe. The bishop's residence would be within the curtilage of the new cathedral when it was built. During the weeks leading up to the Conference there was much speculation as to where this would be. Strong contenders for the honour were Croydon (a County Borough) and Kingston (seat of the County Council), but people everywhere favoured Guildford, because of its central position. And throughout the summer, the people of Farnham asked of each other—what was to become of the castle?

In August, the War Memorial Committee reported that some £900 had been raised by public subscription and added that they had come to the end of their capabilities on that front. More money was needed; the *Herald* accused the public of a lack of gratitude towards the brave soldiers who had fallen during the war. The architect had finished his design of the cross, and, in October, Major Patrick's tender in the sum of £400, was accepted by the Council for its erection in Gostrey. Work was commenced in December, and was expected to take about three months. Patrick's also landed a War Graves Commission contract for the supply of 400 headstones for British soldiers' graves in France. Each stone was to be inscribed with the name and number, the crest of the dead man's regiment, and an emblem to his religion. If they wished, relatives could add a personal inscription.

The houses at Sheephouse were coming along well. There were snags, of course —materials were held up by strikes, and plasterers, it was said, could earn as much as 2s. an hour on jobs elsewhere—but in August the Council advertised for tenants. By October, 18 of the houses had been tiled, and 30 had their brickwork up. Rents were provisionally fixed at 17s. a week inclusive. In November eight were ready for occupation; the fences were up and the plants in. By the end of the year, 10 of the houses were occupied. The Council were proud of their copy-book estate.

The rooms in Brightwells House were being sorted out for their future public purposes. A Mr. Kemp was taken on as gardener and his wife as caretaker; they were given living quarters in the house. The St John Ambulance Association were allowed to keep their motor ambulance in the coach house until such time as the Council might need it for their Ford truck.

The Chamber of Commerce tried to interest the Council in the growth of light industries in the town, but such palavers had little effect . . . The Traction Company increased their fares, and started a new service between Aldershot and Alton . . . The planning applications in August included one for the Lion Brewery Memorial Hall in Babbs Mead—which was passed provided the building of it would not interrupt work on Council houses. Harold Falkner was arguing about his bill for £164 14s. 0d. in respect of architect's fees to date for the Hale Ward housing schemes. These were still proving awkward; Caesar Bros. had opted out of the old army hut conversions, and Mr. Wilkinson undertook to do them all.

Swain and Jones sought leave to install a Bowser long-distance, self-measuring petrol pump at their East Street garage. This was agreed, providing the swing arm was at least eight feet above the pavement . . . Further changing accommodation was necessary at the swimming baths before boys up to the age of 14, and accompanied by their sisters, would be allowed to bathe during 'ladies only' hours.

Government subsidies became available to the builders of houses in the private sector, subject to a limitation in cost. The subsidies ranged from £230 to £260. Often the Council, who issued the necessary certificates of entitlement, helped in borderline cases to bring the estimated cost within the prescribed limit with a few deft touches.

In October, the Defence of the Realm Act was exhumed to deal with the coalminers' strike. Fuel supplies were again controlled, and street lighting reduced by 50 per cent. Just like wartime all over again.

Sir Johnston Forbes-Robertson lectured at the Church House on 15 October on *The Heroes of Shakespeare* . . . 'Brewer' White, Farnham's wicketkeeper, and his team-mate, F. Hutchings, were selected for a trial match at the Oval on 31 August, playing for the Young Professionals against the Young Amateurs . . . J. S. Holroyd of 'Sunnyhurst', East Street, set up a motor-cycling world record at Brooklands on 20 September, doing an average of 50.19 m.p.h. on a Blackburne 22 c.c. machine over a distance of 451 miles 1,207 yards in nine hours.

At the Winchester Diocesan Conference on 11 October, it was unanimously resolved to divide the existing see and a committee was formed to consider ways and means and report back in six months' time. The future of Farnham Castle was discussed at length. Delegates wondered how it could be used for Church purposes, rather than letting it fall into private hands. The ancient ties between castle and town, and the freedom with which bishops had always allowed the townspeople to use the park were now in jeopardy.

The bowling green and tennis courts scheduled for Brightwells at an estimated outlay of £400 met with opposition, for the cost had risen in the meantime to £1,050. This was disappointing, for the councillors had been looking forward to a grand opening in the spring. Not to be outdone, they borrowed the money from the Law Union and Rock Insurance Co., Ltd., at 6¾ per cent., repayable partly in 20 years, the rest in 60 years.

Lionel H. Smith moved his hairdressers' business from 103 West Street to 1 The Borough . . . James Eggar, M.B.E., son of Farnham's auctioneer and estate agent, was made a C.B.E. in recognition of his important contribution in the Office of Works to the defence of London during the war. Whilst not mentioning J. Alfred Eggar by name, the *Herald* of 13 November did cautiously venture the following information regarding the Armistice Day two-minute silence:

> Now that this solemn observance has become part of the national life, it is interesting to recall that it was in Castle Street, Farnham, that such an interval of silence, during which the thoughts of the people might go out to their brethren overseas, was, we believe, first instituted.

In 1920, the ritual was more formally organised by having the Hants Cadets on hand to sound on their bugles 'The Last Post' and the 'Reveille'. There was a large gathering of councillors and townspeople in Castle Street.

The 131st Venison Dinner took place at the *Bush* hotel on 18 November, with Ernest Jackson in the chair. There was some talk on the town's failure to become a borough.

The surveyor reported good progress on the re-surfacing of roads in the district following the havoc wrought by army traffic. Mr. E. Lord, caretaker at the Council offices, was made road foreman, in succession to Mr. Greenaway, who had left for Woking, at £3 10s. 0d. a week, plus cycle allowance. An indication of the seriousness of the prevailing unemployment is shown by the fact that there were no fewer than 56 applications to fill Lord's place as office caretaker. Mr. B. F. Bryant got the job, at £2 10s. 0d., and a cottage in Brightwells. Freddie Bryant had done his bit in the war, and, like most soldiers, had a fund of memories. One concerned a troop train somewhere in France during an unscheduled halt, when many of the passengers took the opportunity to hop off and obey the call of nature. Their undignified scramble, in various stages of undress, to catch up with the train as it moved off was a delight to the eye.

Mr. Cass had been caught out doing a private job of road surfacing for someone living outside Farnham, whereas, in his terms of employment, he was required to devote the whole of his time to the Council. He promised never to do so again.

The lead-up to Christmas was wet and warm—the rainiest and mildest within recent years, according to Colonel George Chrystie of 'Shortheath Lodge', unfailing editor of the *Herald's* weekly weather record. Yet, despite this, shopping was brisk and the people went through the festive motions. Even the workhouse was gaily decorated for the occasion.

1921

That this Council respectfully urge upon the Government the grave necessity for stringent economy in administration in their various departments owing to the gravity of the financial position of this country.

Farnham Urban District Council: February 1921

AS NEVILLE CHAMBERLAIN once put it—in war, whichever side may call itself the victor, there are no winners, but all are losers. When the drums were beaten, it had been 'Thank you, Mr. Atkins', now it was back to 'Tommy this and Tommy that and Tommy go away'. But Thomas wouldn't. On all sides he could see evidence of the affluent world from which he was barred. The newspaper advertisements aimed motor cars at the rich at anything from £100 to £500! 'Why let the new motor tax deter you?', exhorted Heath and Wiltshires, whose 1921 G.N. was guaranteed to do 60 miles to the gallon and cost only £276 12s. 6d. Ladies needed fur coats when motoring on chilly days, said Whites of Aldershot, who had a large selection of them. He had only to walk along the golden mile of The Borough and West Street to notice the goodies in shop windows, the opulent banks, the exclusive *Bush* hotel, the glitter of gold and silver in Borelli's shop.

The rich were not without a conscience, of course. They nursed a conventional sense of gratitude towards the lads killed in the war, and had contributed money to pay for Mr. W. C. Watson's expensive memorial cross which, in mid-January, went on display in Patricks' window in East Street. The Council were advertising for the names of those who had died. The list, so far, contained some 202 names— 64 in the town area, 105 in Hale, and 33 in Badshot Lea. By the time the list closed, so that Patricks' might set about engraving the names on the panels, the number had risen to two hundred and sixty-seven. That was about 13.3 per cent. of the 2,000-odd men of the urban district who had served in the forces, or 2 per cent. of the district's entire population. Lieutenant-General the Earl of Cavan, K.P., G.C.M.G., K.C.B., M.V.O., G.O.C. Aldershot, was booked to unveil the cross at 3.50 p.m. on 10 April 1921. Gostrey Meadow was closed at 1 o'clock, and the relatives of the dead men were allowed in before the general public. A band of the Royal Artillery played; all the top brass of Church and laity were present—everyone who mattered, except those whose names were on the panels.

Watson's 23ft. high, hexagonal, Portland stone monument was a handsome work, befitting its purpose well. One compelling effect of a war memorial, even after a lapse of 60 years, is that, whenever you happen to pass one, you know at once what it is and why it is there, and according to your philosophy, you are consumed by a sadness or by a revulsion against the events responsible for it being there. This cross bore the arms of Farnham together with a pelican, symbolic of the mythical bird which plucked its breast in order to give blood to its offspring. The captions ran: IN GRATEFUL MEMORY OF THE MEN OF FARNHAM WHO GAVE THEIR LIVES FOR THEIR COUNTRY, and WHAT I GAVE I HAVE. At the last minute, the Earl of Cavan could not make it because of military duties arising out of the industrial crisis. Major-General Sir Walter Campbell, i/c Administration, Aldershot Command, deputised. The band played; a choir sang under the direction of Mr. G. C. Macklin; solemn tributes were paid to the fallen; there were pregnant silences, and here and there tears. Thus Farnham got its war memorial—two years, five months and five days after ceasefire.

But right now in the early weeks of 1921 it was the living, not the dead, who were causing all the ferment. For many ex-servicemen were still without jobs; others fortunate enough to be in work bitterly complained that they were not getting a living wage. Flag-days were held in Farnham; the do-gooders placed £500 at the Council's disposal for financing job-creation schemes. Some of the money went on paying unemployed men to paint the Council offices and renovate the caretaker's cottage in Brightwells.

Outwardly, life went on as usual. The Diocesan Board were now embarked on meetings to consider (a) the boundary of the new see, and (b) the fate of Farnham Castle. The Farnham Parochial Church Council set up a watch committee to monitor everything said about (b) . . . Mr. W. H. Osborne, the retiring stationmaster, was replaced by Mr. H. J. Towning from Feltham . . . The London Joint County and Midland Bank opened a branch at 33 The Borough, with Mr. C. P. Lewis from Cardiff as manager . . . Mr. R. M. Sargent delighted the Council by qualifying as an inspector of meats and other foods . . . Mr. P. A. Foster, the rat-catcher, asked threepence for each one destroyed . . . Councillors Clist and Varney raised the dust by ventilating the fact that much of the Council's business was conducted with local firms in which certain councillors had a financial interest.

Mr. Midgeley Taylor reported favourably on the Hale Ward drainage work to date. There was no shortage of labourers for this; they were two a penny. A further loan of £17,000 was necessary for the final phases of the scheme; government refused sanction for this because of the crisis, but did agree to sufficient expenditure to enable the sewers already laid to be brought into use. The Minister was reminded that the Council had originally made application as far back as 1914 and was told that any interruption of the work would mean that part of the Hale Ward would have to continue using earth closets or cesspits, also that the workforce would have to be disbanded. Mr. Chassereau, the Clerk of Works, left for a post in Shanghai, and Leonard Starling, Mr. Cass's assistant, took over the job. Six of the old army huts at Hale had now been converted, with six more promised shortly. Tenants were selected at rents of 10s. a week. The oval at Sheephouse was being cleared of builders' rubble and levelled for grassing.

William Kingham and Sons, owners of the ancient *Lion and Lamb* building, were quite sure that they had 'a very interesting old place' on their hands and were planning to restore it. Robert and Alfred Kingham were enthusiastically encouraged by 'the unofficial Town Restorer', Mr. C. E. Borelli.

A cow being driven to market took a wrong turning and poked its head through Mr. Bentall's side window in Bear lane . . . Ian Hay (John Ian Beith), the popular writer, was booked to lecture in the Church House on 11 March . . . John Victor Macmillan, who had commenced his career as a curate at Farnham parish church under Canon Thory Gage Gardiner, and was currently vicar of Kew, was appointed Archdeacon of Maidstone and a Canon of Canterbury Cathedral. He was later to come back as a Bishop of Guildford.

The report of the Medical Officer of Health for 1920 listed his inspections at 24 factories, 33 workshops, 18 bakeries, seven slaughterhouses, five laundries, one lodging-house, three houses in which outworkers lived, and 22 cowsheds, dairies and milk-selling places. Of these, 18 factories, 29 workshops and 11 bakeries were found to be up to standard, and defects in others had since been rectified. The abattoirs were in good condition, but only one of the laundries. Of the milk centres, not one was found to be in first-class order—10 were dirty and nine had dung heaps close by. The situation was a danger to health and called for action under the Milk and Dairies Consolidation Order 1915.

Councillor Barnard resigned membership for reasons unstated and paid the two-guinea 'customary fine'. John Hawkes, member for Hale, had been absent from meetings 'without cause of illness or other approved reason' for more than the statutory six consecutive months (he had attended only three of a possible 21 Council meetings) and his seat on the Council was therefore declared vacant under the Local Government Act 1894. Those due to retire in 1921 were Councillors Bentall, Borelli, Baigent and Mitchell, the first two of whom were to seek re-election. Mr. Baigent crowned his valuable public service with a seat on the Magistrates Bench. Mr. Mitchell was warmly thanked for his 18 years' stint as a councillor. He was now an ill man and, on 23 April, he died at the age of seventy-two. His 40 years in Farnham had been fruitful. Son of Frank Mitchell of Capel, Dorking, where he had learnt the trades of carpentry and of brick and tile manufacturing, he formed the Farnham Flint, Gravel and Sand Company, and was instrumental in opening up the local gravel and sand industries—a welcome successor to the dwindling hop cultivation. Tom Mitchell had brick and tile works at Crondall, potteries at Old Park, and lime works at Seale. He farmed Costleys Farm in the Tilford Road. He played a big part in developing

Farnham as an elite residential centre, especially on the south side of the town, where his own house, 'The Lindens', was one of the first to be built in the Great Austins Estate. All this, as well as being a councillor and an ardent Congregationalist. His widow, Mrs. Miriam Mitchell, duly added his portrait to the Council Chamber gallery. At the election on 2 April, no poll was necessary in the Hale Ward, for only three candidates came forward for the three offered seats.

Town Ward

Eliza Barnard, 'Burlington House', South Street	264
Hamilton Kendall Bentall, 'Rozel', Tilford Road	620 (re-elected)
Charles Ernest Borelli, 35 The Borough	656 (re-elected)
John Lewis Jones, 'Cheveley', High Park Road	644 (elected)
Edward Maxwell Perceval, The Grange	608 (elected)
Henry Sanders, 'Sanfield', Lancaster Avenue	506 (elected)
William George Taphouse, 45 Downing Street	463

Hale Ward

Alfred Rose Robins, Park Farm, Badshot Lea
Ernest James Varney, 'Beverley', Upper Hale
Georgina Charlotte Watkins, 'Heath End House'

There was some surprise that Mrs. Barnard came bottom of the poll; she had been expected to make it on the strength of her husband's record (some suggested that he had resigned in order to make room for her); however, Women's Lib again triumphed with Mrs. Watkins of Heath End. Councillor of the Year award went to George Murrell, with a 100 per cent. attendance at council and committee meetings; Mrs. Stroud was a close second, with 95.6 per cent. Mr. Murrell became Chairman for 1921/2, with Councillor Swansborough as his deputy.

The coal miners' strike broke out on 31 March and went on and on until 4 August. There was nothing that the government could do under the Coal Strike Emergency Powers Act 1920, apart from rationing fuel in diminishing lumps to householders and maintaining minimal supplies for essential purposes. In the days before electricity became the chief source of energy, the effects of a coal strike showed up in the most unlikely places. In June, for instance, the *Herald* apologised for a reduction in format because the production of the newspaper was dependent on gas.

In May, it was learnt that Noel ('Boy') McCormick had at last persuaded Joe Beckett to accept his challenge for the British heavyweight title. In doing so, it was said that the 'Boy' was conceding about 36 pounds in weight, though his superiority in speed and skill was generally expected to compensate for this. Having once beaten Beckett, McCormick planned to challenge Carpentier for the European title. He was thought to have a fair chance; Jack Dempsey, who knew the 'Boy' well—they shared a house in the States—was all for him. The fight with Beckett was arranged for Monday, 12 September 1921 at the Royal

Opera House, Covent Garden. Throughout the summer, Farnham's attention switched from cricket, tennis and bowls to the unaccustomed sport of prize-fighting. For 'Farnham's Champion', as the townspeople preferred to call him (with his approval) had decided to train in the town, and the Church House was put at his disposal. Here, watched by adoring fans, McCormick sparred with minor stars in the boxing firmament under the watchful eyes of his trainer and masseur, George Dipple of Aldershot. McCormick, it was said, was sometimes asked by reporters and others why he had adopted Farnham as his pad, rather than live it up in the metropolis. His answer was that he had a strong dislike of the kind of lionising and publicity found in large cities. Farnham was quiet yet cheerful, and the people friendly but undemanding. He had made a lot of friends and he liked the town so much that in July he persuaded his parents to come over from Ireland. He bought a house, 'Uplands', Ridgway Road, which he re-named 'Ringside', as the family home; the *Daily Chronicle* described it as 'an estate at Farnham'. Excitement mounted as September approached. Concern was expressed about McCormick's lack of weight, though he became the general favourite, and, in particular, the darling of the 12,000 men, women and children of Farnham.

Having patched up the wartime ravages in roads through Heath End and Weybourne, work delegated to the local authority by the County Council (who now reimbursed the Council to the tune of £2,537), the Highways Committee turned their attention to the streets in the town centre. Always high up in the repertoire of Harold Falkner's conversation pieces was the state of the road outside his house at 24 West Street. In the summer it was a dust bowl, and in the winter a sea of mud. The Council decided on dressing the street with asphaltic macadam. They then took a long hard look at Crondall Lane. This was routine from long ago, for the narrow, windy lane only led to a village in Hampshire, passing Harold Falkner's Dippenhall relations on the way, and it hardly seemed worthwhile spending good Surrey money on it. But now, with the decline of hop-growing releasing land for residential development, Crondall Lane would soon require the treatment.

The clinic at Brightwells was now in full swing, the quarterly report claiming treatment of some 593 babies . . . The Sanitary Inspector claimed a fairly average total of 80 lbs. of unsound beef, and 7 lbs. of diseased pork during the month of March . . . Twelve huts at Upper Hale were now converted, and 10 occupied. They were named Gorseland Cottages.

Suggestions were invited from tennis players as to the feasibility of forming a Brightwells tennis club, with the exclusive use of the courts, say, on three days a week. Four offers were received, ranging from £6 to £20. There was feeling over this undemocratic use of the courts, but the £20 bid was accepted by eight votes to seven, for exclusive use on Mondays, Wednesdays, and Fridays. The swimming bath, due to re-open on 30 May, had a deficiency of £71 on the last season's trading. Season tickets for the 1921 season were priced at 10s. 6d. adults, and

5s. for children; casual bathers, sixpence and threepence. Mr. G. May was appointed as superintendent.

Mr. George Elphick, one of Farnham's longest-rooted tradesmen, died on 19 May, aged seventy-seven. He came from Walham Green in 1881 and bought the drapers' and outfitters' business of Chilton and Scammell at 13 West Street, which he extended. A churchwarden and staunch follower of the Conservative Club, he was a notable swimmer and a founder of the Bush Bowls Club. He left one son and three daughters.

As from 12 June, postal deliveries on Sundays were discontinued . . . The licence of the *Surrey Arms* in East Street was snuffed out by the Justices . . . New bus routes brought Upper Hale and Badshot Lea into touch with civilisation . . . There was planning application for a billiards room at the *Railway* hotel.

Major-General Edward Perceval, recently elected to the Council, took up an appointment in Berlin and was unable to fulfil his obligations as a councillor. He was told that he should either resign, paying the two-guinea fine, or absent himself from meetings and be thrown out with ignominy. In the same letter, he was congratulated on his appointment and his departure regretted! In July the Council voted a £100 contribution towards the Grammar School's purchase of adjacent allotment land for the purpose of extending the school; also £230 for land at Badshot Lea as a future burial ground. There was a reprieve for the final phase of the Hale drainage works, helped by a drop in wages and cost of materials. The Broomleaf estate was re-sold in lots at a public auction on 19 July, but the Council again decided against buying the area traditionally used as a place of public entertainment. They also lost the opportunity of acquiring Lot 6, a piece of land in the Tilford Road which was already rented by them as allotments.

On 2 July, the Coal Emergency Committee (Councillors Clist, Mardon and Ransom) held an inquest on the local effects of the Great Miners' Strike. Stocks at the railway station on 7 April had been 53½ tons of household coal, 50 tons of steam coal, and 150 tons of anthracite. By 28 April, the household coal had dwindled to 16 tons; then the brewery had placed 100 tons at the disposal of the Urban and Rural Councils. This had been distributed in rations of ½ cwt. per week per household. By 20 June, the stock was down to 10 tons, and the ration reduced to ¼ cwt.; 6,500 permits had been issued. On 7 June the Committee had purchased a truckload of coke, and this had kept the bakeries going until the Gas Company, who had run out, were able to resume distribution. With the end of the strike now in sight, stocks were not quite exhausted.

Admiral Molteno submitted a plan in August by Harold Falkner for the blocking up of the front entrance of his house, 'Chestnuts', East Street, and making a new principal doorway at the side, in the private road acquired by the Council when buying Brightwells. The admiral already had a right of way, but this, the Council pointed out, would considerably increase his easement.

During his absence on holiday, discrepancies were discovered in the books of the Accounts Clerk, involving what appeared to be in the region of £250.

Accompanied by his father, the clerk attended a special Council meeting on 23 August. The father begged for merciful treatment and offered to repay whatever sum was missing. City accountants were called in to straighten out the 1920/1 accounts and advise on a foolproof system for the future. The guilty officer was sacked, but no further action taken against him. In November, out of 42 applicants, Mr. Richard Watson of Northwich was given the vacant post at a salary of £175 a year. With the passing of time, he became the Council's Treasurer.

A petition signed by 40 devotees prayed that the bowling-green be made available on Sundays. This caused a major storm, for the issue involved was of greater consequence than the mere winning of a right to enjoy a few pleasant and decorous games of bowls. The petition knocked at the foundations of orthodox traditionalism and was one town's expression of the public's interpretation of St Mark 2.27—'the sabbath was made for man, and not man for the sabbath'. It was an outcome of the war's emancipating influence and marked a breaking away from the stranglehold which the Church had exercised over the townspeople ever since civic affairs were first controlled in the Vestry under the benevolent yet watchful eyes of the clergy. Bowing to the popular trend, the Council sanctioned bowls between 2 p.m. and 6 p.m. on Sundays, a decision which wrung from the Rev. E. J. Buttifant of the Emmanuel church a copy of a resolution passed by his Select Vestry, recording profound regret. 'Such a course', declared the Select Vestry, 'is dishonouring to Almighty God, prejudicial to the best interests of the town and a deplorable example to the rising generation'.

The world stopped on 12 September for the epic fight at the Royal Opera House, Covent Garden, between Joe Beckett, heavyweight champion of Britain, and Noel ('Boy') McCormick of Farnham, Surrey, light-heavyweight champion of Britain and America. Many famous people were at the ringside, including Charlie Chaplin and Mum and Dad McCormick. In the 'Boy's' home town, Len Davies had arranged for a running commentary to be telephoned from Covent Garden to Oakley Brothers' paper shop in East Street. A crowd, estimated by a *Herald* reporter at between two and three thousand, gathered outside the shop. Beckett's superior weight told from the start. He roughed up McCormick a lot, especially in the fourth round with a block-buster which almost sent his opponent somersaulting over the ropes. But the 'Boy's' speedier and more skilful tactics were a joy to watch, and the crowd bellowed their unanimous support—especially one spectator who kept shouting 'Farnham, Farnham'. After the fourth round, the fight was mostly Beckett's. In addition to pressure from Joe, McCormick was feeling the effects of a hand injury received a few days earlier. Any other man would have retired, but he stuck it for 12 rounds. His was a magnificent achievement; the verdict was unpopular, and Beckett was almost lynched. Back in Farnham two days later, McCormick was given a hero's welcome. He would, he said, from the steps of the Church House, challenge Beckett to a return match. He was sorry to have let his Farnham friends down on this occasion. In the 1930s, when the McCormick legend had subsided, his trainer, George Dipple, lived with his Irish wife in Cambridge Place, off East Street. They were familiar habitués on the local scene. George had two main topics of conversation: 'Boy' McCormick, and 'I'm the only man round here who's been in the French Foreign Legion'. Both were good for a pint.

News was received in mid-September of the death of Bishop Neville Talbot's wife—formerly a Miss Eastwood of Chichester—in Pretoria. There were two children, a girl of two and a boy born recently . . . The Memorial Hall in Babbs Mead was ceremoniously opened on 21 September. In later years, when the brewery had departed from Farnham, the Council took it over, but eventually it became a white elephant . . . The decline in wage levels was quite remarkable. In October, the Council were able to reduce the wages of their workmen by 15 per cent. The Clerk and Surveyor also suffered the same treatment. Altogether, a saving of £500 a half-year, and a drop in the general rate poundage for the half-year from 3s. to 2s. 8d.

That intrepid body of volunteers, the Farnham Fire Brigade, was funded by the Urban (three-quarters) and Rural (quarter) Councils, plus contributions from Frensham (£35 p.a.), and Seale (£16 p.a.). The Joint Fire Brigade Committee met on 13 October to take stock and in particular to consider urgent steps to replace the somewhat run-down appliances. These consisted of—(1) fire escape, bought in 1893 (now out of date); (2) steamer, bought in 1896 (boiler condemned; (3) manual engine, bought in 1903 (in working order); (4) tractor, bought in 1917 (in running order).

The old Merryweather steamer, which had cost £479 in 1896, had done yeoman service. On the very day of its launching ceremony outside the Town Hall, presided over by Mrs. Fitzroy of Hale Place, it had been called to one of Farnham's worst-ever fires, and had limped home the next day badly blistered and with all the polish burnt off. The latest report of the Boiler Insurance Company had disclosed the fact that to all intents and purposes the boiler was worn out and no longer insurable; instructions had been given for it not be used. The tractor was an old type Delauney motor car, converted in 1917 by Heath and Wiltshires. It was used for carrying 1,000 feet of canvas hose, stand-pipes, fittings, and appliances, as well as towing the manual engine. With a full load, it had to draw about five tons, plus its own weight. Currently, it was the only means of traction available to the Brigade. It seemed possible that in the event of a fire, the Brigade would have to catch the next bus and pour buckets of water over the flames. A replacement boiler for the Merryweather would cost in the region of £300; moreover, it would have to be fitted to an appliance which was already 25 years old. The extravagant, though sensible, alternative was to lash out on a brand new up-to-date fire engine. They grasped the nettle firmly and voted for a 50 h.p. Merryweather chassis, fitted with a 300–350 gallon capacity plunger pump, with a 35–40-feet extension ladder—the lot to cost between £1,900 and

£2,000. This would be a complete fire-fighting unit. The existing equipment could be retained for emergencies.

J. W. Wright had a heart attack in his office on 12 October, generally thought to be due to overwork. At a special meeting on the following day, the Council considered a letter from Dr. Ealand which concerned the state of the Clerk's health and the need for his rest from duties over a period of three months. The doctor had safeguarded his patient's interests in stipulating that the Council should assure Mr. Wright of their combined confidence in him, and, secondly, that all financial work should be kept up-to-date so that, on returning to the office, he would find a clean slate. The Council responded with good grace and genuine sympathy; they straightway drew a cheque for three months' salary and wished the Clerk luck. The problem now was to find someone qualified and willing to act as *locum tenens.* Ernest Crundwell and the Clerk's son, G. F. Wright, couldn't manage it because of the effect on their law practices. The Urban District Council's Association were unable to help. They again approached Mr. G. F. Wright with an offer of a lump sum of £152 12s. 0d. if he and his partner, Mr. Kempson, would undertake to act as joint acting clerks. Kempson and Wright gave way provided that the sum offered was equal to the salary normally payable to Mr. Wright, senior, and that a separate accounts officer be engaged as they could not undertake to keep the books.

The British Labour Party was emerging as a force to be reckoned with, and continued on a local scale to show its face in orderly, law-abiding groups. The Farnham Party organised a meeting between the councillors and a deputation of unemployed, headed by a Mr. Dowling, on the subject of job-creation schemes. The Council were impressed, for the men had several good suggestions to make—cleaning out the river bed, widening Crondall Lane, repairing council houses, rounding-off dangerous corners at street junctions, re-surfacing roads, finishing off the Hale drainage works, etc. Relieving unemployment had the enthusiastic support of the government, who promised grants to local authorities equal to 65 per cent. of loan interest or 60 per cent. of wages. It was a fine way of getting things done on the cheap, though the initiative should have come from the Council. The package decided upon included corner improvements, the re-laying of an effluent drain in Water Lane, the widening of that lane, and the long-delayed making-up of roads in the Great Austins estate. Was it a sign that the war was receding in councillors' minds when it was voted that these jobs should be given to men with families, but not necessarily ex-service men?

Arthur Rose, the seed merchant in East Street, whose private residence, 'Montrose', South Street, abutted the Council's depot, reached the end of his endurance when a stone-drying and mixing plant, used in preparing the top-dressing for re-surfacing roads, was added to eccentric, and usually noisy, contraptions peculiar to a local authority. He got Ernest Jackson, his solicitor, to write to the Council and complain. Patience, implored the Council—the work would only take another four weeks; then the offending machine would be removed to a site on the sewage farm.

Mr. Hall, the postmaster, wanted to suspend the third delivery on Saturdays in order to provide further relaxation for his postmen. What cheek! Right on top of cutting out Sunday deliveries! When suggesting the pruning of Wednesday's third delivery instead, Mr. Hall was firmly told that he should take proper measures for the postmen's relaxation without curtailing public services.

Brigadier-General E. F. Brereton of 46 Castle Street, who had replaced Major-General Perceval as District Scout Commissioner, was given permission to erect a flagstaff in Castle Street to mark a saluting base at an inspection of the local Scouts and Guides on Sunday, 20 November, by Sir Robert and Lady Baden Powell.

The Farnham Ruridecanal Conferences were now debating whether Farnham should be included in the proposed new Diocese of Guildford, or remain in Winchester. Dramatic press headlines such as 'Has Farnham been Betrayed?' wrung anguished denials from Bishop Talbot, who took every opportunity of mentioning 'his dear beloved Farnham'.

John D. Wood and Co., the estate agents, reported that, at an auction held in London on 11 October, bidding for Moor Park had failed to reach the reserve.

A health week was launched from the pulpits on 9 October. On Monday, Sir Allan Perry lectured at the Church House on public health generally, with particular emphasis on the right sorts of food to eat. Mrs. Colman addressed the mums on Wednesday and, later in the week, spoke to Miss Murrell's Girls' Club. Major Coulon talked to the St James's Boys' Club, to an audience of two or perhaps three boys. Throughout the week, five of the town's six doctors visited schools. Reporting the event, the M.O.H. remarked that 'the inhabitants of the town did not appear to have any interest in the preservation of the Public Health'.

Despite urgent pleas, the Minister of Labour moved Farnham's employment exchange to Aldershot. Next to go to the rival town were the functions of the local War Pensions Sub-committee. Ironically, the County Council, who had turned down the Council's bid for higher status, were asking for help in opposing the Royal Commission's proposal to enlarge the area of the London County Council at the expense of a slice of Surrey, which threatened to take half the County's population and rateable value.

Wilkinson's final account for converting Gorseland Cottages came to £4,870. All the huts were now occupied . . . Loan sanction was received for the new fire engine in the sum of £1,400 . . . Surrey Federation of Chambers of Commerce grumbled about the increasing number of street traders (they did not even pay rates) and urged that these parasites should be brought within the provisions of the Registration of Business Names Act 1916.

Superintendent Arthur Simmonds resigned after 43 years in the Force, the last 24 as Farnham's police chief. He had done a lot to change the face of the town. In the famous Brewster Sessions of 1901/2, he had been the front man who, as each pub licence came before the Bench for renewal, declared 'I object, your Honour'. He became known throughout the country as the 'Universal Objector'. It was reliably stated that since 1901 he had objected on grounds of redundancy to some 40 pubs in his district. Another of his feats was the abolition of the Castle Street fairs. These traditional fairs, held three times a year from time immemorial, had got out of hand and were a source of contention between the Council and the Town Hall Company. Simmonds organised a campaign of police harassment, with the result that the fairs were relegated to Broomleaf Field in Waverley Lane. Arthur Simmonds was due to retire on 31 October. He did so in yet another blaze of publicity; for, on Sunday, 30 October, one James White, delivering milk at Mr. Ralph Carver's residence, 'The Highlands', Shortheath, discovered the body of a girl lying in the garden. Kathleen Violet Mansfield aged 14 years and 10 months, had been foully outraged and done to death. In service with Mrs. Stovold of Broomleaf Farm, she had visited a weekly auction sale at the Assembly Rooms on the Saturday and was, it seemed, on her way to her parents' home at Maffields, Shortheath, close to the scene of the murder. There were unconfirmed rumours involving a soldier or soldiers. Superintendent Simmonds, instead of spending his last day at the station, feted by gift-bearing constabulary, was chasing around the neighbourhood in the company of a Scotland Yard detective. He was even slightly injured in a car crash at Weybourne. It was not until two or three days later that he handed the case over to his successor, Mr. Lucas, from the Woking police. The new superintendent had already done time in Farnham as an inspector, and was therefore no stranger to the town. He walked straight into one of those spine-chilling murders which the press of the time delighted in dramatising for the enjoyment of readers.

In the tight, God-fearing little community of Farnham there was a growing feeling that, despite his fan rating, 'Boy' McCormick should not be allowed the use of the Church House. Opinion was divided—some of the clergy, in fact, argued that boxing was a healthy form of sport, just like tennis or football, or bowls, provided it wasn't on a Sunday. Furthermore, McCormick had charged the public entrance fees to come and watch him training, and had given the money to the Church House Trustees. But boxing was rough—they hit each other, didn't they? When the 'Boy'—or Mac, as he was more often called these days—announced that he would be fighting Ted (Kid) Lewis, the middle-weight, at the Royal Albert Hall on 17 November, and asked for the use of the Church House, his application was politely but firmly turned down. Mac understood and was quite happy about it, being the nice friendly person he was. The brewery let him use their Memorial Hall. This time, McCormick would have no disadvantage in weight. Both boxers had to weigh in on the night at not more than 11 stones 9 pounds; in fact, Mac would have to reduce a little. He had a new trainer, Rud White of Wales. Dipple had set up in business, on his slice of the Beckett fight proceeds, as a chiropodist and masseur in The Borough, though he continued to tend Mac's feet muscles. The 'Kid' had a formidable reputation; he had beaten Johnny Basham three times, and was known as 'the demon fighter'. McCormick's loss to Beckett had lowered his standing somewhat, but, if anything, the odds were on him. The fight was not for any boxing trophy, but was one of a series to produce a challenger for Georges Carpentier. It, nevertheless, attracted a wide and influential audience, which included Billy Wells and Tom Webster, the *Daily Mail* cartoonist. They slammed at each other for 11 rounds with the outcome remaining in doubt. In the 12th, the 'Boy' had the 'Kid' at his mercy, dazed by one to the head, and with his guard dropped. This was the moment for the k.o., a certain victory for Mac. He didn't take his opportunity—just stood there as if intentionally giving Lewis time to recover. His chance did not come again; in the 15th round the umpire stopped the fight and declared Lewis the winner.

In November, there were rumours—soon to be confirmed—that Lloyd George, the Prime Minster, was negotiating with agents to buy part of Lord Ashcombe's estate at Churt and was planning to build a retirement home near the Devil's Jumps.

George Lansbury, editor of the *Daily Herald,* and prominent in Labour circles, gave a long pep-talk at the Corn Exchange to local brothers hosted by their now entrenched candidate, T. H. Marshall. Mrs. Philip Snowden, suffragette, temperance reformer and wife of the Labour politician, was a speaker at the Farnham Field Club, her subject being a journey through Bolshevik Russia. The storm clouds were gathering.

The rain fell in torrents on Christmas morning.

The Kid Lewis v. Boy McCormick fight, 1921; a cartoon by Tom Webster, reproduced by permission of the *Daily Mail*.

1922

'A little cottage down in Surrey—not much of a place; in fact it is so small that when the revolution comes no revolutionary commissary will think it worth while confiscating.'
David Lloyd George, Prime Minister, describing his
newly-built house at Churt, near Farnham

THE GROWTH OF THE TOWN as a residential centre is discernible along its exit roads and in off-shoots from these. Once upon a time, there were only two exits which really mattered—the one which went eastward to Guildford and on to London, and the other westward to Alton, Winchester and on to goodness knew where—for few ever travelled that far. There were byways going to north and south along this thoroughfare, but as these were narrow country roads leading to villages like Crondall, Frensham, Tilford, or Elstead—communities that shared Farnham's desire to be left in isolation, having a deep mistrust of strangers—there seemed little point in improving them to B-road specifications. Two king's highways, anyway, were quite enough for any town to have to keep up.

Such was the general policy adopted by successive Vestries, Local Boards, and Urban Councils up to the later years of Victoria's reign, when outbursts of what is quaintly termed population explosion inspired speculative builders to indulge their fancy, first in the abandoned hop-fields between the eastern exit road and the Bishop's park, then on the southern slope of the valley above the railway, with Alfred Road, St George's Road and Tilford Road (west). These two estates at St Cross and Waverley had absorbed the town's explosion debris for the past 30 years or more. They were Farnham's contribution to the Victorian domestic scene, now in the 1920s lacking in modern conveniences. Also, Farnham was 'moving with the times'; the exploding population demanded houses with three-down, three-up, and built-in bath and a lavatory; rather than two-down, two-up, one round the back, and no bath. Most delectable of all undeveloped land was the gently-rising expanse of pastures east of the Tilford road and part of the untouchable Waverley Abbey estate. Then in 1921 came news that Broomleaf Farm was in the market. The opportunists went and saw Swain and Jones about new cars; their wives went and saw Mr. Borelli, the jeweller. The package deal to a potential resident would, desirably, include a nice 36-ft. wide roadway all ready to move into, rather than the narrow lane which wound its way to the Abbey. One resident frontage owner made an offer to the Council of a free strip of frontage, and on the other side of the lane, Major Rupert Anderson offered a 10-ft. wide strip, his only condition being that, when completed, the new road should be called by its former name, Waverley Lane. Thus to have had depths of frontage handed to them on a plate, without having to fight resident frontagers tooth and nail, was a treat which, one would have imagined, could be counted on to shock any local authority out of their slumbers into sending the roadmakers in at the double. These frontage owners, they decided, must be joking; there was a snag in it somewhere. Pressed to take advantage of this offer, the surveyor was told to get out facts and figures for both the Waverley and Tilford roads. These came to £9,400, payable in the long run by the ratepayers at large. So the Council took no action, beyond suggesting to the middle-man involved that it might be a good idea to inform purchasers of building plots that they would possibly at some future date be required to surrender depths of frontage for the purpose of road-widening. The reply was that this course would 'prove to be a clog on the ready sale of the land'. It did not, however, stop the builders moving in. On 21 January 1922, the *Herald* mourned the passing of an interesting local landmark with the demolition of the oast houses at Broomleaf Farm. Passersby, the paper said, would miss the old weather-vane. And so, on the south-east, Farnham loosened its green-belt. The villas that arose—too many villas, George Sturt grumbled in 1925—were neat, functional in all respects, detached each from its neighbours, and not without enduring charm. They increased in size and status as they climbed the slope of the hill, but without any sharply demarcating line, so that all who came to live there had varying tastes of the good life.

Hardys had completed their work on the Hale drainage and the surveyor issued his final certificate in the sum of £19,084 14s. 2d. Mr. Cass was warmly thanked for taking over the role of consulting engineer; he was voted a gratuity of £250, though he had saved the Council a much greater sum. Notices were served on property owners to connect up to the new sewers. The Council were certainly keeping their word to the Hale Ward. The 10 permanent houses, named Heathyfield Cottages, were finished at a cost of £7,400, and ready for occupation in February.

About 500 people attended the Popular Lectures Committee's enterprising fixture at the Corn Exchange on 23 January, when George L. Mallory gave a lantern lecture on the attempt that he and his team had made on Mount Everest.

In February, their rural cousins passed plans by Philip Fielder of London for Lloyd George's house at Churt. J. W. Woolnough of Eastbourne was the contractor. It was rumoured locally that the P.M. was spending some £15,000 on it, though a figure more like £5,000 was mentioned. L.G. had been down recently putting plants in. When the house was finished in the autumn, it was named 'Bron-y-dee': a *Herald* reporter thought this was Welsh for 'Breast of the East', which might be construed as 'Facing the Dawn'—though one correspondent from Wales suggested it meant 'On the Brink'.

The landlord of the *Cricketers,* Downing Street, had been caught out serving drinks after permitted hours and lodged an appeal against the Justices' refusal to renew his licence. In the magistrates annual report, it was stated that in the Farnham Urban District there were currently 48 licences, including off-licences, or approximately one to 252 population.

Ernest Jackson, solicitor, of 'The End House', Castle Hill, died at the age of sixty-four. He was a son of the Rev. Charles Jackson of Bentley rectory. His wife had recently become Farnham's first lady magistrate.

On 28 February, Councillor E. M. Perceval was duly expelled for having been absent for more than the prescribed six consecutive months. Earlier, his colleagues had congratulated him upon being given a knighthood in the New Year honours.

The efficiency of the allotment system was improved by the designation of certain trusted tenants as unpaid prefects in controlling lettings, collecting rents and advising the Council on such anti-social practices as unofficial sub-lettings or cases of neglect . . . Consent was given to a Mr. Arrann to ply for hire in a 30-cwt. 14-seater omnibus between Farnham and the *Pride of the Valley,* Churt, via Tilford Road . . . Harold Falkner was busy enriching the elite Great Austins estate with houses of quality, though Sturt saw fit to describe him as 'the evil genius of the countryside'.

The Council election on 3 April followed the by now established pattern of Tories versus Labourites. Excitement mounted during March as nine nominations were received for five vacancies in the Town Ward, and four for two in Hale. Retiring members who were seeking re-election were Clist, Figg, and Mardon. Newcomers were John Carter of the *Carlton Temperance* hotel, Downing Street, who was standing as an Independent; F. T. Dowling, tailor (Labour); W. G. Taphouse, greengrocer of Downing Street; and the pick of the Conservatives— Joseph Ewart, solicitor; Mrs. Philipson-Stow; and Brigadier-General Brereton. In Hale, W. F. C. Aungier, manager of Caesar Brothers; J. J. Chuter, described as a railway employee; William Norris, a contractor; and H. E. Bide of Alma Nurseries were in contention. It was said at the time that every vote solicited by a Labour candidate during the energetic pre-election campaign ensured two votes from Conservatives determined to keep them out. The results read as follows:

Town Ward

Edward Fitzgerald Brereton, 46 Castle Street	751 (elected)
John Carter, 49 Downing Street	280
Harry Clist, Alfred Road	645 (re-elected)
Francis Thomas Dowling, 1 Myrtle Villas, Crondall Lane	320
Joseph Ewart, 'Acacia House', Ridgway Hill Road	609 (elected)
Arthur James Figg, Long Garden Walk	636 (re-elected)
Arthur George Mardon, 'Hawarden', Firgrove Hill	715 (re-elected)
Elizabeth Willes Philipson-Stow, 'The Old Vicarage'	385
William George Taphouse, 45 Downing Street	393

Hale Ward

Walter Francis Charles Aungier, 'Holberry Cottage', Hale .. .. 255 (elected)
Herbert Edward Bide, Alma Nurseries .. .. 308 (elected)
James John Chuter, 'Winton Cottage', Hale 209
William Norris, 'Perseverance Cottage', Upper Hale 134

The Philipson-Stows had taken over the antiques business at the Spinning Wheel in The Borough from Miss Paget. Mr. Mardon became the new Chairman, with Mr. Murrell as Vice-Chairman. Councillor of the Year went to Mrs. Stroud, with attendances at all 23 council meetings.

The new fire engine arrived on the day of the election. Arrangements were made for its civic reception—just a quiet gathering of the two constituent councils and other local dignitaries, and a few well chosen words by the Chairman of the Joint Fire Brigade Committee, and perhaps the Chief Officer. Mrs. C. F. Falkner, the Chairman's wife, was asked to perform the launching ceremony in the time-honoured way with a bottle of champagne. At this point, Councillor Atkins was heard to remark that in his opinion the liquid employed on this part of the ceremony could be put to better use. And so, in the evening of 3 April, Mrs. Falkner lifted the bottle of bubbly that was suspended by a red ribbon on the front of the resplendent new fire engine and smashed it down on the radiator with the words 'I have much pleasure in christening you *The Princess Mary*'.

Aldershot obtained their Charter in April; instead of gloating over Farnham, the Mayor-elect, Arthur H. Smith, manager of the Army and Navy Stores, had some kind things to say. He and his three brothers, he said, had once sat at the feet of Charles Stroud at the Farnham Grammar School, and he was a keen member of the Old Boys. Farnham, he said, should really be a borough by virtue of ancient traditions. The Council had played it all wrong; before submitting their petition, Aldershot had argued it out with the Hampshire County Council, so that at Privy Council stage it had been a *fait accompli* at local government level. Farnham, their own petition now a dead duck, were well represented at Aldershot's Charter Day celebrations on 18 June.

News filtered through in the local press from time to time concerning the future of Farnham Castle. In May, for instance, there was the possibility of it being used partly as a residence for the Bishop of Guildford, the rest being put to some diocesan purpose or other. The building contained 64 rooms and 14 staircases; there were 2 miles of carpets, and Mrs. Talbot had said that it took a ton of coal each day to keep the place moderately warm. The bishop's salary, then £6,500 a year, was quite inadequate. In some optimistic quarters, it was even suggested that Farnham should become the Cathedral City and that the parish church should become the new Cathedral Church.

News concerning 'Boy' McCormick was now less frequent. Following his two major defeats, he had been travelling round Europe, giving exhibitions, refereeing fights, and earning a crust here and there in the way peculiar to boxers on their way out. He had had no fight now for six months, though

Carpentier had promised him a match in Paris sometime, and was letting himself grow stale.

All this time, a domestic upheaval had been brewing in the Council offices concerning the accounts for the year ending 31 March 1922. It came to a head with the arrival of the District Auditor, a routine yearly visitation which, in the ordinary course of events, entailed nothing more than a few ticks here and there, a bit of rubber-stamping and walks up to the *Bush* for expense-paid lunches. The 1922 audit was, however, different; a firm of accountants had worked it out at a difference of £302 0s. 11d. That this had been repaid by a sorrowing father was neither here nor there. The auditor came down to see justice done. His name was Mr. G. G. H. Stone, and he had a heart of the same material. Mr. Stone's report to the Farnham Council dated 4 May 1922 could be regarded as one of the auditorial greats. It opened with the observation that he had found it impossible to make a satisfactory examination of the Council's accounts because some of the necessary books could not be found.

Take tennis and bowls, for instance. There was no ticket system in force; people using the courts and greens were required to enter the amounts paid by them in a little book. This book, however, could not be found. At the inquest, the clerk explained that the groundsman, being illiterate, was unable to conduct any system of counterfoil receipt book-keeping. At the swimming baths, the unused rolls of tickets could not be produced to the auditor. In the public conveniences, pennies were collected by an attendant who entered the totals in a little book; he had failed to make any entries since 18 June 1920. No stockbook was kept for supplies of Glaxo sold at the Welfare Centre. Here Mr. Wright pointed out that this service was conducted by voluntary ladies, who, like Caesar's wife, were above suspicion. No separate accounts were kept for payments to contractors: everything went through the wages book. Payments which should have been certified by the surveyor were not so certified, rendering it an easy matter for discharged workmen to be retained on the payroll, and for their fictitious wages to be pocketed by a dishonest clerk.

The existing system of 'Cash Receipts and Payments' might have served the purpose well, say, in the Church Vestry before 1866, but nowadays it was all the thing for a local authority to speak in terms of 'Income and Expenditure'. This meant the same thing, but sounded different. Also, Mr. Stone wound up, the time had come for a qualified accountant to be appointed—one who would not be content to jot his transactions down on his shirt cuffs, but would act to the dictates of the various M.O.H. Financial Provisions Orders. Most of the blame rubbed off on to Mr. Wright, who combined the offices of clerk and accountant. He was stung into voicing the impossibility of acting in both capacities unless his duties were altered to enable him to spend one week in each month on the accounts. The Council could not run to the expense of a qualified accountant, so they tightened things up as best they could and left it at that. They did go over, though, to the 'Income and Expenditure' line of thought.

For good measure, they also decreed that in future all outgoing correspondence should be typewritten, and carbon copies kept.

The summer of 1922 was pretty poor weatherwise, as well as being thin in events of any magnitude. The garden fetes and village flower-shows held their occasions; cricket, tennis and bowls ran their accustomed courses. The Gostrey Meadow bowlers formed themselves into a club, with H. J. Tadd of East Street as honorary secretary—they competed for a pair of woods presented by the late Tom Mitchell, and Mr. Kempson gave a challenge cup. W. F. Rankine, Chairman of the Badshot Lea United Sports Club, won £10 from the Council for improving the village green. 'All the live murmur of a summer's day.'

The job-creation package—in Water Lane and at dangerous corners—had an unhappy sequel. When applying for government grant towards the cost of £1,126, this was rejected because the workforce had been recruited from the local jobless and not through the official Labour Exchange. Can one sense a reluctance to treat with the Exchange since its removal to Aldershot? There might have been the possibility, for instance, that Aldershot men were taken on instead of Farnham's. As if arising from Farnham's go-it-alone attitude, Aldershot Borough Council convened a meeting of local authorities within the Employment Exchange area to discuss urgent matters. Member councils were asked to submit schemes for work in their districts to provide jobs for the 1,712 unemployed men in the area, 275 of whom lived in Farnham. Ideas included a new road from Hickleys corner to the southern end of the railway bridge in Firgrove Hill, the continuation of Alfred Road from St George's Road to Firgrove Hill, various other road improvements, the cleaning of the river bed and the making-up of the Great Austins roads.

Tommy Hill, the Downing Street electrician, installed an internal telephone network in the Council offices for £21 10s. 0d. The surveyor prepared an estimate for wiring the offices for electric lighting.

It was such an expensive business for householders to go on the sewer, what with piping the 'small room' into the intercepting chamber at the gate and installing the necessary furniture. Nevertheless, the Hale residents were responding with enthusiasm; probably there was a feeling of oneupmanship amongst neighbours. The Council, of course, had powers to enforce connections in the long run, but for the time being they were content with persuading people. At Badshot Lea, two publicans and the Rev. H. P. Metcalf of St George's vicarage had to be jogged on the elbows.

The Council were worried somewhat about certain tenants moving into the Gorseland Hutments. Some came from dwellings which were decidedly frowsy; it was hoped that 'better living conditions' in the huts would improve their standards, but one could never tell.

A fire in June at Henley, St Cross, the residence of F. A. Mitchell, tobacconist in The Borough, provided a further opportunity to point the finger of scorn at the long-suffering water company. When directing the hose at the flames, it was found that, instead of a good 60 lbs. per 3-in. main pressure necessary to gush water in force, the merest trickle emerged—about 35 lbs. per 3-in. pressure, guessed the Chief Officer of the Brigade.

At the inquest in July, three questions were asked—had there been a delay on the Brigade's part?; had all reasonable care been taken?; and had the water pressure been adequate? The answer to question one revealed a somewhat antiquated system of summoning the fire brigade. Mr. Mitchell, on telephoning the fire station, had been told that, as it was after closing hours at the Council offices (of which the station then formed part), he should inform the police, who would then alert the brigade. Receiving the call at 10.30 p.m., the police had tried phoning the Council offices, where, by luck, 'Mr. Sargent just happened to be around'; it was he who called the firemen. The engine arrived at the scene of the fire at 10.45 p.m. The manager of the water company was very definite that no call had been received at his works asking for the pressure to be upped. Whilst no bid had actually been received from Charlie Chaplin for the film rights, the spectacle of the Council's brand new fire engine dribbling cupsful of water from its hoses must have had its funny side. All the blame was put on the water company, who received the full majesty of the Council's wrath. It was clear that the company held no promise of improvements in the town's water supply, but, on the contrary, 'sought to shelter themselves behind their Provisional Order of 1886. It was idle to accept that an order made 36 years ago, when the population was barely 5,000, still applied'. In view of the serious situations which arose from time to time, it was the Council's bounden duty to take steps to exercise their powers under the Public Health Act 1875 to provide their district with a supply of water sufficient for all public and private purposes.

A recent Diocesan Conference had clarified the position regarding the Castle with the resolution—

> that the Diocese of Guildford be invited to undertake the responsibility for the upkeep of Farnham Castle and that the consideration of this responsibility be referred to a committee consisting mainly of representatives from the area proposed to be included in that Diocese. And that the future use of the Castle be referred to the same committee with a view to their considering the possibility of its use as a residence for the Bishop of Guildford and a Diocesan House for conferences, retreats or in any other way.

The War Memorial Committee, their work now finished, handed over to the Council their final balance sheet and surplus cash. As from now, the memorial—'one of the Town's treasured possessions'—would be the responsibility of the local authority. Met entirely from public subscriptions, the expenses were as follows:

	£	s.	d.
The memorial: Messrs. H. C. Patrick	489	10	0
Inserting names and carving panel: H. C. Patrick	103	0	0
York stone paving, alterations of ground and gates: H. C. Patrick	165	0	0
Planting yew hedges: Bide and Sons	13	0	6
Architect's fees: W. C. Watson	57	12	0
Advertising, stationery, etc.	35	18	9
Donation to Bourne Memorial Fund	10	10	0
	£874	11	3
Balance to F.U.D.C. for maintenance costs	35	15	4
	£910	6	7

On that Armistice Day of 1922, the people gathered round the Cross, paying homage to the dead and keeping a deep silence for two minutes. They had paid £232 for poppies from street-sellers. Those who had lost husbands or sons, thought of them. Then the gun fired and the bugles sounded, and the traffic flowed again.

Lloyd George had lost no time in entering into local affairs. He had an entry in the Goat Show at Dogflud on 12 August, organised by the West Surrey Goat Club, but was unable to attend in person. Then, on 19 October, he resigned his government and handed over to Bonar Law, and Farnham and all other towns were plunged into a general election. Polling day was 15 November. In the Farnham Division, the Labour candidate, Thomas Humphrey Marshall, M.A., put up a determined fight. He scored 5,321 votes against Arthur Samuel's 14,557, no mean feat in a Tory stronghold like Farnham. Marshall was heard to say afterwards that, in his reckoning, the Labour Party would be in power, not in the next election, but in the one after that.

A strike of local dimensions occurred at Mr. Saunders's hopground at Burrows Dene in September, when the pickers downed tools from 11 a.m. to 3 p.m. on the opening day because of the remuneration offered—2½d. a bushel. They won 3d. a bushel . . . It was fitting that a branch of Toc H. should be formed, on 25 October, in the home town of Gilbert Talbot. The Rev. P. B. (Tubby) Clayton, padre at the old house at Poperinghe during the war, was in Farnham to get the branch started.

McCormick, back from a three-month tour of Germany, had many kind things to tell of the late enemy. Germany was 'a land of plenty', labour was cheap, and the workers gave of their best. More than once, people had said to him 'you state that you have won the war, but we have won the peace'. The girls were not up to British standards, being more masculine in character. Three German women of high rank had proposed marriage to him. As if to offset an impression of soft living, the 'Boy' let it be known that he had cabled a challenge to Siki, who had beaten Georges Carpentier. In the meantime, he was training at Manchester for a contest with Arthur Townley.

At the Venison Dinner that November, the bishop mentioned that he had given instructions for the herd of deer in the park to be killed off, and so in future the promoters of the dinner would have to look elsewhere for a fat buck. There had been deer in the park since time immemorial, and the town was rather shocked by this new evidence of episcopal economic stringency. Mr. Mardon launched an appeal for the preservation of the herd, and the bishop willingly cancelled orders for its suppression. The deer did, however, eventually disappear from Farnham Park and venison dinners came to be provisioned from the herd in Petworth Park. Another matter mentioned at the dinner, by Mr. Mardon, was that the Farnham Market House and Town Hall Company were willing to surrender the company's rights in Castle Street on the understanding that no fairs would be held in that street in the future. This opened the door wide for the formation of a public market elsewhere in the town. The Gostrey Meadow frontage in Union Road was put forward as one suggestion. In the new year, meetings were held to foster the idea.

Councillor Gertrude Stroud initiated a Christmas Gift Fund for distribution to unemployed families, and a committee went to work on it. A sum of £118 16s. 3d. was collected and vouchers were issued to some 150 households for 7s. 6d. to 25s., according to the number of children under fourteen. These were exchangeable for commodities such as meat, groceries, or coal. The fund became a regular Christmas feature in the years to come, until changing conditions rendered it superfluous, and the thought behind it needless.

1923

The papers grow more and more excited, or say gaspy, with promises, day by day, of new things in 'wireless', 'broadcasting', 'television', and so on. Truly the things promised are very new; we are, for instance, to see with our eyes what is happening in the Arctic Circle, or to hear with our very ears the roar of lions in Central Africa.

George Sturt

IT IS INDEED DIFFICULT for those who, at the touch of a button, are able to watch a test match being played in Australia, to understand fully the sheer amazement which greeted the advent of sound broadcasting in the first years of the 1920s. Formed in October 1922 to consolidate earlier experimental, spasmodic and rudimentary services, the British Broadcasting Company began regular transmissions a month later from London, Manchester, and Birmingham. The public were invited to install receiving sets on payment of a 10s. licence. Of course, everybody knew that, even before the death of Queen Victoria, ships at sea had communicated without visible means, and that wireless telegraphy had spanned the oceans some years before the Great War. But all that, as far as the public was concerned, were things that seafaring community and post office authority got up to—it didn't make sense. Suddenly to be told that they, the public, might also listen to voices and sounds from a distance was carrying matters a bit too far. And yet who would once have thought that carriages would run without horses? Or that man would travel through the air, instead of going by train as Nature intended? Tentatively, intensely curious and with rapidly-growing enthusiasm, the people made their first advances towards this new-fangled source of entertainment.

At first, people went to 'Wireless Concerts' organised by tradesmen like electricians—Hales in The Borough played a leading role—who saw in the cult an obvious means of livelihood. Others followed—in January 1923, Heath and Wiltshires were advertising valve sets at five guineas each; the B.B.C., they said, had successfully transmitted acts from the Grand Opera at Covent Garden. One's first-ever 'listen-in' was a moving experience. The gathering of people around a bandstand in a Hampshire town on 23 April 1924 included many who, like the present writer, were interested more in the magic of wireless than in the gravelly voice of King George V which came over it opening the British Empire

Exhibition at Wembley. Suddenly a town lost what remained of its insularity. Improved travel facilities and, in dormitory areas such as Farnham, the cosmopolitan character of wealthier residents had already eroded the defences. Now the Voice of London effectively broke down the remaining barriers. Whether wireless was a good thing has never been established.

*   *   *   *   *

It was perhaps obvious that, upon its release by the Master of Waverley, the eastward spur of the ridge which separates the valleys of the Wey and Bourne, would be pounced on by the Upper Crust as the ideal location for their grand houses. The long, wide tableland which formed this delectable site was called, appropriately enough, by the field-name Great Austins. It was divided into 720 building plots; down on the lower terraces of Farnham, a similar area of land would have accommodated, at a rough guess, about 10 times as many houses. Most swingeing of the rude shocks experienced by settlers on virgin soil is the bill that the local Council sends for making-up and taking-over the estate roads; even with 720 frontagers to share it, this can be quite an item. Furthermore, no-one is particularly interested in the road beyond the front gate, which, if it comes to that, is more generally used by the public at large.

The councillors found themselves confronted by a close-knit body of more powerfully-corridored, higher-officered gentleman settlers who pointed out that the estimated cost of the work was excessive, that the main estate road was already much used by the public and had suffered from the haulage of materials to a recent Council building site, that pavements and kerbs were unnecessary, for it would be better for the roads to retain their rustic character—and more in like vein. The Council gave way on several points and modified the estimate. Even so, the matter went to a three-hour sitting of the Bench. In the end, the bill was reduced to £6,320. The average per house of about £88 was, in those days, quite a considerable sum.

With so many job-hungry men about, and the government footing 65 per cent. of the wage bill, the Council were taking the golden opportunity to add all kinds of finishing touches to Farnham which transformed a somewhat backward town into a place of charm. W. German and Sons were engaged to repaint 24 street name-plates, and supply 18 additional ones. Electric street-lighting was tried out with an experimental lamp at the *Royal Deer* corner, but the old gas-lamp won on points. They bought 11 acres of land from the Farnham Gravel Company for an extension of the sewage farm. The railway people were persuaded to run fast commuter trains to Waterloo, taking about 60 minutes.

There was a resurgence of effort in the town; it showed in unexpected quarters —the approach to the down platform at the station, for instance. Waterloo was profusely thanked by the Council for beautifying this; no longer would strangers arriving by train get the impression that, owing to a signalman up the line pulling the wrong lever, they had alighted at some up-country depot in Darkest Africa.

The improvements coincided nicely with the recent beauty treatment that the Council had given Tilford Road up as far as Alfred Road. But it transpired that the treatment on platform two owed nothing to Waterloo, who were indifferent to such matters—they had yet to start competitions for the best-kept railway stations. It was the inspiration of a rare breed of stationmasters, our Mr. Townley. He won a mention in the Council minute-book.

McCormick reappeared. His fight with another Mr. Townley—Arthur—had been called off because Townley had a damaged eye. The 'Boy', however, made up for this by beating Wild Burt Kenny of America in four rounds at the White City, Manchester, on 9 February.

Thirty-two of the 34 Sheephouse tenants produced a petition which led to the banning of games on the oval played by persons under the age of 14, thus abating a nuisance caused, presumably, by the two households not signing the petition . . . Caesar Bros. asked £3,300 for building 10 three-bedroom houses on a two-acre site at the *Elm Tree*, Weybourne, a total outlay of £4,270, which called for economic rents of 11s. 8d. a week. Caesars also contracted to build public conveniences on Hale Recreation Ground for £215 10s. 0d.

Major Patrick won an order from the War Graves Commission for 681 head-stones for the graves of unknown soldiers in Flanders, and, in July, a further order for over two thousand. The stones were to be lettered A SOLDIER OF THE GREAT WAR. KNOWN UNTO GOD. Mr. Courtenay Welch of the Army College, Heath Road, promised two guineas if the Council would start a fund with which to pay the expenses of poor people wishing to go to London to join parties of bereaved relatives on visits to the graves of their kin in Flanders.

Dr. Sloman reported on his Health Week held in October 1922. This time there had been less truancy in the schools. Emphasis had been laid by two speakers from the National Council on the dangers of venereal disease.

The Public Market Committee reported in March. Their three suggested sites were the auction mart in South Street, a meadow between the river and Darvills Lane, and a triangular piece of land at the rear of the *Waverley Arms* public house. Capital outlay should be in the region of £3,000. Approval of the general public was required under the Public Health Act, 1875, for a scheme of this calibre, and a public meeting was arranged for 6 April.

Items considered and approved by the ratepayers were:

(1) To provide a market place and construct a market house and other conveniences for the purpose of holding markets.
(2) To provide houses and places for weighing carts.
(3) To make convenient approaches to such market.
(4) To provide all such matters and things as may be necessary for the convenient use of such market.
(5) To purchase or take on lease land and public or private rights in markets and tolls for any of the foregoing purposes.
(6) To take stallages, rents and tolls in respect of the use by any person of such market.

The Town Hall Company said they first heard about the scheme in such detail when they read an account of the meeting in the *Herald*. Particularly they did not like item (5), which threatened the Company's sovereignty in Castle Street. Reaction was swift: the Company withdrew their earlier support for a public market which they had anticipated would have been on no greater scale than the occasional stall or two. Further opposition came from the owners of the sites suggested in South Street and Darvills Lane, who flatly declined to sell. The Councillors were by no means masters in their own house.

The Wey Valley Water Company, who supplied water beyond the area of the Town Ward, had been caught trying to increase their charges by 75 per cent. They were immediately sat on by local authorities concerned, and had to settle for rises of 50 per cent. The Farnham Water Company, who operated in the Town Ward, had always been a moribund lot. Now the news came that they were seeking a merger with the Wey Valley people. If this took place, consumers would face rises in water charges of about 19s. 3d. a year, and, as whipping boys, the Council would get the stick for this. The alternative was for the Council themselves to take over the town supply. A figure of £17,000 was bandied for lock, stock and barrel, including the Company's outstanding loan debt of £5,000. Roughly, if the Council took it over, charges would go up by about twelve shillings. They would still get whipped, but not so hard. There were advantages, of course, in the Wey Valley taking over, for they were specialists in the field. Their water was immaculate, and its pressure faultless. The Council, on the other hand, were not used to piping water, though they did have tremendous confidence, and could find themselves deep in the stuff. In the end, all three sat round a table to see if a scheme could be devised that was beneficial to the consumers—and least painful to the councillors.

Chairman Mardon spoke glowingly of the Council's record over the past year. The *Herald* made it sound even better and the press cutting was pasted in the official minute-book. It was entitled 'Something Attempted, Something Done' and set out in considerable detail the work of 18 council and 95 committee meetings.

The election on 26 March, however, was fairly low key. It lacked the good clean fight put up by the Labour ranks in 1922. The retiring members, Councillors Mrs. Stroud, Murrell, Ransom and Sanders, all stood for re-election. There was one newcomer, Lieutenant-Colonel Vallentin of 'Bethune House', West Street. He knocked out Harry Sanders. No poll was necessary in Hale. The score-card read as follows:

George Murrell, 'Albany House', West End Grove	..	..	..	973 (re-elected)
Arthur George Ransom, 'Highwick', The Fairfield	..	..	..	677 (re-elected)
Henry Sanders, 'Sanfield', Lancaster Avenue	..	..	..	518
Gertrude Annie Stroud, 'Elmsleigh', Station Hill	..	..	..	571 (re-elected)
Henry Edward Vallentin, 'Bethune House', West Street	..	..	696 (elected)

Mardon and Murrell were chosen as Chairman and Vice for a second term.

Dame Margaret Lloyd George made her debut in local society by opening a sale of work at Farnham Institute, organised by the Congregational church. The ex-Prime Minister was to make few appearances on the domestic front; he was more often seen in the hot dry summers of the 1930s, beating out the flames, as they neared his house, of the many heath fires.

That spring, with unbounded enthusiasm, the townspeople made preparations for a grand carnival to be held in the mad, merry month of May. They had put the town down for a donation of £2,000 towards a large-scale programme of extensions to the Royal Surrey Hospital in Guildford, and £2,000 was what they intended to raise. It would be no hardship. Ever since Shakespeare, perhaps earlier, Farnham folk had loved dressing up in motley and playing the fool. With uninhibited abandon, they loved pageants, processions and any excuse for letting their hair down; it was in their nature. This occasion heralded their first opportunity of throwing off the war clouds; the 'Roaring Twenties' were beginning to roar. Who better than the ebullient Willie Loe of the Farnham brewery to mastermind the revelries? Not on Sunday, 6 May, of course; this he left to the clergy, who made full use of it with a United Services procession and an open-air service in Gostrey, attended by the councillors in full regalia. Monday and Tuesday were devoted to sports, with a boxing tournament, athletics and football matches. Wednesday, 9 May, was Procession Day, with a battle of confetti and an evening performance of *Midsummer Night's Dream* in Brightwells by the Frensham Players. On Thursday, there was a revival of the old Farnham Fair in Castle Street. Friday was declared the Day of the Children. After it was all over, Mr. Loe received requests from various towns in the country for copies of the official handbook. They had been impressed by the pictures and paragraphs appearing in the daily newspapers and were eager to study the Farnham pattern.

The weather was kind; the little rain which fell on Wednesday morning did nothing worse than lay the dust. Tuesday morning dawned fair. After breakfast, the town centre, gaily hung with bunting, filled gradually with pleasure-seekers, many of them in fancy dress. Just before 10 o'clock, a man hove in sight up Castle Street. He was not dressed in anything—he was 'starkers'. To give Mr. Loe the benefit of any doubt that may have passed through the minds of some spectators, this surprise item was not part of the official carnival programme. From evidence later pieced together, it was due to unrelated circumstances. The nude man, of Lowndes Buildings, Castle Street, a painter employed by the brewery, had a history of mental trouble back in the war years which had since been cured. Active in local football and cricket circles, he had been married as recently as 10 days previously, and it was thought that perhaps the excitement of this, together with other factors, had brought on a recurrence of the trouble. He had escaped from the house, tearing off his clothes as he went into Castle Street. A tall, well-built man, with long hair streaming behind him, he ran down the street, repeatedly shouting 'Get thee behind me, Satan'. It seemed that Satan didn't do this, preferring the front view. Ladies stood aghast; young girls took shelter in doorways. Turning at the Town Hall corner, he proceeded into The Borough. A small black dog, also nude, trotted at his feet.

Making his way majestically westward along The Borough came a policeman. He was doubtless savouring the fresh May morning, uplifted, possibly, by the happy carnival mood and thinking about whatever constables think about whilst on the beat. There comes a time in every copper's career when, despite his training, he finds himself at a loss. He stood nonplussed. But not for long: he went to arrest the 'streaker', who became obstreperous. With the help of a bystander and Dr. Ealand, who was quick to arrive, he whisked him into Frisbys' shoe shop (though a trouser shop would have been a wiser choice).

Farnham did not send the Guildford Hospital a cheque for £2,000. They sent £4,257 13s. 4d.

The Tories acknowledged that not everybody wanted to live in a council house with their Housing Act of 1923, which implemented a council's powers under the Small Dwellings Acquisition Acts to advance loans (repayable over 20 years) to prospective owner-occupiers of houses up to specified floor areas in size. Gradually at first, and then with burgeoning effort, the fields around the town, once the focus of Farnham's great hop industry, sprouted rows of neat, loved, owner-occupied bungalows and houses. 'The spirit of property doubles a man's strength', wrote Voltaire in 1764. In Farnham, the 1921 census had revealed 18 cases where families of two to five persons were living in one room, 122 cases of two to nine persons in two rooms, and 132 of three persons in three rooms. During the building boom of the later '20s and throughout the '30s, people such as these sorted themselves out into decent living standards. In no way could this have happened simply by building council houses.

Baths superintendent J. Greenwood was mentioned in despatches for diving in fully clothed to rescue a lady in distress . . . The *Herald* of 2 June reviewed George Sturt's new book, *The Wheelwright's Shop* . . . June's plans included three for houses in Waverley Lane—from Mrs. A. M. Mitchell, Lionel Mitchell, and Archibald Smith . . . Major Rupert Anderson now offered frontage depth on the left-hand side of Tilford Road to enable a 36-ft. roadway to be constructed.

Surgeon-General Owen Edward Pennefather Lloyd, V.C., a son of Major M. P. Lloyd of the 59th Regiment, and a boarder at the grammar school in 1863–5 under Charles Stroud, was awarded a K.C.B. He had won the Victoria Cross at Fort Suna, later Fort Morton, during an attack by the warlike Kachins.

The County Medical Officer put Farnham well down in the charts as regards infant mortality rates—worse, he said, than some industrial towns in the Midlands. Figures for 1922 had revealed a rate of 8.9 per cent. He blamed bad sanitary conditions in Farnham.

There was a plan in July for alterations to the *Marlborough Head,* which transformed that pub's unexciting exterior... Shoreditch Council sought support for a recommendation to the government to ban the practice of some bakers taking customers' stale bread in part-exchange for fresh loaves, this being a potential source of disease . . . Further thought was given to renewing application for a boundary extension which would take in the remaining portions of the old Farnham parish (the Bourne, Wrecclesham, part of Rowledge, Tilford, and Dippenhall) . . . On 12 July, the National Assembly of the Church of England formally approved the Diocese of Winchester (Division) Measure 1923.

On 7 July, a big Labour rally was held in Farnham, with visiting brothers from far and wide. J. Ramsay MacDonald was the guest of honour. The park and other local amenities were placed at their disposal. Instead of storming the castle, the visitors were conducted over it by one of the bishop's staff as if they had been royalty.

Mr. L. H. Poole, editor of the *Farnham Herald* for many years, and a familiar figure in the Council chamber, handed over a 1785 copy of *The Gentleman's Magazine* which contained an account of Farnham's bid for the restoration of parliamentary representation. Later in the year, Mr. Poole became ill and died.

There was concern about the dangers to horse-drawn traffic caused by excursionists tying balloons to their charabancs, throwing out streamers and otherwise signifying their passage through the town. A complaint to the County Council reached a higher level, for letters were received from the Under-Secretary of State and the Ministry of Transport to the effect that a sub-committee of the Departmental Committee on Licensing and Regulation of Hackney Vehicles were busy working on it.

In July, news leaked that Bishop Talbot was retiring. The departure of an overlord at the castle, and the arrival of his successor had, since the 12th century, been to the township at its gate an event perhaps of greater significance than, say, a change in the monarchy. The emancipating effects of the Great War had tended to liberate the townspeople from their feudal loyalties, and the pattern of relationships between castle and town now rested on other considerations. Dr. Edward Stuart Talbot had been in Farnham for 12 years. During that time, he had endeared himself and his family to the people by a friendly disposition and neighbourly behaviour. The bishop referred to the castle and town as his dear, beloved home; he and Mrs. Talbot had kept open house as well as giving up all privacy in the park. They had taken a big part in local affairs. Now, in a special message to his 'Farnham friends', Dr. Talbot said 'The time has come for me to go'. Who would be his successor? One Fleet Street paper tipped Dr. Cyril F. Garbett, the Bishop of Southwark. And would he come to live at Farnham Castle? Yes—quite possibly from choice—for he had been at Farnham Grammar School in the 1850s, and may have had yearnings to end up in the citadel.

George Baigent, the builder, had now started on the development of the new road, Bridgefield . . . Sensing the need for an architect on the staff, Mrs. Stroud proposed Mr. Sargent, who dodged this by pointing out that his duties as sanitary inspector would suffer . . . The age limit of boys privileged to enjoy mixed bathing at the baths was reduced to eight years . . . Mr. G. A. Hale suggested holding 'wireless concerts' in Gostrey Meadow . . . 'Boy' McCormick was downed by David Magill of Belfast at the Liverpool Stadium on 20 August.

G. S. Nicholls of the Cambridge Garage, Hale Road, sought permission to store petrol and 'inject it into motors by means of an overhead swing-arm pump'. Means of injecting a different sort of liquid into horses now began to disappear from the streets, though, here and there, a horse-trough was retained as an antiquity. An ornate trough designed by Harold Falkner several years previously, presented to the town by Miss Paget, but rejected by the unanimous disapproval of the inhabitants, still languished somewhere in the council yard. Now Hewett and Lee expressed their willingness to mount it in their market place in South Street.

Sir Edward Perceval arrived back home from Berlin at the end of August, his spell of duty with the War Graves Commission completed. He had headed a team charged with the task of tracing British solders reported missing during the war, and seeing that they were decently buried. He had been able to identify some five thousand. Commenting on the Germans, Sir Edward said that generally they were well disposed towards the English, but had no time for the French or Belgians. They had tended British graves conscientiously. They seemed to be adopting our games and were becoming especially keen on football.

Philip Snowden, already high up in Labour corridors, purchased 'Eden Lodge', a 16-acre property at Tilford.

In mid-September, Dr. Talbot's successor was named as the Rt. Rev. Frank Theodore Woods, M.A., D.D., Bishop of Peterborough. The moment of truth had arrived for Farnham Castle. At a special meeting on 26 September, Chairman Mardon told his fellow councillors that he had received an invitation to attend a meeting of the committee appointed by the ecclesiastical authorities to consider problems in connection with the future of the castle and park. Mr. Mardon wished to take with him the wishes of his Council in the matter, especially upon the question of whether, in the event of the authorities deciding to dispose of the castle and grounds, an effort should be made to secure them for public use. His own feeling was that if the Council took no action, and the park was eventually alienated from all public rights of way, then future generations in Farnham would not hold them guiltless in the matter. After a full and frank discussion, every member identified herself or himself with Mr. Mardon's views, and it was unanimously resolved:

> that the Chairman be empowered to say that, should it be found necessary in the ecclesiastical interests to dispose of the Park, this Council, as representing the town and district, desire to have the opportunity of exhausting the possibilities of acquiring it for public uses before any action for its sale is actually taken by the authorities.

> That with regard to the future of Farnham Castle, this Council desires with great respect to express the hope that it may be found possible to continue the connection which has existed for so many hundreds of years between the

> Castle and the National Church, but that failing, they trusted it might be possible to use the residential portion for the purpose of a College, a School or similar institution rather than as a private residence.

News was received in October that the new Bishop of Winchester had been persuaded to take up residence in part of the castle for a temporary period of one year. Meanwhile, throughout the remaining weeks of summer, Dr. Talbot had been moving around his diocese bidding farewell. In his home town of Farnham, this called for more than a sermon from the local pulpit. Always effusively polite towards the long succession of bishops at the castle, the townspeople felt a special relationship with the Talbots. They were in effect likely to be the last of that long succession. They and their three sons had professed a love for the town, not merely tolerating an unwieldy and expensive home on sufferance. More as friends, than as 'my lord and lady at the manor,' they were entertained at the Corn Exchange, where Dr. Talbot received a replica of the silver cup presented to the bailiffs and burgesses of Farnham by John Byworth in 1623.

Reporting on one aspect of the mini-civil-war inflicted on the public by the London dock strikers, the food inspector, vetting consignments at the railway station, had found it necessary to condemn 700 lbs. of bacon, 46 lbs. of salt beef, 24 lbs of imported beef, 9 lbs. of prawns, and 12 jars of preserved meat.

Mr. E. W. Langham submitted plans for an extension at 114 West Street . . . 130 applications were received for the tenancies of the 10 new council houses at Weybourne . . . Two additional tennis courts were completed in Brightwells . . . The Public Market campaign fizzled out with an offer from Hewett and Lee of the use of the cattle sales yard in South Street on any one day a week, except Mondays, for the purpose of a weekly produce market.

The 133rd anniversary of the Venison Dinner took place at the Corn Exchange on 25 October. The Earl of Midleton who, as St John Brodrick, had once been Farnham's member of parliament, was thanked for his provision of a fat buck from Peperharow Park. In responding to the toast to the ladies, Councillor Mrs. Watkins felt flattered in being the first woman ever to make a speech at the dinner.

W. H. Smith and Sons moved into their new shop at 12 South Street. Their old bookshop, at the corner of South Street and Union Road, was taken by G. R. Sherrington, the tobacconist—there was a steady flow of council office staff across the street for packets of cigarettes . . . The London Joint County and Midland Bank changed their name to the Midland Bank.

After a special meeting on 1 November the Council plunged into the deep end with an offer to the moribund Farnham Water Company of £22,000 (£17,000 share capital and £5,000 mortgage debt). Mr. Crundwell, acting for the company, had, however, been doing his sums in greater detail; his total, including dividends and compensation to directors and servants, was £24,950. Moreover there would be the expenses of promoting a Bill, holding public meetings, etc.

And once the undertaking had been acquired, they would have to spend at least £5,000 to bring it into the 20th century. They upped their offer to £23,500, plus compensation of £153 to the company's manager and £37 to the secretary. E. C. mentioned the Council's liability for payment of dividends during the interim period of transfer—something, he had to confess, which hadn't occurred to him earlier. It was clear to an observer that the Council were getting deeper and deeper into problems. They called in Midgeley Taylor as their adviser—for catching rainwater up at Old Park and delivering it around the houses was, they had discovered, easier said than done.

The primitive conditions in the Hale Ward had not altogether ceased with the laying in of sewers. Certain properties did not lend themselves to connections, being below the level of the sewer. So such people had to continue to pig it with earth closets or other archaic methods, and night-soil carts had to make special calls. Then the Council had a bright idea. If a substance called 'dry-soil' were used, instead of whatever the householders did use, then the mixture could be put in the dustbin.

The committee appointed to revive the urban district extension bid recounted past abortive moves. Following the Hale Ward takeover in 1913, the Council had prayed to the County Council for the transfer of the remaining areas of the old rural parish. Consideration of this had been adjourned until after the war (what actually did happen was that County accused Farnham of presumptuousness), and had since been further postponed, at their own wish, to allow time to deal with Hale's pressing needs. There seemed no good reason for further deferment. The 1921 census showed that the areas under discussion had a population of 5,100—almost an urban density. The benefits they derived from the Rural Council were minimal apart from highway maintenance. There was a complete absence of drainage, no provision for cesspit emptying or scavenging of privies and earth closets, and no dustmen called. All sewage and refuse, if not buried by house-holders, was deposited, open to the sky, on the nearest stretch of wasteland. There was no street lighting—though this might be regarded as an asset, for it cloaked the nocturnal activities of the furtive bucket-emptiers. The inclusion within the urban district of these backward villages would secure for them most of the advantages of modern civilisation, together with higher rate demand-notes. Appalled by this picture of rural England just across the border, the Council hesitated no longer, but sealed a petition praying for the transfer to the Farnham Urban District Council of the Parish of Farnham Rural, being that part of the Ancient Parish of Farnham which had not been transferred to the Farnham Urban District by the Order sealed by the Surrey County Council on 29 July 1913.

Sales of poppies on 10 November (Armistice Day being on a Sunday) raised £214 7s. 9d. . . . At another kind of sale, at Farnham Castle, Hewett and Lee auctioned remaining furniture and effects, including several paintings, left behind by Dr. Talbot . . . Sale posters at least 100 years old came to light during alterations at 1 The Borough. They were stuck on an original oak window frame, long since walled up. Other timbering in Lionel Smith's new premises was being exposed.

The difficulties the government were having in carrying out Bonar Law's policy of protection for British industry led to the dissolution of parliament in November. The Liberals this time fielded a Captain Christopher Williams of Kensington; the Labour candidate was a Mrs. Anne Elizabeth Corner of 'The Junipers', Milford. Farnham rocked to observe that their Chairman, Mr. Mardon, was in Mrs. Corner's corner. The poll on 6 December netted: Conservatives, 12,534; Liberals, 4,979; and Labour, 3,520.

At the meeting on 4 December, the Council recorded the death of Mr. Watts, who had been foreman at the sewage farm during all the 37 years of its existence. They presented £52 to the widow, and advertised for his successor. There were 30 applications, and Mr. Cecil Choate of Byfleet was chosen. His hobby was motor-racing—he was a steward at Brooklands—but the main reason for his endearing nature was a dry humour and a fund of questionable anecdotes connected in sundry ways with his profession.

News which shocked his declining circle of fans came through that 'Boy' McCormick had been sentenced at Manchester, with two other men, to 12 months' imprisonment for assaulting two girls. McCormick had burst into tears and told the court, 'I am known throughout the world as a clean-living man and I have the sweetest wife in the world; I never laid a finger on the women'. When appealing against the sentence, he declared that the women had demanded money, and that the whole thing was a plot to discredit him; if the sentence stood then his career as a boxer would be finished.

The Surrey Educational Committee asked whether Farnham had yet done anything about forming a public library under the Libraries Act 1919. Because, if not, County were thinking of taking advantage of an offer by the Carnegie Trust and establishing a rural library scheme in Surrey, which would, of course, take in Farnham. The Council were delighted. Reading was still the main occupation outside working hours, and borrowers had their pick in several commercial libraries in the town—Smiths', Boots', Sturts' and others. Never at any time had the county been so well off for first-rate authors. The more libraries, the better. This one would be free to borrowers, and would doubtless hit the commercial libraries. (Public or commercial, libraries are the bane of writers who enjoy only a limited circulation. For each copy in a lending library might be read by as many as a hundred borrowers, many of whom might otherwise reward the writer by buying copies of their own.)

Mrs. Stroud again launched a Christmas Gift Fund appeal, and some 305 poor people in the town benefited.

1924

Farnham be a queer place, that's t' say there be some queer folk in it. Some of us be straight, and some of us be crooked, but if anyone deals crooked wi' us, we deals crooked wi' 'im.

Historical Episodes (E. Neville Lovett, Rector):
words addressed to Bishop Sumner on his arrival at
Farnham Castle in 1828. Staged in August 1910

THE ARRIVAL OF A NEW BISHOP in Farnham, even when eroded of much of its significance by changed concepts at the castle, was a signal occasion and one which still ranked as a very special event in the annals of the town. The Bishop of Winchester was a public figure of national dimensions, high up in the episcopal order. He owed his first allegiance to his far-stretched See, but his home was in Farnham. Here he lived with his family, enjoyed domestic privacy, slept, ate food bought in Farnham shops, entertained or relaxed from the cares of Church and State. Dr. Talbot was one bishop who had insisted that he was as much 'a citizen of Farnham as any of the town's inhabitants', whom he made a point of calling his 'neighbours'. He had been a frequent worshipper at St Andrews, which he looked upon as his parish church. He was a benign father-figure to whom the town's elders could turn for guidance in an emergency.

The strong special relationship which existed between the castle and town spelt different things to their respective occupants. To the bishop it was important to keep one's own doorstep clean. To the 20th-century model townsmen, it represented something which was of increasingly less practical value, and more of a hangover from the feudal past, coupled with a civic pride in being able to count a Lord Bishop among the local ratepayers. The natives had always been pleased to see the steady trickle of illustrious strangers—statesmen of renown, famous men of letters, the arts, science, medicine, or commerce, and, of course, distinguished men of arms who lived for a time within the district. According to their rank, they would be recognised in many ways, such as roping them in to give lectures or chair at social functions. A Bishop of Winchester was always of special interest. He was a worthy of the special treament which, from time out of mind, had been dispensed by generations of natives. As this could be expected to follow traditional lines, it was imperative, as a matter of urgent curiosity, both for an arriving bishop and the

77

townsmen, to lose no time in discovering what sort of person each would have to deal with and to assess the likely situation before coming to grips with it.

Over the years, the welcoming ceremony, though observing the basic principles, had shed much of the fine careless rapture of former times. Several bishops ago, the village headman would have made speeches in the prevailing patois; then the carriage would be unhorsed and, preceded by a band, strong men would haul the bishop and his lady through the streets between lines of cheering yokels. Outside Fox's Tower, the cavalcade would pause for more speeches until the bishop could make his getaway, retreat indoors, and pour himself a stiff cocoa.

Dr. Frank Theodore Woods moved into the castle on 31 December 1923, before his enthronement at Winchester Cathedral on 5 January 1924. His civic welcome was arranged for 22 January in the Corn Exchange. In the meantime, preliminary reconnaisances were made on both sides. Mr. Macklin and his church choir went up to the castle and sang carols to them. Mrs. Woods handed out invitations to at-homes. Then she took refuge in her bedroom with 'flu, and left it all to her husband. He was, he said, 'very happy to make the acquaintance of so many of his neighbours'. At 6.40 p.m. on 22 January, Farnham's important people assembled in the old boardroom at the Exchange. Letters were read from the Rev. J. M. C. Crum, rector, and Mr. Wright, Clerk of the Council, regretting their inability to attend because of illness. At 6.50, Mr. Mardon and Mr. Murrell met Dr. Woods at the door. Being still in hiding with the vapours, the doctor's lady was represented by a Mrs. Lunt, her cousin. After some polite exchanges, the company made their way to the main hall where there were a goodly number of 'all classes of the community'. Chairman Mardon made the first speech, presenting the bishop to the people. The occupants of 'the house on the hill', he said, had always been their neighbours in the truest sense of the word. He went through the conventional phrases, finally touching on the poignant topic of the coming split in the Winchester Diocese and its implications for Farnham Castle. When Mr. Mardon sat down, Lilian Warren, young daughter of J. H. Warren of Broomleaf House and a pupil at Elmsleigh School, handed Mrs. Lunt a bouquet for Mrs. Woods. Then Mr. Kempson spoke in his 'usual bright and breezy manner'. He regretted that the first speaker had said all the things there were to say, and proceeded to say a lot of them again. Now it was the bishop's turn. He had, he said in several different ways, already found Farnham such a homely place. He gave praise to his predecessor, Dr. Talbot—now recuperating in Rome (where he had had his pocket picked of a purse containing £40). The chairman briefly responded and ended with a warning to the newcomer that, if he should decide to cut down any of the trees at the castle, then he had better consult 'a certain townsman' first. This reference to Councillor Borelli's love of trees, Farnham's stock joke, never failed to bring the house down, and, possibly, a frown to the face of the stranger who wasn't in on it. As the people filed from the hall, the bishop shook the hand of each. That was how Bishop Theodore Woods became a citizen of Farnham. Speaking the following month at a meeting in Guildford, he compared the castle in that town with Farnham's. Guildford's, he believed, had once been used as a gaol; during the revolution, it had not been considered important enough to defend. Farnham Castle had a much wider history; during the Civil War, it had been besieged by Cromwell's men; royalty down the ages had been frequent visitors (one bishop had even asked his sovereign whether he regarded the place as an inn). 'I have', said Dr. Woods, 'already fallen in love with Farnham'.

*   *   *   *   *

As if jealous of the big event taking place in Church of England circles, the Roman Catholics leaked a resolution to build a new Church of Saint Joan of Arc in Farnham. Asked when, Father Robo replied—not for a long time yet; we've got to save up first. They had the land between the Tilford and Waverley roads. They raised the first £1,000 by the autumn.

Farnham's wartime air force prodigy, J. F. A. Higgins—now ranking as an Air Vice Marshal—was appointed Air Officer in Command, H.M. Forces, Iraq. The *Herald* recalled that he had once lived with his parents at 'The Chestnuts', East Street. Following the armistice, Higgins had represented the Air Force at the Washington Conference for the limitation of armaments.

The tenant of 5 Adams Park Road was given permission to install 'a wireless apparatus', provided his insurance company had no objection.

Lime and plane trees were ordered for planting on the new pavement on the east side of Tilford Road. Further up, over the brow of the hill, modest improvements to the road were planned as far as Greenhill Road. It was found that a bank of trees would block progress; rather than fell these, land was acquired to the left so that a new roadway would skirt them. One sees the hand of Mr. Borelli in this; as watchdog of the town's amenities, he came in for a good deal of good-natured chaff during his long spell on the Council. During World War Two, an unlikely story circulated that a pilot sent aloft to report on the town's vulnerability to air-raids claimed that he couldn't see the place for trees. The legacy left by Mr. Borelli has remained Farnham's greatest asset; but for him, the town would probably have been vandalised to the point where its character was indistinguishable from that of so many other places—a sprawl of uninviting houses surrounding a central belt of repellantly-fronted shops, with a self-conscious square of tortured grass the only concession to nature.

A Mr. H. H. Wolstenholme applied for permission to run a 14-seater motor omnibus between Farnham and Rowledge . . . The vicar of the Bourne was campaigning for an open space in the Ridgway, big enough for football or cricket . . . A circular from the High Commissioner of Australia invited immigrants from the United Kingdom under the Empire Settlement Act, 1922.

In keeping with their reputation for picking only the right people, the promoters of the 'Pop' lectures booked Walter de la Mare for a talk on Egypt on 14 March. He went down with 'flu at the last moment; but never mind, a week later, Hilaire Belloc lectured on Joan of Arc; it was his third appearance in Farnham.

Captain Strickland, Head of the Grammar School since 1919, caused surprise by resigning in March. He was taking up a partnership in a firm of tutors, W. Nichols and Marcy of Chancery Lane. His successor was appointed in April. Mr. Francis Arthur Morgan, M.A. (Oxon), M.C., came here from the Whitgift Grammar School, Croydon. 'Moggy' was to stay in Farnham for the rest of his scholastic career.

Meanwhile, in the Water Company takeover issue, much of the stuff had flowed under the bridge. There had appeared to be an element of collusion between the company and the Wey Valley Water Company which threatened the Council's intentions, and caused them to press forward with a deadline not later than 24 June 1925. John White Lewis, the F.W.C.'s manager, died, thus saving £156 in compensation; they also persuaded Mr. Crundwell to waive directors' compensation (£300) during the transition period. Finally, on 24 March, an amended draft agreement was signed and the file passed to the Minister.

The two new roads which spanned the Tilford and Waverley roads were now in the throes of development. The higher one ran through a field formerly called Little Paradise. It was a sensible practice of the Council to perpetuate field-names by bestowing them where possible on development roads running through. This was not always practical, of course—there was one field in the district which bore the name of 'Dirty Hole'. Stanley S. Dawes of Heath and Wiltshires, one of those having a house built in the road, objected to the proposed name of Little Paradise Road. One can see his argument. Alternatives like Manor Rise or Manor Ridge, after the nearby Manor House, arose—conjuring up street-names from scratch was a mind-bending exercise. Then the Chairman suggested Menin Way—after the Menin Gate Memorial at Ypres, on which his son's name would appear. The lower road was named Longley Road, also for a personal reason.

The town's magnificent fund-raising effort for the Guildford Hospital Appeal was rewarded with an invitation to the Chairman to attend the opening of the extension—a new out-patients' wing—by the Duke and Duchess of York.

The election on 5 April ended the membership of Councillors H. K. Bentall, J. Lewis Jones, and Mrs. G. C. Watkins, who did not seek re-election. Mr. Ewart and Mr. Borelli were returned, together with newcomers E. S. Crow, a builder in Hale Road, Alexander Grange of High Park Road, and A. R. Robins. Sir Edward Perceval and Harry Sanders tried to make a comeback, but failed. Mr. Crow informed his audience that he was not much of a hand at public speaking, but was full of ambition to do all the right things. For the third year running, the top two posts went to Councillors Mardon and Murrell.

As a moderately law-abiding community, with a quota of petty offences probably no greater than that of the average small town, it was curiously out of keeping that Farnham should possess the capacity to stage at intervals some grievous crime of the sort sensationalised by Fleet Street. William Edward Hall, married, 28 years of age, was on the staff of Lloyds Bank, Castle Street: as part of his duties, he manned the sub-branch at Bordon at certain set hours during the week. Lance-Corporal Abraham (Jack) Goldenberg of the 2nd East Lancs., stationed at Bordon, had a small account there; he was planning to marry and needed funds. On 3 April, he took an officer's revolver, went to the bank, shot Hall and helped himself to the contents of the till; he buried the money outside his barrack-room. Goldenberg was sent for trial at Winchester Assizes on 19 June. His appeal against the death penalty was dismissed at a later court. A petition signed by 100,000 people and 70 M.P.s was sent to the House of Commons. As an outcome, bank clerks no longer manned sub-offices unless accompanied by a colleague.

The main event of the day for Farnham, however, was the fruition of the Council's petition for a takeover of the remaining villages in the old ecclesiastical parish of Farnham. The primary object was, of course, drainage, and the Surveyor had prepared a tentative scheme at a guesswork figure of about £60,000. This cost was so high because of the need to lay connecting sewers through undeveloped land between the isolated communities and the town. The Rural Council, whose district would be decimated if the proposed transfer went through, devised a scheme of their own which was in no way as good as Mr. Cass's—even the Tilford residents declared that, whilst they had no wish to become urbanised, being truly rural in character, they preferred the town scheme. The County Inquiry was held at the Corn Exchange on 8/9 May, when it was emphasised that time was of the essence, so that, if approved, the takeover should be expedited. The reason for the hurry was that, owing to an easement of the unemployment problem, the government was setting a deadline on its 65 per cent. of wages grant.

The regions recommended by County for transference to the Urban District were the Bournes, Wrecclesham, Rowledge, and Dippenhall. That left Tilford—the delectable jewel in the crown—expressly excluded. The view taken by the Court was that, whereas the areas ceded were more or less contiguous with the town, or soon would be at the current rate of building development, Tilford was an isolated village, rural in all respects and surrounded by a broad belt of open country which, praise be to the Lord, looked like remaining immune from devastation. The cost of bridging with sewers the wide, ratepayerless approaches to the village would add considerably and unjustifiably to the drainage bill. Mitchell Banks, representing the Council, continued to press for the inclusion of Tilford at the Ministry of Health inquiry. He dangled before the Commissioner the Council's offer to sewer Frensham (though not included in the application) as an attraction. But no—the Commissioner was a hard man. Finally, a line was drawn on the map from Old Frensham Road, near Pinehurst, in an easterly direction to the river, then to Waverley Mill, and, keeping to the road, in a north-easterly direction to the parish boundary. If the Council would accept this ruling, then the Rural Council would drop further opposition.

It took time, of course, for all this to be translated into a Confirmation Order, and for this to arrive via the County Council. Throughout, the Government's

Unemployed Grants Committee had been kept alerted with a draft application for a grant towards the huge wage bill anticipated. On 31 July, a chilling letter was received from the Committee stating that it appeared, on the facts before them, that the situation had not been accelerated to such an extent as to render it eligible for a grant. With admirable restraint, this letter was recorded in the Council's Minutes as having caused 'keen disappointment'. They tried again, tactfully pointing out to the U.G.C. that the delay in starting the proposed drainage works in the added areas had been due to the government dragging their heels. Back came the Committee's true reason—namely that the proposed works were not *primarily* promoted for the relief of unemployment, but as a scheme which would have to be carried out in any case. One senses that this snag should have occurred to those responsible when doing their sums earlier.

Statistically, the boundary extension would increase the population of the Urban District from 12,307 (including Hale) to 17,737, and the area from 3,214 to 10,660 acres. There were many more mouths to feed; that grant of 65 per cent. of the wage bill would have come in useful. As an added blow, about this time the Privy Council came through with the belated information that they could not entertain Farnham's petition for a Charter unless the town had a minimum population figure of 20,000. It just wasn't their day.

It was, on the other hand, Major H. C. Patrick's day. Visitors to First World War cemeteries throughout the world might find, on closer inspection, the signature H.C.P. on many of the memorials. In May, the firm secured orders for carved tablets in the cemetery in Jerusalem; in July, a contract for four 18-ft. high memorials to the Indian forces who fell at Mesopotamia, to be erected in Alwiyah and Baghdad, inscribed in Urdu, Hindi and Gurmukhi. They also carved inscription panels on New Zealand memorials for the Twelve Tree Copse and Hill 60 cemeteries at Gallipoli. Major Patrick had carved his own niche—a house by Harold Falkner in Browns Lane. Nearby, Mr. Stedman designed one for Mr. E. W. Langham. More and more, the town's prosperous businessmen were staking out their minor estates in the desirable residential areas to the south-east. The semi-rural aspect of this part of Farnham was not accidental; it was contrived, with the help of Nature, by thoughtful architects during the first quarter of this century, and one should be thankful for them.

Mr. H. J. Varey, B.A., from Uxbridge County School, took the place of Mr. E. G. Hunt on the staff of the Grammar School . . . A meeting was held at the Corn Exchange in June in an attempt to form a local branch of the British Fascisti, whose intention it was to combat the growing amount of communist propaganda then flooding the country . . . The Chamber of Commerce was campaigning for more public conveniences, especially in the town centre, and Mr. Sargent was hunting for likely sites.

The Council seconded Enfield Council's plea for legislation controlling the plethora of advertising hoardings increasingly despoiling the countryside. A joke in *Punch* depicted a man gazing at a village almost completely hidden by a giant hoarding which informed him that it was a 'Beauty Spot'.

The tragic deaths of Mallory and Irvine 28,000 feet up on Mount Everest prompted a letter in *The Times* which recalled that Leigh Mallory, when a master at Charterhouse, had travelled in all weathers to Farnham in order to take classes under the Workers' Educational Association initiated by his friend, Mr. Morgan.

The Diocese of Winchester (Division) Measure 1923 passed through the House of Lords early in July and was presented for Royal Assent. The Diocesan Board was still talking about using part of Farnham Castle as a bishop's residence and the remainder as a Retreat House. They had now decided to sell the park, except for a small area in the proximity of the castle.

The final bill for the Water Company came to £33,180. This included £7,500 for new works, replacements, high-level water tower, etc. The Council became the owners of the undertaking on 1 July, pending official confirmation. The rest of the year was spent in overhauling the complex. A. H. Ball and Co. laid pipes along new roads or replaced defective mains; up-to-date machinery ousted the worn-out equipment; Crosbys renovated the engineer's house. A new engineer was appointed in November, out of 189 applicants; he was L. C. Wright from Romsey, until a few years back a second-engineer on a Union Steamship Company boat. With the added area—or 'Outer Ward', as it was termed—and the Water Undertaking, not to mention the expansion of admin. work occasioned by the development currently taking place throughout the district, it could be said that, all at once, the Council were in big business. Your Council officer is long suffering; he will plod on, year after year, his duties increasing almost imperceptibly little by little, without any noticeable increase in salary. But the bulk increase in the autumn of 1924 was far from imperceptible, and the staff began to make noises.

In the public health department, the Medical Officer, Dr. Sloman, was nearing retirement, and in no mood to take on 5,000 additional potential clients. Dr. C. E. Tanner, his counterpart in the Rural District, had given notice (he was accorded a terrific send-off in October at Waverley Abbey, with tributes paid from the platform by the Archbishop of Canterbury, Dr. Randall Davidson, and the late Bishop of Winchester, Dr. Talbot). It began to look as if at any time the health of the town might be at risk.

In rating circles, too, there were rumbles. Alf Thorp, holder of the dual appointments of Assistant Overseer (which entailed collection of the town's Poor Rates) and the Council's Collector of the General District Rates—the two were consolidated in 1929 as the General Rate—was not a man given to rumbling. Being stone deaf, he remained in silent isolation. Each time a new property was built, his work went up by one more assessment; now, with the Outer Ward, the rateable value had shot up by £33,703, bringing the total to £102,915. Alf Thorp used to tell the story about the village rate collector who, under contract with the Rural Council, was paid a commission based on a percentage of the small amount of rates he collected. A manufacturer chose his village as the site of a gigantic factory and the collector's commission, on this one assessment alone, came to about £500 a year. In the end, after much pressure, he agreed to retire on a pension of £300 a year. About this time, A. J. Nash, of 41 Castle Street, parish Poor Rate collector in a neighbouring area, resigned, ahd Thorp found himself in a unique position to córner the local market in rate collection, not only in the town but throughout a considerable slice of West Surrey. He played hard to get; the world was his oyster.

Bourne Mill, Guildford Road, came on the market and the Council bought the house and mill, five cottages and 29 acres of land for £4,500. A large area of frontage was re-sold to the County Council for road improvements, and land at the back to the Guardians for a probable extension of the workhouse. Enough land was left for a housing estate and allotments. One sees the hand of Mr. Borelli in the careful preservation of the house and its adjoining cottage, unique amongst Farnham's antiquities.

The 1920s were blissfully still an age when children were expected to be seen but not heard. The Council had by no means neglected this sector of the community, having provided Gostrey Meadow and other romping areas. Brightwells, on the other hand, had been earmarked as a quiet place of public walks, pleasure gardens and discreet games areas for the enjoyment of more sober age groups. The kids, it appeared, had taken over, and the noise was shattering; people working in the house had to shout at times to make themselves heard. So up went the notices.

Tenants in part of the house—the War Pensions Committee—gave notice as from 29 September 1924, not because of the bedlam outside, but for occupational reasons. They had the large room on the ground floor; it was re-let to an architect at £50 a year. Later, this room became the public library.

On 7 October, the councillors welcomed the six country cousins transferred to the Urban District Council under the Surrey (Farnham Urban District) Confirmation Order 1924. These members from the Outer Ward brought the official strength of the F.U.D.C. to twenty-four. The six new gentlemen were Councillors R. C. Avery, C. F. Falkner, S. Lathey, H. A. Skerry, A. Julius Stevens, and E. Tully.

There was yet another general election in October. This time, there was no Liberal candidate in the Farnham constituency, and Arthur Samuel well and truly pushed Mrs. Corner into the corner with 18,272 votes against 4,613. Farnham's M.P. was still doing well; in December, he was appointed Parliamentary Secretary to the Department of Overseas Trade. He took the oath in the Jewish fashion, wearing the hat.

East Street—that melancholy thoroughfare which could have modelled for Tennyson's 'long, unlovely street'—had always been a thorn in the side of Farnham's immaculate town centre. Over the years, the street had become a Tin Pan Alley of such eyesores as the gas works, hospital, cinemas, and the like, though, by so being, rendering a valuable service to the rest. Now with the motoring age the street had sprouted commercial garages and was a repository for a growing number of clapped-out motor cars. All this, plus the considerable flow of passing traffic had led to intolerable congestions. East Street was the responsibility of the County Council, so Farnham wrote to Kingston, suggesting that it might be tidied up a bit, the kinks straightened out, the congestions eased and generally made to look more respectable. County came back with a revolutionary idea—why not have a brand new by-pass road, branching off, say, at the *Albion* hotel and running through the meadows south of the town centre? Mr. Cass, the Surveyor, was told to mull over it.

But Mr. Cass had other plans. In the field of local government, the officers in the Town Hall, being in the front line, are the ones who take the knocks. For they are in direct contact with the parishioners, who pull faces at them or attack them in the bazaars. The life-span of an L.G.O. expires, unless he expires first, at the age of sixty-five. Long before this dotage is reached, however, disillusionment sets it, and cases are known of an officer showing the whites of his eyes and biting. Biting a ratepayer is taboo, and the only outcome is for the officer to strike his tent and steal silently away. That is what Mr. Cass found it expedient to do, with effect from 10 November 1924. At his going, he was conventionally thanked by the Council for 27 years' excellent service, given fully paid sick leave for three months, and thereafter retained as consultant surveyor at £156 a year. How many of Farnham's admirers ever spare a thought for those who, back in the formative years, set the town on its path towards Utopia? Robert William Cass came to Farnham from Pudsey in 1897. With Yorkshire relish, he went to work on the one-horse dustbowl which offended his eyes. When he retired in 1924, Farnham was on the tourist maps.

Mr. Leonard Starling was confirmed as Acting Surveyor, at a salary of £400, plus a 'mechanical traction' allowance of £30. The Clerk was still unwell; in December, Mr. Arthur Minns was formally appointed Deputy Clerk, with power to act in Mr. Wright's absence. Thus a new staffing pattern began to emerge.

Robert George Wilson arrived from Sleaford, .Lincs., in October to be the new postmaster . . . The Council took over maintenance of the castle steps and footpath . . . A putting-green was planned for Brightwells . . . A supplementary rate of 2d. in the pound was levied in the area of the Council's water supply; this was additional to water rates, and, on the face of it, a clumsy manoeuvre to disguise the fact that, in total, consumers would pay more or less the same as those in the expensive Wey Valley Water Company's area.

Everything now centred on the newly-acquired Outer Ward. At grass-roots level, the staff were taking over from their country cousins. Mr. F. W. Parratt, for instance, the Wrecclesham *enfant terrible,* was currently converting an unsuitable granary into a dwelling house without the formality of submitting plans. And new refinements were being thrust upon the villagers in the shape of house refuse collection and street-lighting. A. H. Ball and Company's tender of £3,253 was accepted for phase 1 of the drainage works. The Council were third time lucky with the Unemployment Grants Committee over the Outer Ward drainage grant. This time they enlisted the co-operation of the Aldershot Employment Exchange and a deputation journeyed to London and were interviewed by the U.G.C., who gave way, subject to the work being commenced within 18 months from 1 December 1924.

Opening talks on feasibility, County stressed that the need for a by-pass round Farnham was not a pressing one . . . The Electricity Company were asked to extend their wares to the Hale Ward . . . December's plans included no fewer than 19 new houses in the private sector. George Baigent submitted drawings of his extended lay-out in Bridgefield . . . Farnham Theatre Company wanted alterations at the *Palace* theatre, East Street.

A further 125 council houses were planned for various sites. For a start, Mr. Sargent was directed to prepare drawings for 30 houses on a 3½-acre plot off Firgrove Hill (Arthur Road) that Mr. Mardon was willing to part with for £200 an acre.

At Christmas, 200 poor families benefited from the Gift Fund. On Boxing Day that ancient coaching house, the *Bush* hotel, revived an old custom with a boar's head on the sideboard. Visitors were invited to cut themselves a slice. In the evening, the company danced to the music of Cyril Fisher's band. On 28 December, the river overflowed its shallow banks and poured into the basements of cottages in the low-lying streets.

1925

Not since February 1900 has Farnham experienced such a flood as that which covered Bridge Square, Longbridge, Union Road, Lower Church Lane, Vicarage Lane and Downing Street on Friday and Saturday in last week . . .

Farnham Herald: 10 January 1925

THE WATER ROSE 14 inches in the ground-floor rooms of the houses in Lower Church Lane; in Vicarage Lane, they had it up as far as the fourth stair. The flood waters surged across Gostrey Meadow into Union Road and Downing Street, marooning the buildings there in a depth of six inches. In Longbridge, a horse in the shafts of a cart belonging to E. Beale, the corn merchant, slipped and fell. It was a heavy horse, and efforts to raise it failed. They held its head above water until, in the end, they were obliged to shoot the poor beast. Floods in Farnham, whether on a big or moderate scale, go back to the dawn of history.

Once upon a time, itinerant pilgrims seeking a night's lodging at Waverley Abbey mostly resisted the temptations of the town centre by the simple means of avoiding payment of the toll, and, leaving the road under the eyes of the bartender, made their way downhill, past the entrance to the church, to the river. They forded this and, forking left, climbed the slope to the path which led to Waverley. By the time Henry VIII had put a stop to the need for this pilgrimage, the town was possessed of a well-trodden way across the valley, the broad bottom of which was of the sort marked on the maps as being 'Liable to Floods'.

The natives had perhaps been rather silly building their church on the declivity south of the main street, instead of looking towards the gently rising, flood-free area on the north side. They did, however, have the foresight to build it on a shallow mound—though this is said by some to consist of an accumulation of human bones. For where there's a church, there usually follows a fashionable backwater. In Farnham, the precinct had become not so much a backwater as an underwater. But having already started on the downward slope, there seemed little point in not making use of the well-trodden path of the pilgrims, and so came Downing Street, the lower end of which was subaqueous at times. On the further bank of the river, the beaten track was developed by what came to be called Bridge Square, Red Lion Lane, and Abbey Street, an isolated suburb of of Farnham which divulged no reason for its existence—unless it was that the pilgrims halted here to dry out after fording the river, and the locals, having failed to lure them into the town, set up toll-free souvenir stalls.

Colonel George Chrystie saw to Farnham's rain; he had been seeing to it for the past 25 years in his garden at Shortheath Lodge, which was never under water. Before him, the Rev. T. W. Sidebotham had also done it for 25 years in his garden at the Bourne vicarage. These two gentlemen, whose pluvio-metrical exertions had overlapped for a period of five years, must presumably have had a love-hate relationship with the gentle drops from heaven. Colonel Chrystie informed the public that, during his time, there had been a yearly average of 29.24 inches of the stuff; that the heaviest rainfall in any one year was that of 1903, with 42.85 inches, and the lowest in 1921, with 14.32 inches.

It had always been the keen desire of authorities along the river to ensure that, by hook or by crook, all the water entering their district, plus their own, should pass on intact, without spilling any, for the chaps downstream to cope with. The River Wey came in full measure from across the Hampshire border, but, instead of leaving on the other side and flooding, say, Godalming, it overflowed the shallow banks through Farnham and spilled itself over the adjacent townscape. This didn't often happen, of course—only when it rained hard, and that was often. It had worried the Council and their predecessors in office for time out of mind. No government had ever established an authority over waterways above the point where they ceased to be navigable, so that, when a river took to the road, the local council were without powers to tackle the problem. The Council would clutch at straws. Riparian owners, that is to say, people with the river at the bottom of their gardens (and at times with their gardens at the bottom of the river) would be unfairly charged with blocking up the river bed with rubbish, and told to clean it out. In Farnham, such riparians included people living in big houses along West Street, and the Council could not lean on them too much. Another culprit was the rector, and all one could expect from him was *Song of Solomon: 8/7*. The laundry in Darvills Lane also came under fire, for they used a system of sluices which diverted the water into their premises. On leaving, the water took the dirt with it and deposited this on the river bed, causing shoals to form.

The Thames Conservators, who looked after the Thames from Teddington westward, were well pleased with a situation in which the Wey tributary spilled itself over Farnham instead of adding to their problems by discharging its full load into the Thames at Weybridge. It was, however, whispered that the Ministry of Agriculture were thinking of setting up a River Wey Drainage Board, so the Council appealed to them for help. The reply told them that the Surrey County Council were in process of promoting a Bill through the Commons to require the authority to control waterways within their county. For the time being, the Chairman opened a subscription list in order to buy coal for distribution to the poor so that they could dry out their cottages. Within a week he had received £14 and supplied 40 homes.

*   *   *   *   *

January's plans included one from the Midland Bank for new premises at 33 The Borough . . . Mr. R. Courtenay Welch of Heath End undertook to plant six young trees, grown from seeds taken from trees at Verdun, to form a background to the Hale war memorial . . . A lay-out plan was studied for an extension of Beavers Road to link up with the Hart. The Deputy Clerk was one who built a house there . . . The new houses in Arthur Road were estimated at about £15,000. Tenders were accepted from H. Punter (for 16) and F. le Clercq (for 14).

Dr. Sloman expressed no wish to retire, even after 48 years as Medical Officer. With both urban and rural areas now to cope with, his salary increased from £137 to £250, a point which may not have escaped his attention.

Mr. Starling's appointment as Surveyor was confirmed in February, at a salary of £400, rising to £500. Mr. Cass's son, George, became his first assistant. Alf Thorp had played his hand with skill; he was now in the rate collection business with a total stipend of £600, out of which he was required to provide his own office accommodation. This was at 9 Downing Street; over the mantlepiece hung a rifle—for pleasure only, for Thorp was a keen amateur marksman. So a new generation of 'gentlemen at the Town Hall' was emerging; public servants whose letters after their names qualified them to sort out the problems of the ratepayers and to advise their masters, the councillors, on how to run the town.

An old boy himself, Mr. Langham gave excellent publicity in his local paper to the doings of Grammar School pupils, past and present. One of many who had distinguished themselves in one field or another was Professor James Kendall, M.A., D.Sc., LL.D., F.R.S., who was currently Professor of Chemistry at Columbia University. Later, in 1928, he was to hold a similar post at Edinburgh University. At the old school in West Street, 1901-1907, he had been one of the early scholarship boys.

On 13 February, Canon E. Neville Lovett was inducted as Bishop of the proposed new Diocese of Portsmouth. During his reign as Farnham's rector, he had distinguished himself by promoting fund-raising pageants against a background of the castle walls—*Historical Episodes* which depicted somewhat imaginative renderings of past occasions between castle and town, which, nevertheless, brought in the money for enterprises such as the Church House.

More floods in February—though of a minor nature . . . F. Sweetzer, the Farnham golf club professional, holed out in one at the sixth hole—156 yards . . . J. F. Smallcombe of 76 Castle Street sought permission to sling a wireless aerial at a height of 50 feet across the street to the house opposite; his object was to obtain a clear signal . . . Miss C. N. Williams, Head of the Girls' Grammar School, was off to a better-salaried headship at a girls' school in Ipswich. Her successor was Miss Doris Marjorie Drought, M.A. (Oxon.), from the Modern Languages Department of the Godolphin School, Salisbury.

Meanwhile, the acorn dropped by a throw-away line from the County Council—'why not by-pass East Street'—had germinated. In March, the surveyor made a tentative report on the proposal to introduce 'a new road by which motorists might avoid the tortuous gauntlet of East Street'. County, said L.H.S., favoured a route through the park, where it would not clash with any built-up area. He also reported on a possible highway constructed from Junction Bridge, along Guildford Road and East Street, as far as Castle Street. The latter suggestion, surely, would have entailed the replacement of the sacrosanct Borough bottleneck. A member of the public suggested moving back the existing buildings to widen the street by emulating an engineering feat recently successful in the United States—'you jacks 'em up on trolleys and someone blows a whistle'. The Chamber of Commerce, worried that by diverting passing traffic through the park the travellers might escape the clutches of Farnham shopkeepers, protested against the whole idea of a by-pass. An alternative route through the meadows south of the river was also in their minds. Mighty oaks from little acorns grow.

That ubiquitous item of street furniture, the telephone kiosk, made its appearance in Farnham with an application in April to erect one on the footpath at the South Street corner . . . A licence to store 30 gallons of petrol was issued to Mr. James Corpe in Ivy Lane . . . W. Kingham and Sons asked to build warehouses at the back of the *Lion and Lamb* buildings (which were now being restored to something like their original charm) . . . G. B. Hersey and Sons, Ltd., quoted £19,691 3s. 11½d. for work on the Outer Ward drainage scheme—even half-pennies in those days had a value.

The election on 6 April filled four vacancies in the town and two in Hale. Of the five candidates in the town, Councillors Figg and Mardon were re-elected, and Mr. Philipson-Stow regained a seat. The fourth successful candidate was Alexander Selfe Marsh, a singing and elocution teacher of 'The Jungle', Abbey Street. William Arnold, described as a retired coach-body builder of 'The Bryn', Menin Way, was unsuccessful. In Hale, there was one nominee, Herbert William Bide, for two vacancies, but Mr. Aungier, one of the retiring members, was persuaded to stay on.

'We have made history', declared Mr. A. G. Mardon in his winding-up speech. He hoped that the latest extension of the district would prove a wise measure. The water undertaking, he regretted, was costing more than anticipated, but at least the town was now protected against fire. He was jubilant about housing development, in both public and private sectors. And he had kind words to say about Mr. Minns, the Deputy Clerk, who had carried on during the long illness of Mr. Wright. Mr. Ransom declined the offer of Chairmanship for health reasons. Mr. A. G. Mardon was—for the fourth year in succession—sent to the Chair, again with Mr. Murrell as Vice.

Miss Doris Jefferies, daughter of H. J. Jefferies of 'The Ridges' in the Bourne, and solicitors' clerk at Hollest, Mason and Nash, was congratulated on passing the final examination of the Law Society. She became a partner of Lipton and Jefferies in Jermyn Street, Piccadilly.

A letter from the Diocesan Land Surveyor in April puzzled the Council. It enquired whether there was any prospect of the town wanting to buy part of the park for the purpose of a by-pass road. The Clerk wrote at once saying that the Council had been assured that they would be kept fully informed about all developments for the disposal of the park, and had been given first refusal. Now it seemed as if they were being left out of the picture, excepting insofar as land for a new road, which would be subject in any case to compulsory purchase if necessary. The Diocesan Surveyor put their minds at rest with the assurance that the Council's option would be honoured. One member suggested buying the park without further ado. It was a weighty matter, involving great expense.

The King's speech on 9 May, which re-opened Wembley Exhibition for a second year, was relayed to the town through three loudspeakers by G. A. Hale in The Borough. Wireless was still a novelty; perhaps in the not very distant future, commented the *Herald,* we may have scenes as well as sounds.

The summer season opened in Brightwells on 16 May, when the new bowling green and miniature golf course were used for the first time. The bowlers taking part were later presented with a photograph of the event. Putting was a craze which swept the country briefly in the '20s, and was prolonged hopefully in an exaggerated form by seaside authorities.

Pre-demolition photographs were taken for posterity of the buildings on the Bourne Mill Estate which stood in the way of road improvements. The Council, doubtless at the instance of Mr. Borelli, had recently resolved upon this excellent practice. So much of the town's ancient past had been lost forever.

There were complaints about the street musicians, those victims of the post-war unemployment problem. Instrumental or vocal, singly or in groups, these performers would solicit one's small change at frequent intervals along the street. The renderings of the solo vocalist were an art form intended for passers-by rather than a static audience. For the sounds bore no resemblance to any known song, but were ululant expressions with neither words nor tunes which ceased only when a policeman hove in sight.

Mr. Sargent was presented by the councillors with an armchair on the occasion of his marriage to Miss Newton . . . Mr. William Ayling of East Street gave a demonstration in Gostrey Meadow of the capabilities of a motor mower . . . Family bathing was introduced at the baths on Sunday afternoons between 2 and 4 o'clock, under the watchful eye of the superintendent. The idea was to teach the kids to swim; if the mums and dads had other ideas, then that was just too bad . . . Farnham Grammar School old boy—Reginald R. Tomlinson, A.R.C.A. (boarder, 1899–1903)—was mentioned as having leapt from being Principal of Cheltenham School of Arts and Crafts to Inspector of Art Work for the London

County Council, at a salary which, the *Herald* exclaimed, must be in the region of £1,000 a year.

The latest in the extraordinary success story of Air Vice Marshal J. F. A. Higgins, C.B., D.S.O., was that, in the Birthday Honours, he had been made a Knight Commander of the British Empire. He lived at 'The Chestnuts' Uxbridge—was this house named after his childhood home in East Street, Farnham?

The Council put their house in order with an Order made under the Local Government Act 1888. The district was divided into six wards, and the total number of councillors fixed at twenty-one. The new establishment was as follows:

Ward	Area in acres	Number of houses	Number of voters	Councillors
Castle	2,387	1,034	2,272	5
Waverley	1,265	680	1,443	4
Hale	1,415	817	1,824	3
Badshot	1,485	312	716	2
Bourne	899	846	1,691	4
Wrecclesham	884	515	1,152	3
	8,335	4,204	9,098	21

Several residents in Castle Street petitioned against the parking of motor cars in that street. The Council asked the police to sort it out, but nothing was done—at any rate over the next half-century and more. Perhaps the best way of ending this desecration of the town's most glorious heritage would be to paint double yellow lines up each side and pass the problem back to the motorists.

Street accidents were now established as a regular feature, taking the place of wartime casualties in the local paper. Many involved cyclists, who had yet to learn to take evasive action at the approach of a motor car. A workman named Stapley, for instance, who was cycling down Firgrove Hill one June day, had the foolhardiness to make his way through the windscreen of a motor van coming up the hill. In the same week, and almost at the same spot, another bicycle attacked Mr. Sargent's motor-cycle. Later in the month, a motor-cyclist and his pillion passenger were killed at Coopers Corner, Runfold, in collision with a lorry that jack-knifed. Drivers in those days did not have to study and pass a test before taking a car on the road; they just got in and drove. The men took care to some extent to avoid trouble. From accounts in the press, the female of the species was the deadlier. The ladies, it seemed, had a way of putting their foot down.

Mr. L. Hodge, whilst manning his post office in East Street one day, was surprised to see a cow walk in. This sort of cosy incident, and the fact that it could still happen, proved that the car had not entirely taken over, and that there was still some room left for humanity, and bovinity.

During alterations to the *Nelson Arms* in Castle Street, workmen found hidden on a rafter 11 ivory fish, from one to two inches long, as well as parts of broken churchwarden clay pipes. The fish were similar to a set of 11 tokens found 20 years earlier at the post office. The *Herald* correspondent wrote that these small dummy fish were at one time asociated with the ancient sport of angling. Anglers, who are traditionally 'as thirsty as a fish', would make for their favourite pub at the slightest hint of rain, there to carry on their sport by fishing for these tiddlers in a bowl of ale. The 1 April would be club gala night, when 11 tokens would be immersed in ale specially brewed for the occasion. If the larger fish floated above the smaller, then this would forecast good fishing prospects for the coming season.

In their urbanisation of the Hale Ward, the councillors undertook to give names to the jungle paths. Hitherto, more often than not a resident's postal address would be 'near the (here followed the name of the nearest pub)'. At least two of the lanes, Alma Lane and Ball and Wicket Lane, were, in fact, named after pubs. The name now suggested for the main thoroughfare was 'Hale Street', but this was altered at the request of General Roy to 'Upper Hale Road'. When name-plates were ordered from the Never Rust Metal Co., Ltd. (whose products never rusted), it was found that the charge was 1s. 1d. per letter. If the General's recommendation had been as short as his own name, then this would have been economically sound.

The Council had had time by now to assess their capabilities as suppliers of water and to come to recognise some of the malpractices of the consumers. People got up to all sorts of things. Workmen on building sites, for instance, helped themselves to water without paying for it, and otherwise honest householders had a way of using the stuff to water their gardens. There had been a heavy drain of supplies, and increased pumping became necessary. But on the whole the councillors were satisfied that they had got away to a cracking start; at least they were achieving all the things which, in the old days, they had tried in vain to make the Water Company do.

Mr. Langham wrote on 19 June—

> Dear Mr. Mardon,
>
> I am about to buy the land belonging to the Trustees of the Late William Cox in the Ridgway Road. I am buying it with the intention that it shall be be kept as an open space and be used by the public as a recreation ground.
>
> With this end in view, my wife, my daughter and I myself wish to offer it to the Urban District Council as a free gift, and if the Council will accept it and undertake that it shall be kept as an open space forever, arrangements can be made for the land to be conveyed forthwith from Mr. Cox's Trustees direct to the Council.

Mr. Langham's solicitors intimated that it was their client's wish that the land should provide a playground for young children, and that he would like to impose a condition that no games or otherwise should be allowed to restrict the use of the land by children. If the Council disagreed with this condition, then Mr. Langham would give the land without restriction. In thanking the donor, the Council readily complied with his wishes. The ground was called the Langham Recreation Ground. Mr. Langham was perhaps wise to leave this indelible mark upon the town he loved, for his better-known memorial, the *Farnham Herald* newspaper, may cease to be attributed to him by future generations.

The 10-ton monster steam-roller which clanked its way over the 40 miles of roads within the urban district, and lived in a little house built for it just inside the entrance to the Council yard, was now too heavy for the modern methods of re-surfacing roads with bituminous macadam. Accordingly, a 6-ton 'Advance' roller was ordered from Wallis and Stevens of Basingstoke for £666.

The hopfields and farmland were falling prey to the get-rich-quick developers, and Farnham was losing its long tradition of husbandry to that of a commuters' paradise. Plans were coming in these days, not only for single properties, but for whole roads or estates at a time. One new road at Wrecclesham was named Stickhams Road, but this was changed by popular request to Echo Barn Lane because of an old barn there which emitted spooky noises at night. This building was bought at an auction sale by General Kays for £47 2s. 0d.

Following Mr. Langham's example, Chairman Mardon gave a piece of land adjoining a new housing site off Firgrove Hill. Solicitors on both sides waived their charges . . . The Farnham branch of the Middle Classes Union begged the Council to reduce their rates, even at the sacrifice of some part of their programme . . . Hales in The Borough asked permission to stage a wireless demonstration by the Marconiphone Company in Castle Street. It was eventually held in Brightwells, which was gaily decked in fairy lights. Reception was loud and clear.

At a big Labour rally at Camberley in August, Mrs. Elizabeth Corner blotted her copybook by attributing her defeat in the past two general elections to the 'damned snobbery' of the Farnham people. Mr. J. Beckett, Labour M.P. for Gateshead, who was present at the rally, described Arthur Samuel as one of the 'good, fat, rich gentlemen of Farnham', who weren't fit to lick the boots of honest workers in Durham. In October, it was announced that a Woking schoolmaster, Arthur Duncan Campbell, B.Sc., L.C.P., F.R.E.S., had become the prospective Labour candidate for the Farnham Division.

Ernst Crundwell, senior partner of Potter, Crundwell and Bridge, died on 31 August. Born near Tunbridge Wells in 1858, he had come to Farnham in 1884 to join Henry Potter. He had involved himself in a wide range of local activities—one of his part-time jobs was Clerk to the Rural Council—and had remained in harness right up to his final illness in July.

In September, another firm of solicitors, Kempson and Wright, moved from 121 West Street to premises opposite the Council offices in South Street which they had bought from A. H. Guyer, the architect. No. 121 West Street was sold by the executors of William Wells to H. E. Bide. It was later converted from offices into a shop.

In an effort to control the increasing street traffic, white lines were painted experimentally on the road at the corners of South Street and Downing Street, and in Bridge Square. They were successful and soon others were added at Crondall Lane, Hale, and Runfold.

With such large chunks of the Rural District now urbanised, the Joint Fire Brigade Committee was replaced by a committee of the U.D.C. only. The brigade lost no time in making demands—one was for central heating in the fire station, which entailed a larger boiler, and another was for a recreation hut, which was duly imported, equipped with billiards table and bar.

Mr. Borelli's constant pleas for a museum finally bore fruit. At the October meeting, he illustrated his prayer with a heart-rending account of an incident which had recently befallen the town. Major A. G. Wade of 'Ash Cottage', Bentley, had written to *The Times* about his recent discoveries. A director of the Metropolitan Museum, Washington, holidaying in the south of France, happened upon a copy of the paper and read the letter. In due course several priceless ancient implements were shipped across the Atlantic. 'It appears', said Mr. Borelli, 'that America is far more interested in Farnham things than Farnham is'. He got his way—a Museum Committee was established.

That autumn, the Outer Ward emerged from the Dark Ages with 35 street lamps, fitted with automatic switches . . . The tender of T. Flower and Co. of Bath, in the sum of £41,555, was accepted for further works of drainage in the Ward . . . Health Week came and went, with Dr. Frank Bedo Hobbs, who had joined the Tanner-Hussey practice, making his debut . . . The Farnham Motor Company, when altering their premises, yielded up a 3-ft. by 70-ft. strip of frontage for widening this narrowest part of East Street.

The Joint Isolation Hospital Committee, with a past record of big spending, agitated for a 25/30 h.p. Huddart hospital ambulance, costing £770 10s. 0d., to replace their horse-drawn ambulance. They were asked—why not just buy a second-hand chassis and rig up a body on top? The Council suggested a Sunbeam chassis that was then available. But the Committee were concerned about the comfort of their clients and dug their heels in. Balloon tyres were the things now, and Morris-Cowley were fitting four-wheel brakes as a standard feature.

The councillors displayed little interest in the Venison Dinner held at the *Bush* hotel on 31 December. Could not the speeches be shorter? asked Mrs. Stroud. That of Lord Midleton contained a reference to the dormant petition for incorporation. The County Council, he said, were coming round to the idea in view of Farnham's now enlarged district.

1926

Cold though it be, the gentle snow
Doth over all her mantle throw,
And every form a beauty takes
When, covered by her pearly flakes,
She hides awhile all ugly things
Where'er she spreads her pure white wings.
Thus to mankind the wintry sky
Preaches the grace of Charity.

Rev. Stanhope E. Ward:
Farnham Herald, 23 January 1926

THIS TIME IT WASN'T FLOODS; the pearly flakes spread their white wings. The townsfolk looked out and saw the snow lying round about, deep and crisp and even. In the words of one Farnham councillor, the likes of it had not been seen for getting on for 20 years. The irritating thing about excessive weather, and about snow in particular, is that it must be dealt with without delay. By contrast, man-made situations enable a council, with strategic deferments, to ward off the evil day for as long as they like. Public opinion concerning snow varies from the views of kids, who enjoy romping in it, to those of councillors and their staff whose unwanted task it is to deprive the youngsters of their snowball material. A heavy fall does, however, provide a unique opportunity for a council to put themselves on public exhibition with their impressive impedimenta, so demonstrating their real strength to sceptical ratepayers whose normal concept may be limited to the weekly visit of the dustcart and the half-yearly bill for its maintenance. For the modern fleet of snowploughs, grit-spreaders, road-sweepers, ancillary lorries, troop-carriers, staff limousines and mobile canteens which erupts from the council fortress to do battle with Dame Nature is indeed a fine spectacle.

In 1926, however, the half-yearly rate bill was much lower, and the anti-snow fleet correspondingly less impressive. It was limited to a few hired carts and one-man-power shovels. Spare men were, like the snow, in abundant supply though shovels were scarce; and operations were usually bedevilled by the non-arrival of hired carts. Even so, in January 1926, no fewer than 77 handlers were at work in the streets of Farnham. There were, of course, problems. Where to dump the pearly flakes was one; grit was another. The little roadside heaps

96

of grit that were a feature of the countryside in the 1920s were there for such emergencies, but had long since been kicked around by small boys, and lost in the surrounding undergrowth. More seriously, the frosts had lifted the road surfaces and split them open. Man could not win against the elements; there was only one real remedy for snow, and that was a thaw, in Nature's own good time. And that usually produced a flood.

Little Rene Smith, aged 22 months, whose parents lived at 60 Downing Street, fell into the swollen river by the bridge in Gostrey Meadow. She was rescued by the wife of Alan Bateman of the Farnham Motor Company. Her plucky action, diving fully clothed into the river, was recognised in the Council Minutes. It was thought that Rene had been attracted to the water's edge by the ducks on the river. Currently, these ducks were causing a minor problem, for it was not only children—dogs, too, were attracted. After a debate on the subject, the surveyor was instructed to reduce the number of ducks to eight.

A closing order under the Housing Act 1925 was served on C. White of 17 Downing Street requesting his departure, and that of 16 other persons who shacked up with him. Once the *Sun* inn, one of the pubs closed by the Licensing Justices on grounds of redundancy, the house had fallen on hard times.

During the building of W. Kingham and Sons' warehouse at the rear of 16 West Street, a lorry knocked down part of the churchyard wall, displacing gravestones and tablets. After an argument as to whose wall it was, Kinghams agreed to pay Patricks £62 15s. 0d. for replacements. There was a good living to be made out of the dead. Out of a field of several hundred monumental masons, Patricks were singularly honoured with a contract for the name-panels on the Menin Gate memorial, then being erected at Ypres to the design of Sir Reginald Blomfield. They also won an order from the Imperial War Graves Commission for headstones in East Africa.

R. G. Wilson, the new postmaster, was proving to be an amusing raconteur of tall stories. Giving a talk on the funny side of his job, he told of a colleague who had carpeted two linesmen following a complaint from a lady about bad language. 'Well, Sir, it was like this 'ere—'Arry was up the pole and I was standing at the bottom, when he accidentally dropped some hot molten lead on me. So I says to 'im, "You really must be more careful, 'Arry'.".

A Mr. N. Maughan, M.I.C.E., was engaged, with two assistants, to speed up the drainage works in the Outer Ward, for the Unemployment Grants Committee said they would only pay out on work completed by 1 June 1926.

Having got central heating out of the Council, the fire brigade now agitated for greatcoats. These cost £1 17s. 9d. each from Huggins, Son and Co., of Bristol. Chilly folk, firemen—never happy away from a fire.

The Isolation Hospital Committee insisted on ordering an expensive ambulance, letting the Council in for a £400 share of the cost. How different had been an appeal launched by Willie Loe for voluntary subscriptions with which to buy a new ambulance for the St John Ambulance Association. This arrived and was ceremoniously handed over by the Bishop of Winchester in Castle Street on 13 March. These keen voluntary bodies collected in the streets for the refinements they wanted. The Curative Post Committee, for instance, were doing a fine job of work. They had saved up £500 towards electrical equipment, and the Council had promised them a building in Brightwells, together with £200 still wanted.

The Diocesan authorities, through their Farnham Park Disposal Committee, hinted strongly that the Farnham Council were expected to make preliminary overtures for the town's acquisition of the park.

Mr. P. J. Turner, H.M. District Auditor, doubtless with Farnham's 1922 criminal record in mind, had probed with devastating accuracy in his 1925 audit, the report of which now came through. There were three minor financial errors connected with the transfer of the Water Company which needed to be put right. It was when Mr. Turner had discovered that the Council were paying the former surveyor a retainer of £156 a year that he reached for his blue pencil. Cutting the amount down to £50, he surcharged the Council with £14 4s. 7d., being the amount overpaid to Cass to date at the higher figure. Government sanction had not been required for the retainer, and they fought the auditor tooth and nail, even enlisting the aid of the Ministry of Health. Government departments must stick together; whilst confirming that he was not officially involved, the M.O.H. agreed that £50 was enough, but, in the circumstances, he would waive the surcharge. So the Council fought the Minister as well, reminding him that Mr. Cass's services in the Hale Ward drainage works alone had saved something like £1,000 in professional fees. Had he not, they could have added, once given the country the idea of using tarred macadam on road surfaces?

Major Wade dug up a 1st-century Roman kiln at Culverlands, abandoned by the potter when fully loaded for firing. The contents consisted of 100 household jars, wine-strainers, lids, dishes and four store-jars. Many of them had been slipped with a thin colour wash, indicating their second baking. No potter's mark had yet been found, though his fingerprints were discernible.

Arthur Simmonds of 'Normandie', Firgrove Hill, formerly the police superintendent, died in February, aged sixty-seven. His career in Farnham had been an eventful one. He was rewarded in 1917 with the King's police medal for conspicuous wartime services.

They were still toying with the idea of straightening and widening East Street to ease the passage of through traffic. The enormous cost of this—together with the inescapable fact of the Borough bottleneck—prompted County again to recommend a new road which would by-pass the town altogether. Why not, said County, adopt a scheme for Farnham under the Town Planning Acts—all the best towns are doing it nowadays. A town map could embody an approved route for a new road.

The Highways (Plant) Sub-committee, chaired by Councillor Bide, whose purpose in life was to watch over the Council's fleet of implements and equipage, worked out the minimum expense necessary to expand the fleet to meet the needs of the enlarged urban district. The working vehicles of a local authority, being fashioned for specific purposes, are, even when it wasn't snowing, largely of an eccentric design, adding a skittish quality to the street scene. The list ran:

Steam rollers	..	2	Mud carts ..	..	6	Tar boilers	7
Tip carts	.. ..	6	Machine brooms	..	2	Scavenger trucks ..	10
Dust van	.. ..	1	Water cart ..	..	1	Tarmacadam plants	2
Water van	.. ..	1	Horse roller..	..	1		

Parading in line astern, say in some street carnival, these vehicles might have the onlookers rolling in the aisles, but dispersed over 42 miles of urban roads, the fleet tended to look rather thin on the ground. Apart from the steam rollers, they were horse-drawn, and men had been flying through the air now for a quarter of a century. So to begin with, they ordered a Chevrolet one-ton, end-tipping lorry costing £215, a 1,000-gallon Barnes tar-spraying and road-brushing machine for £325, and a Dennis motor-mower for £75.

Dr. Sloman was congratulated on entering into the 50th year of his service as Farnham's Medical Officer of Health, and Mr. Sargent on the birth of a daughter.

Nine of the town's butchers sported sliding glass windows; two, G. H. Hawkins in East Street, and M. Baker, a stall-holder in Castle Street, had no windows at all. This was an improvement on the days, not far back, when most butchers hung their meat outside the shop, where it was coated with dust and grime from the street.

Mr. Starling was given 10 days leave of absence when he married Miss Gladys Mary Layton, daughter of the Congregational Minister. The councillors' present was an electric standard lamp.

Consequent upon their amended constitution, the 1926 election on 29 March heralded in a completely new council of all 21 members. Winding up the old one, Chairman Mardon spoke of their past year's achievements. One hundred and ninety planning applications had been dealt with, 83 of them for new dwelling-houses. The Outer Ward drainage works were in full swing, with £31,000 of the estimated £76,000 already spent, and efforts were being made to complete as much of the work as possible in order to qualify for the Exchequer grant by 1 June. There was little doubt that before long an inquiry would be held by the Privy Council into the town's petition for incorporation.

Councillors Murrell, Ransom, Vallentin, Aungier, Gillespie, Robins, and Tulley decided not to stand for re-election. The 27 nominees for the 21 seats were whittled down to 25, and polls were only necessary in two of the wards—Hale/Badshot and Wrecclesham. Interest in the election on 29 March was consequently lukewarm; the only surprise, perhaps, was that Mr. Bide was voted out in Hale. The score-card was as follows, with an asterisk denoting each member returned.

Castle

   *Charles Borelli, 36 The Borough
   *Arthur James Figg, Long Garden Walk
   *Alexander Selfe Marsh, 'The Jungle', Abbey Street
   *Henry William Philipson-Stow, 'The Old Vicarage'
   *Gertrude Annie Stroud, 'Elmsleigh', Station Hill

Waverley

   *Edward Stephen Crow, 'Tanfield House', East Street
   *Alexander Grange, 'Chamberscroft', High Park Road
   *Henry Sanders, 'Sanfield', Lancaster Avenue
   *Henry Arthur Skerry, 'Brackenfield', Runfold

Hale/Badshot

   *Sidney Kenrick Bacon, 'Hereford Cottage', Hale (126)
   Herbert William Bide, Alma Nurseries (116)
   Charles Binfield, 'Hawthorn Cottage', Hale (121)
   *John William Swansborough, 'High View', Hale (197)
   *Alan Perrett Tice, Badshot Farm (271)
   *Ernest James Varney, 'Beverley', Hale (284)
   *Edwin Winter, 24 Lower Farnham Road (232)

Bourne

   *Joseph Ewart, 'Acacia House'
   *Samuel Lathey, 'Brackendene', Lower Bourne
   *Arthur George Mardon, 'Hawarden', Firgrove Hill
   *Alfred Julius Stevens, 'Twynax', Middle Bourne

Wrecclesham

   *Robert Charles Avery, 'Homewood Gate', Rowledge (106)
   Arthur Brown, 'Sunnyside', Rowledge (65)
   Charles Franks Falkner, Dippenhall (62)
   *Charles Godby, 'Heatherbrae', Boundstone (96)
   *Ernest Hill Wakeford, 'Sunnyfield', Lower Bourne (79)

At the A.G.M. on 20 April, A. G. Mardon was re-appointed as Chairman for the fifth consecutive year, though the decision was not unanimous. Mr. Borelli became Vice-Chairman. The meeting was one of carefree abandon. At the end of two hours, Councillor Swansborough proposed that the members should be allowed to light up their pipes or cigarettes—he drew the line at cigars— adding that he had asked Mrs. Stroud, but the Chairman pointed out that this had never been allowed in the past, and it was perhaps unwise.

The year 1926 was destined to go down in history as the Year of the Great Strike. Being the sort of place it was, Farnham did not suffer unduly, though there were pettifogging disturbances of everyday life, such as few trains, scarcity of fuel, reduction in gas pressure, unreliable postal services, lack of most daily papers, and anxiety about the food situation. Directives sprouted from Whitehall, the army swung into action, local authorities took command, voluntary amateurs rallied to the cause. Between them, they somehow managed to keep the wheels turning; between them, they beat the strikers. Local committees were formed to handle coal distribution, food and other essentials. Someone drove up to London each day and brought back copies of *The British Gazette*, published by the government during the emergency. One of Kinghams' drivers reported being attacked by a picket in London. There was a seemingly unending flow of motor- or steam-driven vehicles through the town, labelled 'Food Supplies', and the streets teemed with special constables. At last, on Wednesday, 12 May, the 1 o'clock news was interrupted with the announcement that the Great Strike was over.

Fortunately, there had been no strike by the men rushing through the Outer Ward drainage. Some 150 labourers were now working on Contract Two. The Arthur Road council houses were finished and occupied. This job had cost £14,410, surprisingly lower by £589 than the estimate, a rare bonus that was attributed to the skill of Mr. Sargent, whose economical design and personal supervision at all stages had reduced the outlay. They gave him a gratuity of 25 guineas and spent the rest on providing cycle sheds for the tenants. In May, sanction was obtained to borrow up to £4,000 to build 10 houses on a £250 site at Weydon Mill. Punter and Le Clercq put them up for £3,550; they became 1–10 Weyside Cottages, Red Lion Lane.

Letters were read at the meeting on 1 June from the Prime Minister, the Divisional Strike Emergency Officer, and the Chairman of the Surrey Volunteer Service Committee expressing appreciation of the efforts of the Council and the townspeople of Farnham during the national emergency. Although the strike had subsided, the miners' dispute continued until the following December and fresh instructions from London, dated 28 May, decreed that supplying coal for ordinary household purposes was prohibited, unless authorised by the local authority on grounds such as sickness or total reliance on coal for cooking purposes. On 3 July, fuel stocks in the railway bunkers were reported to be down to 20 tons, and those of some merchants were exhausted. The Council supplied these traders with 22 tons from reserves in the Council yard, leaving some 60 tons in reserve. At the end of July, stocks at the station were down to 15 tons. The Divisional Coal Officer recommended the purchase of coal from overseas, and some Silesian fuel appeared later.

It was rumoured that a suitable house costing £7,000 had been found near Guildford for the bishop when he came, and that an option had been obtained on it; also that an appeal for funds had been launched. This was disquieting news for the Friends of Farnham Castle.

Mr. L. Milne of East Street set up a new world record at Brooklands, riding a motor-cycle and sidecar for two hours at an average speed of 64.17 m.p.h.

The Rotary Club drew attention to the public library issue; this had died following an initial burst of enthusiasm. Interested parties met on 23 July and were addressed by a Miss Powell, the County librarian. There were, she said,

some 1,000 books available to a branch library in Farnham if they should choose
to form one. One or two meetings followed at which it was half-heartedly
resolved to go ahead, though opposition came from Mr. F. Sturt, who ran one of
the commercial libraries in the town.

The days when the post office existed solely for the service of the public were
numbered. Admittedly this service to date had been exaggerated in that deliveries
of mail were unnecessarily frequent. Tentatively, then with growing momentum,
these services were curtailed. Now—if you please—the postmen wanted Saturday
afternoons off, in exchange for improved conditions at other times. Their demand
was eventually conceded. After all, what could people expect at a penny a letter?

The final years of the '20s and the first half of the '30s were what might be
regarded as the halcyon days of Brightwells Garden. Thereafter, in keeping with
the fickle local character, public enthusiasm waned. The people gathered there,
not only to play tennis, bowls or miniature golf, or to swim, but to use the
pleasant grounds as a forum. In June, Miss Lushington and Mr. Morgan of the
Grammar School were allowed to put on concerts and the popularity of these
led to a pilot scheme for military band performances. They became a regular
fortnightly feature on Wednesday evenings, ending in dance music. The abrupt
falling-off of public interest in the mid 1930s sadly put an end to them.
Nowadays, Brightwells serves mainly as a short cut from East Street to South
Street, or as an approach to the theatre or health clinic. Gostrey Meadow, on the
other hand, has always enjoyed a moderate patronage, being an ideal playground
for children, and, of course, their mothers. When the bowling green was forsaken
by the men for a new one in Brightwells, this became the venue of the Ladies'
Bowling Club.

Plans in July included W. J. Wells's design for a new *Elm Tree* inn at Weybourne, and A. J. Stedman's new shopfront at 1 The Borough for Lionel Smith,
the hairdresser.

There were some 206 men working on the Outer Ward drainage scheme, and
some 50,000 feet of sewers had been laid. Herseys had completed their contract
and, at a special meeting on 28 July at the sewage farm, the Chairman with eight
of the councillors, Mr. Wright, Dr. Sloman, and the Resident Engineer, inspected
the new filter beds and other works. Then the Chairman ceremoniously opened
the valves; it was a solemn moment.

Being a voluntary body with a strong tradition of brotherliness, the fire brigade
called for great tact and diplomatic handling in any situation concerning personnel.
Strictly according to the handbook, members reaching the age of 55 were ready
for the axe, but a kindly higher authority, aware of the personal relationships
involved, allowed the Council to exercise discretion and re-appoint time-expired
men for further periods of up to three years. Chief Officer J. H. Chitty of East
Street was now 62 years old. He had joined the brigade in 1896, was made
foreman in 1908, second officer in 1910, and chief in 1924. First Officer
A. H. Bailey was 58; he, too, had joined in 1896. Fireman A. Budd, just 55, had

been in 32 years. How could one put these long-serving men out to grass? All three were reinstated.

Mr. Sargent was let loose on a large tract of ex-hopground at the rear of East Street. In two phases—of 40 and 36 houses—this in due course became Stoke Hills. Further land for housing was also bought in Hale and Badshot Lea.

In October, permission was given to Mr. H. Cox to build three new shops next to Whitelock's dairy in Ridgway Road, intended for a draper, a butcher and a fishmonger. Heath and Wiltshires submitted a plan for a new shopfront at their premises in Union Road. The tradesmen were responding to residential growth. Normally, relations between the Council and the Chamber of Commerce were excellent, though one minor matter which pinpricked was the over-abundance of low sunblinds—an obvious feature in early photographs of the street scene—for these caused obstructions to shoppers. So the Council invoked the relevant provision of the Town Police Clauses Act, 1847.

Major Wade, that successful archaeologist, had discovered another Roman kiln, half a mile from his earlier find on land belonging to Mr. Langham, off Waverley Lane. In a letter to *The Times,* he described the latest dig as being of more importance, in that not only the oven, but ash pits and the tiled floor of the potter's store and drying-out hut had also come to light.

Casting around for increased office accommodation, the Council were delighted when Arthur Rose, the seedsman who lived in 'Montrose', South Street, decided to move out. Mr. Rose, who house formed one side of the entrance to the Council yard, must have been a long-suffering man to have put up with the clank-clank-clank of the Council's heavier items of impedimenta such as the steam-roller. 'Montrose' was a six-roomed house, with space at the back for a future extension. To gain six more offices for £1,350, plus cost of adaptation, say, £250, and all bordering upon the curtilege of the existing depot, was almost too good to be true. The opportunity came providentially, for the Council were faced with an imminent staff explosion from two causes. The Rating and Valuation Act 1925 had gathered under the Council's umbrella all the piecemeal rate collectors hitherto pecking away in their own backyards, and office space was needed for the setting up of a new Rating and Valuation Department (this was allocated the ground floor of 'Montrose'). The other new department looming up was the Town Planning Department, which—unlike rates (which had come in with Queen Elizabeth's Act of 1601)—was a 20th-century innovation designed to obviate a town's drift towards the higgledy-piggledy in its future development, assuming, of course, that it had not already been higgledied-piggledied in Victoria's reign.

Councillor Borelli had attended a meeting of the West Surrey Regional Town Planning Committee on 23 September, addressed by Mr. Pepler, Chief Town Planning Inspector of the Ministry of Health, whereat a West Surrey Joint Town Planning Committee had been inaugurated. In making his report, Mr. Borelli advised the Farnham Council to become a constituent member of this

Joint Committee, and in December a resolution was taken to that effect in consultation with neighbouring authorities. It all sounded a trifle *avant garde* to the locals. In plain terms, the objects of a town plan were (a) to impress the ratepayers; (b) to stop the antics of irresponsible builders; (c) to plot on a map separate zones for different classes of development (industrial, commercial, residential, etc.); and, of special importance to Farnham, the area designated for the provision of a by-pass road.

Mr. F. T. Wonnacott of 'The Fairfield', wrote in, for the second time, suggesting that the eastern bottleneck of The Borough might be widened by moving the north side bodily to new foundations at the rear of the existing buildings.

The first week in November was Rat Week; people were asked to make a special effort to reduce the rodent population . . . Land for housing was bought from the War Office, measuring 300 ft. by 147 ft. deep, adjacent to Gorseland Cottages, Alma Lane . . . Poppy sales made £366 2s. 6d. . . . Canon Crum preached at St Paul's Cathedral on Sunday, 28 November.

In Stickhams Lane, Wrecclesham, the Echo Barn, once a copyhold of the Farnham Manor, but now enfranchised by virtue of the Law of Property Act 1922, still called for certain formalities connected with the extinguishment of manorial incidents before the building could be cleared away . . . The Three Stiles estate at the top of Beaver's Hill was now being developed . . . The coal strike was virtually over . . . Highways Committee gave thought to a one-way traffic system in the town.

Doctor 'Paddy' Miles of 19 East Street died on 28 November, aged fifty-one. He went down in legend as Farnham's most popular doctor. George Llewellyn Nash Miles was born at Dingle Bay, County Kerry, the son of a Dublin surgeon. He was a cousin of the wife of the Bishop of Liverpool and related to the Marquess of Donegal. He came to Farnham in 1904 to join Dr. Hine, who had taken over the practice of Dr. Coffey. Paddy was enormously popular with the poorer people.

At the Venison Dinner at the *Bush* on 9 December, Arthur Samuel, M.P., spoke again of Farnham's chances of becoming a borough. This had a way of cropping up from time to time without any special solution, and with an apparent loss of enthusiasm at local level. It was still going the rounds in the higher echelons. At the December Council meeting, loud laughter was occasioned by a letter from the Secretary of the London Surrey Society, addressed to 'His Worship the Mayor of Farnham'. This read: 'The Committee of the Society desire me to congratulate you on your election to the Mayorality of Farnham and hope that you have have a successful term of office'. Currently, the situation with Charters of Incorporation was that the Minister of Health was in process of formulating a standard policy on the subject. At a special meeting on 20 December, a letter written by Neville Chamberlain, then Minister, to Arthur Samuel was read by the Council. This said:

> I have looked into the application of the Urban District Council of Farnham for a Charter of Incorporation, about which you spoke to me the other day. As what they want is the restoration of an old Charter, I am, in view of the special circumstances of the case, prepared to recommend the Privy Council to grant their request.

On Christmas Day the weather was fine. Families over-ate and over-drank in commemoration of the birth of a Child. At 'Haven Cottage', Weybourne, a family lamented the passing of an old man. James Pullinger had lived hereabouts for 81 years, starting work at the age of 11 as a stockman on Badshot Farm. When this farm passed into the ownership of the Knight family, he was made supervisor of the farm's machinery and became John Henry Knight's right-hand man in the stables at Weybourne House, and later, Barfields. It was Pullinger who, on 17 October 1895, chauffeured the first motor car ever to run on British roads. They motored from Barfields as far as Castle Street, where they were stopped by the police. Owner and chauffeur each received a summons to appear before the Farnham Bench on 31 October 1895. The case received widespread attention and has since become a local legend. The report in the *Surrey and Hants News*, dated 2 November should be repeated if only to get the record straight.

> On Thursday at the Farnham Petty Sessions, before a full Bench of magistrates, R. H. Combe Esq. being in the Chair, Mr. John Henry Knight of Barfields was charged with permitting a locomotive to be at work in Castle Street, Farnham, on October 17 without a licence, and James Pullinger was summoned for working the same during prohibited hours, namely 3.30 p.m. at the same place and date. Mr. Powell, Kingston-on-Thames, appeared in support of the summonses and Mr. H. Potter (Potter and Crundwell, Farnham) defended. Much interest was manifested in the case because the owner is a well-known local inventor who, on the day in question, was trying a motor carriage, in the form of a tricycle, driven by an oil engine. Mr. Powell, in opening the case, said the summonses were issued under the bye-laws of the County Council of Surrey, which provided that no locomotive other than those employed for the repairing of roads or the purposes of agriculture should be used on the roads of the County without a licence and the maximum fine was £5. There was another bye-law which provided that a locomotive should only be used within certain hours. A locomotive was not only what is generally understood as heavy machinery, but a tricycle driven with other than animal power came under the definition of a locomotive. The locomotive belonging to the defendant was drawn in the same way as a locomotive or a gas engine by the explosion of petroleum vapour and the machine travelled at the rate of from 3½ to 7½ miles an hour. It was more dangerous and less desirable on public roads than an ordinary locomotive or traction engine because the explosion of the vapour caused considerable noise. The machine had been used by the defendant Pullinger without the usual precaution in connection with a locomotive used on the roads. On the 17 October the defendant Pullinger was driving the machine in Castle Street, two persons being on the carriage. The machine was going at the rate of four miles an hour and when it was stopped by the Police the defendant Knight came up and said he would be responsible for the whole thing.

He did not know whether it was going to be contended that this was not a locomotive. The law on that point was settled as long ago as 1893 in the case of Parkins v Priest, which was adjudicated upon by the Lord Chief Justice. The carriage in that case was very light and the wheels were cycle wheels. Mr. Potter interposed at this point to say he had advised his client that it was useless to contend that he was not liable. The case referred to by the learned counsel had not been reversed and he feared until the law was altered such a locomotive as his could not be worked except under the bye-laws. On the day in question, however, he was simply going on a trial trip and was acting in all good faith. He had no intention of committing a breach of the bye-laws of the County. He took great interest in the improvement of carriages of this kind, a premium of a thousand guineas having been offered for the best carriage of the sort. The defendant Knight thought that by paying the Inland Revenue . . .

Mr. Combe, 'Did it enter into Mr. Knight's mind to make this a test case?'

Mr. Potter said this was not being made a test case.

Mr. Knight said his attention had been called to the case of Parkins v Priest just before the commencement of the business. He contended that his machine was not a locomotive within the meaning of the Act and he thought that he was perfectly at liberty to use it. He expected something of this kind would occur, and he had communicated with some of his friends with the result that it had been decided not to make this a test case. The Bench had probably seen what was going on at Tunbridge Wells. He had brought the carriage for the Bench to see and he trusted they would not prosecute him for going home on it. It was the first machine of its kind made in England though there were some 700 in France and on the continent generally. He was sorry he had not seen the case of Parkins v Priest before. The Chairman said the opinion of the Bench was that the case would be met with a small fine. Each of the defendants was then fined 2/6 and costs.

1927

'Wishing there would be a hope for me to make a speak to you, I have notes prepared. They are left in my hotel, so now I find my noise is too poor to do my duty'.

Japanese delegate at the 38th Congress of the Royal Sanitary
Institute, Hastings, 9–16th July 1927
Retailed in Sanitary Inspector's report and preserved for
posterity in Farnham Council Minute-book

IF HE WANTED TO AVOID THE RISK of being run out of town, the editor of a local newspaper should be at pains to navigate the troubled waters which surge beneath the calm surface of his town so as to give the minimum of offence to all his readers. He should cultivate a non-partisan journalism which extols without prejudice the relative virtues of capitalism and communism or beer and lemonade. In any local affray in which the parties may be locked in mortal combat, he should be careful to obtain both sides of the story, shake these up together and publish the more palatable parts. Mr. E. W. Langham of the *Farnham Herald* was adept at this sort of double-talk. His tactful tactics came near to exploding Abraham Lincoln's theory about not being able to fool all the people all the time. There were rare opportunities in inter-war Farnham when it was safe for an editor to throw caution to the winds. The local council, of course, were always good for a knock, for the members were the authorised whipping-boys of the community. But this licence did not cover the doings of the fire brigade who, with the St John Ambulance Association, the Boy Scouts and the town band, were protected. To knock the boys in uniform was editorial suicide.

On Thursday, 30 December 1926, a fire broke out in a bedroom at 'Scotsburn', Rowledge, the residence of Mr. E. F. Ross, whose attention was drawn to the fact by a lady passing by. Mr. Ross rang the brigade at 9.30 p.m., and made three further calls between that time and 9.40 p.m. The fire engine did not arrive until close on 11 o'clock. In the meantime, 'Scotsburn' burnt; the house was, indeed, completely gutted. That, substantially, was how the story got into the local paper. Mr. Ross also told the reporter that, when the firemen did arrive, they were quibbling among themselves as to whether 'Scotsburn' was in the Council's district or in the Frensham parish, for which they were not really responsible—though they would, by gentlemen's agreement, oblige as a generous gesture, etc.

On reading the *Herald's* account, the councillors bristled. At the subsequent inquest, the duty fireman gave evidence, corroborated by his wife, and the post office telephone operator, that the first call came through at 9.55 p.m., not 9.30 p.m. On lifting the receiver, a voice had bellowed in his ear 'Fire Brigade?— Fire! Fire!!', and left it at that. Failing to obtain the address, the duty man had contacted the police and eventually the whereabouts of the fire was discovered. The alarm was given between 10.15 and 10.20 p.m., and the engine got away within five minutes, arriving at 'Scotsburn' some time before 11 p.m. They were there until 5 a.m. the next morning. The nearest hydrant was a quarter of a mile from the house, and 1,300 feet of hose had been used. Thus read a somewhat apologetic account in the following week's paper.

On 22 January, the Chairman entertained some 40 to 50 guests—fellow councillors, chief officers, contractors, and local dignatories—to luncheon at the *Bush* hotel. After a splendid meal of oxtail or tomato soup; fillets of sole Normandie; roast saddle of mutton, or chicken; followed by macedone of fruit Kirch or apple tart, the Royal Toast was drunk. This was followed by a toast proposed by Edgar Kempson 'To the success of the Main Drainage Works of the Farnham Added Area'. Then the distinguished company boarded a chartered Aldershot and District Traction Company's bus and were driven to the new pumping station at Waverley. Here, Mr. Godfrey Taylor, in the regretted absence of his father, Mr. Midgeley Taylor of John Taylor and Sons, Engineers, presented Chairman Mardon with a golden key engraved 'Farnham Urban District Council Main Drainage Pumping Stations. Presented to the Chairman of the Council, Councillor A. G. Mardon, J.P., C.C., 22nd January 1927'. In reply, Mr. Mardon praised 'the beautiful building', remarking in passing that, when it was nearing completion, a lady had enquired as to whether it would be to let. He had great pleasure in accepting the key—which was a handsome specimen of the goldsmith's art—and would one day hand it down to his children. He then opened the door. Inside the station, Mrs. Mardon pressed the electric switch that set the pumps in motion. The company then went on to inspect the other new station at Black Lake. Following this auspicious public occasion, residents in the Bourne, Wrecclesham and Rowledge areas were invited, under duress, to spend a lot of their money on connecting up to the sewers in order to use them on more private occasions.

At the Licensing Session on 11 February, there were objections, on grounds of redundancy, to the renewal of licences for the *White Hart,* East Street the *Cricketers* and the *Bird in Hand,* Downing Street. At an adjourned court later in the month, chaired by Cecil Whiteley, K.C., these three public houses were referred to the Compensation Authority and disappeared from the Farnham drinking scene.

The Council now turned to the intolerable traffic problem. For a start, bus drivers were made to realise that dropping passengers at their individual front doors was no longer possible, and bus stops were regularised at certain intervals along the streets. Drivers wishing to turn around in South Street were requested to do so only at Hickleys Corner or in the station yard, and no longer at the Union Road junction. Private motorists had an established right to park in Castle Street, but there was a chronic need for additional spaces. Private car owners were the ones with money in their pockets to spend in Farnham shops, and had to be cosseted at all costs, whereas the charabanc trippers and heavy lorry fraternity were an unprofitable encumbrance. J. Alfred Eggar, in a letter to the *Herald,* suggested diverting such useless traffic by means of a by-pass road from the *Albion* public house, across the meadows to Hickleys Corner, crossing over South Street by a viaduct, thence under Firgrove Hill and on to rejoin the main road at Wrecclesham. More parking space could be provided for local traffic by the side of this road as it passed through the meadows. Eggar's idea was theoretically sound; a similar route was in due course adopted, with one regrettable modification—his suggestion of a flyover to bridge South Street would have avoided the death of more than one pedestrian.

Land, including the sites of two cottages, was bought at Wrecclesham for £1,050, plus redemption costs, and that village got its recreation ground. The cottages were used for council workmen.

Aldershot Borough Council proposed a conference to consider the establishment of a joint planning authority for the combined areas of Aldershot, Farnham Urban and Rural, and Farnborough. This smacked distinctly of hegemony and Farnham was glad to be able to inform Aldershot that they were already involved in a planning scheme for West Surrey. The borough was also dallying with the idea of taking over the supply of electricity in surrounding districts. Farnham's best defence in these early years of their Hampshire neighbour's self-aggrandisement was the county boundary.

York Road and Lancaster Avenue were the next new roads to be adopted under the Private Street Works Act. Layouts were approved for Little Green Lane, for H. Purchase, and Three Stiles Road off Crondall Lane, for Mr. Figg. The cost of Arthur Road was apportioned between the residents.

Brightwells House was modernised, as far as an 18th-century house could be, by Crosbys for £422, including central heating; wiring for electricity cost £39.

A letter from the Clerk to the Privy Council to Kempson and Wright, acting for the Incorporation Committee, referred to recent correspondence between Arthur Samuel, M.P., and Neville Chamberlain, and the special circumstances of Farnham's application for borough status. As a royal commission was currently sitting to consider the general question of local government areas, and this could have an important bearing on the subject, the Lord President of the Privy Council had come to the conclusion that pending and future petitions (including that of Farnham) should be deferred until the final report of the Commission had been issued. The town's efforts to regain its ancient Charter seemed doomed to failure. Mr. Wright was instructed to contact the royal commission. The 'Aldershot Development Committee' were now trying to involve Farnham in a proposed

Aldershot Command Horse Show. There was already the Aldershot Tattoo—held, incidentally, in Farnborough. Perhaps one way of becoming a borough was to be absorbed by Aldershot.

Vibrations caused by heavy vehicles speeding through the town, especially at night, were rocking the old buildings in West Street. County were asked to impose a speed limit. The West Surrey Town Planners, who were drawn towards Mr. Eggar's by-pass idea, preached patience.

The Council discovered that they had no fishing rights along the river in Gostrey, so they had to prohibit angling there. Were small boys with jam jars exempt?

Small boys—and girls—were themselves keen young fishes. The 1926 swimming bath statistics showed that there had been no less than 2,616 attendances from the elementary schools. Over 250 season tickets had been issued, and family bathing on Sunday afternoons had proved immensely popular. The bath was being used by people from Alton, Hindhead, Odiham, and (Aldershot Development Committee, please note) Aldershot. Further, the more regular bathers were proposing to form a Farnham Swimming Club. This materialised in June; members were granted exclusive use of the bath two evenings a week from 7.30 to 8.30 p.m. The existing bath being found rather small, Mr. Sargent was instructed to prepare a scheme for an extension.

Alf Thorp, now appointed as Rating and Valuation Officer in 'Montrose', South Street, was in process of establishing his departmental staff. Frederic Aubrey Holloway of 'Lynn', Ridgway Road, then on the staff of St Mary-le-Bone Board of Guardians, was selected for the post of first assistant; he took up duties on 4 April 1927, three days after the new Rating Act came into operation. The first result of this Act was a revaluation of rateable properties throughout the country, whilst over a two-year period the old Poor Rate and General District Rate would continue to be collected separately. In Farnham, for the half year from April to September 1927, the Poor Rate was fixed at 2s. 10d. in the pound rateable value, to discharge a precept from the Guardians for £5,668, and another from the Surrey County Council for £10,953. The General District Rate, to cover the local council's expenses, was put at 3s. in the pound. As from 1 April 1929, the two would be consolidated as one General Rate; paying one rate instead of two might fool the ratepayers into believing they were paying less.

The election on 2 April caused little excitement. A. J. Stevens (Bourne Ward) had resigned because of overwork and ill health; in his place stepped the Rev. G. Forbes Wilde. The only poll was in Hale, where four candidates contended for two seats. Mr. J. W. Swansborough was re-elected, and Charles Binfield came on for the first time. 'Charlie' Binfield was to become an unconventional though popular figure on the Council.

In his summing-up, Mr. Mardon said that 1926-7 had been remarkable for the development of Farnham as a residential centre. New estates in the Tilford Road/Waverley Lane area and at Three Stiles were filling up fast. The 201 plans dealt with had included 115 dwellings, not counting council houses. Seventy-six at Stoke Hills and others at Hale and Badshot Lea would, when finished, bring the Council's ownership to a total of 295 houses—one-twentieth of all houses in the district.

This time Mr. Mardon left the Chair, to be replaced by Mr. Borelli, with A. J. Figg as Vice-Chairman. In July, Mr. Mardon was presented with a silver waiter, inscribed, 'Presented to Councillor A. G. Mardon J.P., C.C., by the present and past members of the Farnham Urban District Council as a mark of their appreciation of his services as Chairman of the Council from 1922 to 1927'.

Eight military bands were booked for the 1927 season in Brightwells . . . The old *Sun* inn at 17 Downing Street was replaced by new business premises built by Mardon and his recently-acquired partner, George Ball; they were occupied by Mr. J. Goodrick . . . A Major Maunsell asked permission to tether goats in the Langham Recreation Ground and was told an emphatic 'No'—the surveyor was told to see that goats already in residence moved out.

The *Herald* of 16 April published the first news of an offer made by Courages of Alton to buy out Farnham United Breweries. It was said to be over half a million pounds for lock, stock and barrel, and by the following week it had been accepted in principle. The F.U.B. was the town's only industry of any size. Formed in 1889 by an amalgamation of George Trimmer's brewery and that of the Barrett Brothers in Red Lion Lane, it had been joined in 1910 by J. F. Complin's Brewery of Holybourne. The partnership had 161 tied houses, and branches in Winchester, Eastleigh, Basingstoke, Guildford, and Woking. The departure of their ancient, and indeed only, industry wrung the hearts of Farnham people. What, for instance, was to become of the recently-built Memorial Hall, with its sports ground in Babbs Mead?

On 7 May the *Herald* reported the indisposition of Mr. V. H. Lowry, the electrical engineer at the Farnham Gas and Electricity Company. Could this have been that much talked of occasion when his colleagues conspired together in a practical joke—separately telling Vic how ill he looked, with the result that he ended up in hospital?

In May, the King approved the appointment as Bishop Designate of the newly-formed Diocese of Guildford, of the Right Reverend John Harold Greig, M.A., D.D., Bishop of Gibraltar and Dean of St Paul's Collegiate Church, Valetta. Anxiety deepened as the time approached for the Bishop of Winchester's departure from Farnham Castle. Bishop Woods had been heard to say 'that house shall never be sundered from the service of the Church'. Dr. Randolph, retiring Suffragan Bishop of Guildford, had news of more practical value. A friend, who wished to remain anonymous, had offered to donate £20,000 to finance an experiment over a period of, say, five to seven years, whereby the ancient home of Bishops of Winchester would be used as 'a kind of Spiritual Power House, or Service Station for the Church in the three dioceses of Winchester, Guildford and Portsmouth'. With Dr. Randolph as Warden in overall charge, the castle could be used for such purposes as residential retreats, conferences and meetings, summer schools, diocesan activities, for the use of lay readers, day and Sunday school teachers, bishops' messengers, Scouts and Guides, Friendly Societies, Mothers' Unions, temperance and rescue workers. It might also house the Thorold and Lyttleton Libraries. The £20,000 was not to be invested; it was to be used as capital to pay expenses during the operative period of the experiment. Considerable preliminary work would be necessary to adapt the castle, and the money for this would have to be raised by other means. There was general rejoicing in Diocesan circles that 'someone, unnamed, had so much of the fatal opulence that he should be able to lay down £20,000 to save the Castle from lying shuttered and empty'. There was less rejoicing two months later when, at a conference in Guildford, it was estimated that the white elephant in Farnham would need about £30,000 spent on it in order to bring it up to the requirements of the experiment.

Concerning 'Boy' McCormick, a sad tailpiece found its way from Manchester. On 17 May, his wife was granted a separation order and 'in view of his straitened circumstances' McCormick was ordered to pay 5s. a week and 1s for the child.

E. J. Burroughs and Co., Ltd., the tourist people, offered two 'What to See' road signs, financed by a private donor and distributed on the advice of the Royal Automobile Club. It was nice to be reminded that Farnham was on the tourist map.

The Traction Company were busy extending their network. Four additional Hackney Carriage licences were issued to them in June. The company also replaced an old bus body, which served as a waiting-room at the Shortheath terminus, with a purpose-built article. During 1927, a bitter war broke out between the Aldershot company and smaller one-man operators.

A plan in July led to the conversion of Kempson and Wright's former offices at 121 West Street to shop premises for the International Stores, formerly at 116 West Street. The finished work attracted much praise because of the way in which the firm's architect had retained the old upper facade. The International, commented the *Herald,* had first opened in Farnham at 39 The Borough, which they had occupied until 1900. The company had 525 branches, a substantial tribute to its founder, Hudson Ewbank Kearley.

On 14 July, County considered a communication from the Governors of the Girls' Grammar School which drew attention to the 'growing unsuitability' of the present site and buildings of the school in West Street, owing to the large and increasing volume of traffic. The need for prompt action to secure a site elsewhere for a new school was stressed because of the escalating price, and increasing scarcity, of building land. The Governors were doubtless voicing a long-standing discontent with having to make do with a building cast off by the Boys' Grammar School. At speech day at the end of the year, they were openly talking about a brand new school in Menin Way.

The Venerable Ernest Neville Lovett, Archdeacon of Portsmouth, and once Farnham's dynamic vicar, was warmly congratulated on becoming Bishop of Portsmouth which, like Guildford, had been carved out of the Winchester Diocese.

An impassioned plea from the fire chief underlined the brigade's current difficulties. His argument was that should the appliances in his present command happen to be out at a fire when another call came through, then what would happen? (Actually, the answer here—as all concerned probably knew—was to contact the nearest neighbouring town). Chief Petty Officer Chitty listed the facts. His territory, including by arrangement Frensham and Tilford, was 28 square miles; population 22,800. Equipment, one Merryweather engine bought in 1922, one tractor for carrying 1,000 feet of hose and other fittings converted from a second-hand Delaunay Bellevue motor-car in 1917, and now with a life expectancy of one to two years, and one Shand Mason manual engine, iron-tyred, operated by firemen on each side who jerked a bar up and down to the tune of 'Pump, you blighters, pump!' His personnel consisted of a second officer, first and second engineers, first and second motor engineers, motor tractor driver, 13 firemen, and station duty man. Mr. Chitty's words fell on receptive ears. In October, orders were placed for a Dennis fire tender, with extras such as first-aid tank with hydraulic hose and search lamp, costing £528 10s. 0d., and a Dennis 250-gallon turbine motor fire engine for £400.

Mrs. Poole Berry grumbled about the charabancs which stopped for long periods right outside her house in Castle Street. She wasn't the first, or the last, to complain, with justification, about this fine street being used as a vehicle park. Mr. L. W. Stevens, who sold fried fish in Downing Street, took a different view; the temporary visitors were in his opinion good for business.

*   *   *   *   *

If, indeed, it was at all possible for a relationship which, eight centuries earlier, had first held the people of Farnham in thrall, to be severed forever in the course of a few hours, then that historic event took place on 30 September 1927, when the Bishop of Winchester said goodbye to Farnham. It was true that, somewhere down the centuries, the people—or perhaps a bishop—had cut the umbilical and, at first with faltering steps, then with growing confidence, the townspeople had forged their separate independence. Yet the old ties had persisted intangibly, so that, when the presence of Bishops of Winchester was irrevocably lost from Farnham Castle, it was as if some integral part of the town departed. Tributes followed tributes in the Corn Exchange that day, until at last the final expressions of parting were exchanged. The townspeople's gift to Bishop Woods was a replica of the cup presented to the bailiffs by John Byworth in 1623. In return, the bishop presented an ancient mace, hall-marked 1710 and dated 1742, that had hung on a chapel wall at the castle for nearly two centuries. It was the Council's inscribed address to the bishop, neatly condensing eight centuries of local history into a brief abstract, which conveyed a deeper meaning.

We, the Urban District Council of Farnham, in the name of those whom we represent, desire on their behalf and our's to bid farewell to your Lordship and to Mrs. Woods on the occasion of your departure from this Town. You are leaving a Castle which has belonged to the Bishops of Winchester for 800 years and lands which have been their's since Wessex was a Christian country, and the connection between Winchester's long line of Bishops and this Town is a distinction which we regretfully surrender. Your Lordship's predecessors have always been our friends. We owed to them in the Middle Ages that we were for centuries a self-governing Borough. In later days, the Bishops of Winchester have been neighbours of whom we have been affectionately proud. The severance of so honourable, so long, so kindly a connection costs us a regret which your Lordship will understand and share. And on this occasion we desire to assure you that the unaffected sympathy and cheerful help which you have always extended to any movement for the welfare of the Town adds a deep personal feeling to the reluctance with which Farnham takes leave of her Bishops of Winchester. My Lord, it is with sorrow that we say goodbye to you and to Mrs. Woods. It is with great sincerity that we wish you in your future work Godspeed.

Given under the Common Seal of the Farnham Urban District Council at their Council Chamber at Farnham this 30th day of September 1927.

C. E. Borelli, Chairman
J. W. Wright, Clerk

By comparison, the official welcome given by Farnham to the first Bishop of Guildford, at the Church House on Tuesday, 8 November, was formal, polite, impersonal, and possibly tinged with some embarrassment. For Bishop Greig was engaged in house-hunting elsewhere in Surrey, and he must have felt the implications of this for Farnham. The Guildford Diocesan Board had already collected some £500 towards the building of a cathedral in Guildford. Guildford was the right and proper place to have it; there was no quarrel with that. It was also conceded that, whereas Farnham had hitherto been a conveniently central position in the old Winchester Diocese for the bishop's palace, the town now found itself in a bulge on the extreme edge of the new Guildford Diocese. This, together with the crippling expense of maintaining the castle, made it plain to everyone that Bishop Greig should have a residence that was not only closer to his future cathedral, but would be easier on his purse. Also, the castle could not be expected to stir the soul of a stranger from, in this case, Gibraltar, to the same extent as it had stirred generations of Farnham people for the past eight hundred years.

*   *   *   *   *

There were grateful thanks from Wrecclesham—Mr. W. R. Tanner, spokesman—for the Council's prompt action in providing the village with a recreation ground. A collection of £250 was aimed at towards a football field and facilities for other sports.

Aldershot was not having the same success on the home front that the military town enjoyed in other theatres of war. The borough's next attempt to cross the border into Surrey was a proposed 'Aldershot Joint Sewerage scheme'. Fortunately, Farnham had recently brought drains to the Outer Ward; now Aldershot made overtures to the deprived areas of the depleted Farnham Rural District Council. To associate villages such as Tilford and Seale with a town like Aldershot was unthinkable. Following a lengthy palaver, Aldershot was told to forget it. Had it been possible for The Home of the British Army to act as King Canute and control the flood waters of the River Wey, then it was just conceivable that Farnham might have become a centre for 10-pin bowling, doss-houses, honky-tonks, and other refinements of the 20th century. The river continued to flood the lower reaches of the town unchecked. The Council called in Mr. A. J. Stedman, architect and surveyor. Mr. Stedman was usually to be found on the upper reaches, designing houses for the affluent; the effluent was hardly in his line. But he donned waders and navigated on foot all six and one-fifth miles of waterway within the urban district. His survey produced some interesting statistics.

The average width of the River Wey was 27½ feet, varying from 43 to 15 feet. This, if nothing else, assured anxious people that Mr. Stedman had at all times been within sight of land. The depth of mud averaged 3 to 4 feet, though in some places he had measured as much as 5 feet. The free flow of water was inhibited by several contributory causes, the most serious being the mud, which occupied a considerable volume of the water-course, the overgrowth of weeds on the edges, and the accumulated debris from trees. He estimated the probable cost of clearing all obstacles out of the Wey at £6,270, or 1s. 11d. a foot. Mr. Stedman then listed the 30-odd riparian owners, with precise measurements of their individual frontages, and apportioned this figure between them. Mrs. Soames of Moor Park came out top at £922. Floods had recently caused further hardship and it was time to tackle the problem once and for all. County, who were supposed to have sought powers of river control in their area, maintained a complete silence. Mr. Stedman's report was sent with a covering note to Kingston.

In a drive against the Hale Ward's disproportionate quota of sub-standard dwellings, a closing order was issued in respect of a converted pantechnicon at Hoghatch, lived in by a Mr. Vince . . . The first 40 houses at Stoke Hills were ready for occupation in November, at rents of 9s. a week for three bedrooms, living-room and scullery; 10s. 6d. for a larger edition; and 12s. for those with a parlour and bathroom . . . The new block of 12 houses at Badshot Lea were named Groveside Cottages, but this was later changed to Pine View.

Following minor repair works costing about £100, 'Bourne Mill House' and the adjoining buildings were let to Cecil Hicks on a three-year tenancy at £100 a year . . . Arthur Samuel, M.P., was congratulated on being appointed Assistant Chancellor of the Exchequer. Farnham's member had nursed his constituency well and was very popular in the town . . . Asked when a public library would be opened in Farnham, County replied that owing to demands from 'the more important towns in Surrey', it had not been possible to supply books to Farnham. This snub may have been an answer to the local Council's earlier lack of enthusiasm, engendered by consideration for private stationers in the town who ran commercial libraries.

On 29 November, a special meeting was held to digest the now confirmed disaster that Farnham's last remaining beer industry was to be taken over by Courages of Alton. In the past, the brewing of beer had vied with the castle as a significant contribution to the town's sense of identity. Beer hops and bishops had between them been Farnham's staple industry for time out of mind; to lose both in the same year was a catastrophe, only partially offset by the town's later development as a minor tourist attraction and a home for London-based commuters. Part of the meeting was taken up by debating the fate of the Memorial Hall and sports ground at the Farnham United Brewery premises in West Street. Willie Loe, general manager of the outgoing F.U.B., was anxious that this memorial to the Great War should be retained for the use of the town. His directors hoped that the hall would be handed over to a Trust comprised of Courages and the Council, and leased by the latter at a nominal rent of £1 a year. There were strings attached—notably that the ground must be used for organised sports and not as a public recreation ground.

There was a plan in December from Harold Falkner for the conversion of a building at Deans Farm, Dippenhall, into a cottage. The citation ran: 'The proposed cottage, which abuts hard upon the road leading to the Hartley Wintney Schools, forms part of a larger building or barn, through the centre of which the brickwork has been cut away and a road formed as an entrance drive to a private residence. The roof has been left and forms an arch over the entrance road'.

There was initially some trivial argument with the Council over the damp-course—or lack thereof—but eventually the plan was allowed. One who was privileged to witness the various stages of Falkner's Dippenhall period is quite happy to risk being dubbed a fanatic, by later generations who take it all for granted, when he re-echoes the cry of the time—'thank heavens for Harold Falkner!'. This architectural genius—the description is not a frivolous one—had passed through his bread-and-butter years of designing houses, even council houses, to the requirements, and purses, of his clients, and was now free to indulge his artistry on land owned by his family at Dippenhall, unfettered by the whims of no-one but the Council, of whom he was not in the least afraid.

At the Venison Dinner in December, County Councillor Alderman E. J. Holland assured Farnham that their application for a Charter of Incorporation was still before the Privy Council and that it had the full support of the S.C.C.

'D' (Right Half) Company, 3rd Volunteer Battalion, The Queen's Royal West Surrey Regiment, 1915-19. Back
[Ro]w: Privates T. Patterson, F. Bone, A.P. Crosby, Aldridge, A.H. Larkin, C.H. Crosby. 3rd Row: Privates H. Stacey,
[B]acchus, A. Green, H. Trigg, C. J. Nutt, C. Greenaway, H. R. Huband, L. Shrubb, W. H. Allen, L/Cpl. F. W. Speak,
[Priv]ates C. Ardley, A. T. Daniel, E. Lawrence, C. Pipe. 2nd Row: Privates H. West, W. E. Cox, E. G. McConnochie,
[S]haw, T. C. Turner, W. H. Ashton, J. E. Spencer, J. A. Norris, S. D. Marshallsay, P. C. Barling, G. Goulden, W. Giles,
[D]unn, C. Shrubb, A. E. King, B. Gibbons, A. W. Burningham. Front Row: L/Cpl. J. G. Naish, L/Cpl. W. H. Gunn,
[L/Cpl.] B. J. Turner, Cpl. A. Thorpe, Cpl. C. F. Falkner, Cpl. E. F. Gardner, Sgt. W. Elphick, C.S.M. H. Bide, Lieut. C.
[Ne]therley, Capt. W. G. Wrigley, 2/Lieut. S. C. G. Crow, Capt. W. Stroud, C.Q.M.S. H. Clist, Sgt. A. H. Searl, Sgt. F. A.
[Gu]nn, Cpl. C. E. Borelli, L/Cpl. S. H. Hume, Cpl. C. L. Bentall, Cpl. H. C. Folkard. (*Reproduced by courtesy of*
[Farn]ham Museum)

The two-minute silence was first observed in Farnham: scene outside the offices of J. A. Eggar, whose idea it was.
[Re]produced by courtesy of the Executors of Miss Winifred Borelli)

3. Kilns in Waverley Lane.

4. Customers of the *Jolly Farmer* en a trip to Brighton in 1924.

5. Hale's in 1923: the first radio showroom in Farnham (in the Town Hall Buildings). (*Reproduc by courtesy of G. A. Hale, Ltd.*)

6. Fun fair in Castle Street: no fun for the residents.

Afloat in Lower Church Lane, 33. (*Reproduced by courtesy of E. C. Griffith of Farnham*)

8. The old Town Hall. (*Reproduced by courtesy of Surrey County Library*)

9. The Byworth Cup, 1623—Farnham's 'I Grail'. (*Reproduced by courtesy of Surrey County Library*)

10. The Bailiff's Hall, faithfully restored by Harold Falkner. (*Reproduced by courtesy of the Executors of Miss Winifred Borelli*)

. Edward Leroy and Dr. H. F. Ealand in *The Mikado*, 1928. (*Reproduced by courtesy of Miss Ealand*)

12. Charles Borelli proudly launches the *Golden Hind*, 1931. (*Reproduced by courtesy of the Executors of Miss Winifred Borelli*)

. The Farnham Pageant.

14. B.P. with 'Jam Roll': it cost his Boy Scouts one penny each.

15. The Farnham cricket eleven in the 1930s.

16. The cloud-capped towers of Norman Shaw's Lloyds Bank come tumbling down (*Reproduced by courtesy of the Executor of Miss Winifred Borelli*)

. Mr. Sargent's new swimming pool, 1931. (*Reproduced by courtesy of Mr. R. M. Sargent*)

. Felling the cedars in front of the
stle, planted as seedlings by Mrs.
ownlow North in 1787. (*Reproduced
courtesy of the Executors of Miss
nifred Borelli*)

19. (*above*) & 20. (*right*) Charles Borelli studies a model of the old Market House and Harold Falkner works on one of his houses at Dippenhall. (*Reproduced by courtesy of E. C. Griffith*)

21. Without Borelli and Falkner, Farnham might well have continued to look like this section on the north side of the Borough. (*Reproduced by courtesy of the Executors of Miss Winifred Borelli*)

Two carts and a motor car—a busy time for the policeman on point duty. (*Reproduced by courtesy of the Execu-* *s of Miss Winifred Borelli*)

23.   Anti-flood work on the River Wey, 1935.

24. Opening of the Trapes Housing Scheme by Councillor Arthur Figg in 1933. (*Reproduced by courtesy of R. M. Sargent*)

25. Opening of the new Girls' Grammar School in Menin Way by H.R.H. the Duchess of Gloucester, July 1939. On her right is Mrs. Philipson-Stow. (*Reproduced by courtesy of John Chitty*)

26. A way for the bypass is cleared, 1938. (*Reproduced by courtesy of E. C. Griffith*)

27. 'Winter' by Ursula McCannell. (*Reproduced by permission of the artist*)

28. Farnham Urban District Council Civil Defence: Head Wardens and Deputy Wardens, 1938-1945. Fifth Row: Mr. Webber, Mr. Bate, Sir A. Bagshawe, C.M.G., Lieut. Col. Riddell, D.S.O., Lieut. Col. Murray, D.S.O., Mr. Hirstle, Mr. Hargreaves, Mr. Smyth, Col. Dundas, D.S.O., Mr. Ogbourn, Mr. Weeks. Fourth Row: Mr. Tanner, Mr. Crofts, Mr. Bellairs, Maj. Henley, Mr. Hopkins, Mr. Cox, D.C.M., Mr. Willie, Mr. Page, M.C., Mr. Cook, Mr. Saxton. Third Row: Mr. Lowe, Mr. Ryott, Capt. Hewes, Mr. Roberts, Maj. Campbell, D.S.O., Mr. Armitage, Mr. White, Mr. Kimber, Mr. Macklin, Mr. Patterson, Mr. Hall, Mr. Milne. Second Row: Capt. Mosse, R.N., Brig. Fanshawe, C.B.E., D.S.O., Lieut. Col. Bacon, O.B.E., Lieut. Col. Coxon, O.B.E., Maj. Gen. Newcome, C.B., C.M.G., D.S.O., Lieut. Col. Duke, Lieut. Col. Scale, D.S.O., O.B.E., (Chief Warden), Mr. Hale (Sub Controller), Lieut. Col. Henderson, M.C., (Deputy Chief Warden), Lieut. Col. King-Mason, Lieut. Col. Short, C.B.E., Mr. Aylwin, Mr. Skelsey, M.M. First Row: Mr. Williams, Mr. White, Mr. Cooper, Mr. Hall, Mr. Hills, Mr. Robinson, M.C., Mr. Fry, Miss Hornell, Mr. King, Mr. Cook, Mr. Ayling, Mr. Watmore, Mrs. Hewins. (*Reproduced by courtesy of Surrey County Library*)

29. Victory Dinner, 5 December 1945, in the British Restaurant. (*Reproduced by courtesy of Surrey County Library*

1928

'It has been found from experience that a monopoly is best able to supply the transport facilities of a district because it is best able to maintain a pioneer service at a loss in order to develop the district.'

Spokesman for the Aldershot and District Traction Co., Ltd.,
Farnham Herald, 17 December 1927

'The Bills (measures sought by the Railway Companies to obtain powers to run public transport on the roads) strike at a fundamental point which every Englishman holds dear—the preservation of his existence from the establishment of a monopoly'.

Mr. Shrapnell Smith, director, Aldershot and District Traction Co., Ltd., at a meeting of the Farnham Chamber of Commerce,
14 February 1928

WHEREAS THE ALDERSHOT BOROUGH COUNCIL had no other course than to submit to repeated failure in their efforts to annexe the Farnham Urban District, the Traction Company, because of an outward-looking nature, were debarred from accepting defeat. For in order to survive and proliferate, the company were obliged, by hook or by crook, to project their image north, south, east and west across all frontiers, county or parish. A 'bus war' developed on the roads within a wide radius of Aldershot which escalated into its final stages towards the end of 1927, in which the general public, being the cargo, were directly involved.

When motors ousted horses as a means of transit, the village smiths had to change with the times or perish. Many attempted to augment meagre incomes by running what passed for passenger-carrying vehicles to and fro the nearest town. These small-time operators had proved easy prey for the emerging giant in Aldershot, who effortlessly swallowed up competitors such as D. May of Elstead, who had three buses on the roads, and Arranns of Tilford. Now, at the start of 1928, they had come into direct confrontation with a rival that was more in their own heavyweight class—the Farnham Coaches, Limited. Farnham Coaches was a consortium of Farnham businessmen, which included Councillors Borelli, Grange and Ewart, and was backed by sufficient funds to put up a fight against the aggressors. As local men, they had the sympathy of the Farnham

117

Council, who, as Licensing Authority, had the last say in who could ply for hire in the urban district.

The company had been issued in November 1927 with the right to ply on the lucrative London–Farnham–Bordon route (return fares between Farnham and London were 6s., or 7s. for a period return). On the plum Shortheath and Rowledge routes, their buses raced neck and neck with those of the Aldershot firm until they became a danger to the public. This would not do, so the Council's Hackney Carriage Licensing Sub-Committee called a conference at which the two companies were urged to overcome their differences and to synchronise their timetables 'so as to secure a reasonable service and eliminate the present possible danger to the public from rival services running on narrow country roads in close proximity to each other'. Farnham Coaches agreed, but the Traction Co. responded by putting on yet another bus. So F.C. promptly applied for, and were granted, licences for five more double-deckers on the Aldershot–Shortheath route. This aroused a letter dated 31 December 1927 from G. F. W. George, Secretary of the A. and D. T. Co., admonishing the Farnham Council for allowing another company to ply for hire over routes which his company had been building up for the past 19 years. In reply, he was told to restrict services on the congested Shortheath run or else the Council would hold a full-scale review of the entire bus situation throughout their area.

A. and D. T. Co. fought back with an application in respect of a further 12 single-deckers and six charabancs. They also made formal demand for the transfer of all Farnham Coaches' local services. They won, of course—the Council gave way in May 1928 on all local routes (Farnham Coaches continued to run to London), and restrictions were lifted on the Traction's fleet of 34 double-deckers, 133 single-deckers, and 16 charabancs. Thereafter, the lumbering bulk of a bus in the narrow lanes became conspicuous only by its absence, and would-be passengers learnt the virtue of patience.

*   *   *   *   *

There was skating that New Year's Eve across the church meadows by the river. When the thaw came two days later, the water came in waves, rising 12 inches in 20 minutes. It caused the worst deluge in Farnham, said the *Herald,* since 1900. It flooded the malt kilns at the *Red Lion* brewery to a depth of three or four feet, quenching the fires, and the Co-op and police station were isolated from the rest of the town. From Kingston there had been silence, deep as death, in reply to Mr. Stedman's report. But now, in the face of this renewed violation of people's basic rights, the Surrey Agricultural Committee sent down their Major Harding, the County Land Agent, to a conference on 2 February. It was evident that he had been instructed to see to it that the locals did not start anything on their own initiative that his superiors would not approve. For, as Major Harding pointed out, the increase of flooding over the past few years was not just a local menace but one which affected the whole of the River Wey valley in Surrey and if Farnham did anything to facilitate the flow of the river through their district, then this would swell the floods downstream. A comprehensive scheme at County level was the only course. Certain obstructions were known to exist near the mouth of the Wey where it joined the Thames and these should be attended to first. He did agree, however, to the Council chivvying the Farnham Laundry, whose system of in-flow and out-flow was causing a minor obstruction. There were other contributory factors, such as the smallness of the bridges, and the penstock at Waverley which generated electricity for the Andersons, but nothing could be done about these.

At the Council meeting on 10 January, members paid tribute to Alfred James Nash of 41 Castle Street, who had died on 30 December. Born in 1847 of an old Farnham family who had migrated from Frensham in the 18th century, A. J. was the second son of John Nash who had founded the firm of Nash and Sons, auctioneers, surveyors and estate agents adjoining the market place, where they conducted weekly livestock sales. In 1923, the firm had amalgamated with Hewitt and Lee. Whilst at the Grammar School in Charles Stroud's day, Nash was one of a group of staunch Conservatives who broke up a Liberal meeting in Farnham. He had served as a member of the old Local Board in the 1880s, and had distinguished himself in the closing years of the century by applying for a provisional order to enable him to set up as a one-man electricity supply undertaking.

Mr. Otway McCannell, A.R.W.A., R.B.A., was welcomed as Head of the Art School in succession to W. H. Allen. He was known to be a figure and landscape painter of some renown who frequently exhibited at the Royal Academy and other European centres. His best-known work to date, 'The Devil's Chess Board', was first shown in 1924.

The people of Badshot Lea were lukewarm in their response to the Council's proposal to acquire land in that village for a recreation ground . . . The local troop of the Legion of Frontiersmen were permitted to hold their Easter Monday gymkhana in the Tin Hut Field at Weybourne, which had recently been acquired for a possible extension of the sewage farm . . . The housing programme was continued with six more houses at Stoke Hills, 12 near West Street schools, 12 adjoining Gorseland Cottages, Hale, 24 at Wrecclesham, and 14 near the *Elm Tree,* Weybourne.

Woven into the fabric of these civic activities was the harsh spectre of the town's major worry—the future of the castle. There were disquieting undertones. It was remarked in the local press that Bishop Woods had 'just escaped from the burden of Farnham Castle'. The Guildford Diocesan people made no secret of their inability to undertake any large-scale provision for a Retreat and Conference Centre in Farnham, as had been suggested, because of more urgent calls on their purse. Instead, they were willing, as one of the dioceses in the south of England, to take a minor role in any similar scheme, and would agree to let the castle on a repairing lease at a nominal rent of one shilling a year. Another blow fell in January, when a letter from Bishop Woods in the *Winchester Diocesan Chronicle* told of the appointment as Dean of Salisbury of Dr. Randolph, who had been standing by, with £20,000 in his pocket, all prepared to move into Farnham Castle. At no time was it suggested that the castle might be used for a purpose other than spiritual. Redundant castles had been adapted for civic purposes— there was one in Winchester itself. The Council and their staff were already too big for Paxton Watson's small office block in South Street. Perhaps the breath-consuming climb up Castle Hill would have been too much for ratepayers.

With Farnham Park it was different. There was a real worry that it might fall into the hands of speculative builders. 'Farnham's lung', as someone couldn't help calling it, extended for 295 acres. It had been offered to the Council for £16,000. A deputation of members met Sir Stanford Downing of the Ecclesiastical Commission in London and talked him down to a figure of £10,000. They also persuaded the Commissioners to throw in the area used from time immemorial as Farnham's cricket ground. 'You are going to take away our old Farnham cricket ground', exclaimed Edgar Kempson, one of the deputation, 'if we buy the bulk of the Park, we must have the old cricket ground'. The deal was almost sealed at the March Council meeting, but to be on the safe side it was referred to a public meeting at the Corn Exchange. This was attended by some 500 townspeople. Chairman Borelli outlined the basic facts. He referred to the councillors' own views in favour of buying, and those of many others who were unable to be at the meeting. Not to take advantage of this generous offer would, he said, be nothing short of disaster. Richard Combe of 'Pierrepont', Frensham, had promised 200 guineas and a further 100 guineas from his brewery; Mr. Langham had put his name down for £100, as had Mrs. Remfry of Gong Hill, Sir Edward Perceval, and 'Anonymous'. Kempson and Wrights had offered to do the conveyancing work free. Enthusiastic letters had been received from people like Judge Cecil Whiteley, Mr. Anderson, and Lord Midleton.

Mr. Wright outlined the financial aspect. Because of the desirability of acquiring at the same time additional land fronting the Odiham road, and other extras, the total cost would come to £11,000. Spread over 60 years, this would represent a rate of 1¼d. in the pound. On the credit side, there would be income from grazing rights (£200 a year), the Rangers House (say £50), and sporting rights (about £50). Then Edgar Kempson added his usual folksy observations. Many a time he had trudged through the park, assessing its value to the town. Once, one of his party, the Archdeacon of Surrey, had stumbled into a gravel hole up to his gaiters and was not presentable when they returned to the castle for luncheon. What was £10,000 for 295 acres? Aldershot had paid £30,000 for their park, and Guildford £45,000 for the 150-acre Shalford Park.

Mr. Mardon enlarged upon the threat that, if the town refused the offer, the park might well fall to speculative builders. A lot of people, for instance, had been against buying Gostrey Meadow. Lord Midleton told the meeting to take their courage in both hands. Other speakers followed, and in the end the following motion was put from the Chair: 'That this meeting, having considered the proposal of the Farnham Urban District Council for the acquisition of Farnham Park, is of the opinion that it is desirable in the interests of the town and district and its posterity that they should proceed with the purchase'. Less than a dozen people voted against it. By the end of March a general appeal for funds had been launched.

Maybe it was the decision to buy the splendid park, with its promise for cricket, football and other sports (perhaps a nine-hole golf course, for example), as well as an unlimited space for communing with nature, that turned aside the Council's interest, if, indeed, they ever had one, in the brewery's sportsground in Babbs Mead. This unfortunate white elephant, once a proud memorial to Great War casualties, had become a casualty in itself. It was too far from the town centre. The extent of it was limited to the size of one football pitch. The hall, though useful for dances perhaps, might create an expense on the rates. Courages had offered it to a Trust to be managed by the Council, at a nominal £1 a year; it would be embarrassing to refuse such generosity. But that was what whipping-boys were for; so, in March, it was announced that, 'in view of the Council's present and prospective commitments, the Council regret that they cannot see their way to accept Messrs. Courage and Company's kind and generous offer and undertake the proposed Trust'. This brought letters from the Chamber of Commerce, the local branch of the National Playing Fields Association, and the Elementary Schools Athletic Association, together with visits from Dr. Colman and Mr. Meddows Taylor. Seeing that the heat was on, the Council called for specimen expenditure accounts over the past three years, also a written con-formation of Courages' terms. But their attitude remained unchanged.

Farnham's postmaster, R. G. Wilson, was promoted to the post office at Wigan. During his three-year stint in Farnham, he had made himself popular as the town's funny-man, cum born administrator. He was President of the Chamber of Commerce; he had acted as arbiter in the bus dispute; he had raised £50 for Trimmers Hospital. A sense of humour opens many doors. A Mr. Surplice arrived in due course from Leeds to take his place.

Major Wade had dug up another Roman kiln, this time at Snailslynch. It was stacked with a soft coarse ware, but this was badly crushed, the most intact artefact being in three pieces. On this occasion, instead of going nationwide, or across the Atlantic, the major put the bits on one side, hopefully, for a museum in Farnham.

That busy priest, Father Etienne Robo, was the latest—but not the last—of a long line of local eccentrics who fondly imagine that their writings on Farnham's past are of interest to others. In researching for his *Medieval Farnham*, he asked permission to study ancient records in the Council's custody. In his preface, Robo apologised for what he thought might be taken for undue levity here and there, but hastened to assure readers that accuracy had not been sacrificed to this manner of treating his subject. 'To intermingle jest with earnest', as Bacon once observed, 'is perhaps the best way of sugar-coating a history-book'. Of its kind, Father Robo's was a minor classic.

Gilbert and Sullivan's *The Mikado* opened in Farnham on 28 May. This was the first production of the Farnham Amateur Operatic Society that came into being following an inaugural meeting in December 1927, and which was to achieve great popularity throughout many years to come.

To confront readers with the statistics that, in the Farnham Urban District of 1928, there were 42 miles of highway (main roads, 13 miles 4 furlongs; assisted roads, 3 miles 2 furlongs; unassisted roads, 25 miles 2 furlongs), of which 35 miles had been surface-tarred and the remainder merely patched up; and, moreover, that these roads were lit by 210 street lamps, is perhaps not the surest way of getting their interest. Yet to exclude such details might be a withholding of historically important facts which could only weaken the authenticity of the record.

Of greater human interest—Air Marshal J. F. A. Higgins was in the news again: this time as the commander of a British Expeditionary Force operating against an Arabian tribe from headquarters at Ur. 'Boy' McCormick, reported the *Herald,* on 4 February, was bound over by the Burnley magistrates for assaulting Albert Clifford Lord, a traveller for the firm in which McCormick's estranged wife worked. McCormick had found a note written by his wife to Lord which contained the words 'Bye-bye, darling boy—all my love'.

In February, it was learnt that Bishop Greig had found a rented house—'The Grange', at Cobham. It contained 12 bedrooms, four to five reception rooms, and had extensive grounds. He was planning to move in at Easter. He thought it necessary to explain his extravagance by saying that all his work and entertaining would have to be done at home.

C. D. Quittenton was imported from Stevenage Council as a draughtsman in the surveyor's department at three guineas a week. He later became Town Planning Officer. Dapper in appearance, and of personal charm, 'Quit' was in great demand socially . . . Only one new face appeared at the Council election; this belonged to Miss Rosa Wells, of 2 Stanton Villas, Long Garden Walk . . . Charles Borelli was given a second year as Chairman . . . Falkner's plans for 'Mavins', Greenhill Road, were passed in May. This magnificent house was taken by E. G. Pearson, one-time editor of *The Bombay Times* . . . The park fund appeal reached £1,528, which was considered rather slow going.

The brewery were liquidising their assets. The old *Ship* inn, now a shop at 17 The Borough, was knocked down to Bides, the seed people, for the high price of £3,400; and Jimmy Corpe, the Downing Street garage owner, paid £1,000 for the old *Bird-in-Hand.*

The Council took stock of their first year's trading as water undertakers. Some 78,260,000 gallons of water had flowed through the pipes. Receipts had totalled £23,712, and expenditure was £23,796.

The 30-ft. wide access road to the swimming bath did not extend as far as Brightwells Gardens, so a deal was done with the market people whereby a 6-ft. wide strip on the north side could be taken into the market in return for a 24-ft. road onwards to a gate at Brightwells. This delightful public garden was now in full blossom. A new hard tennis court had been added at a cost of £178, and arrangements put in hand for re-surfacing the existing courts with a red-coloured dressing. Mr. Borelli gave a silver cup for a bowls tournament. A full programme of military band concerts had been arranged for the summer weeks.

Councillors Philipson-Stow and Avery attended a sale of effects at the castle on 16 May and bid £30 for furniture suitable for public offices in Brightwell House. The County Librarian had intimated that a branch library would be formed later in 1928 in the downstairs room of the house. The acquisition of 'Montrose', South Street, however, had released the old committee room downstairs below the Council Chamber, and it was decided to open the library here. In due course, 1,100 books arrived, and the public were given access to them on 5 October 1928. Mr. W. Lightbody of 'Sefton', Shortheath, was librarian; he was assisted by Miss Isobel Gravenor. On that first day, 100 adults and 38 juveniles enrolled. By the end of the year, there were four times as many.

The Rev. J. M. C. Crum was appointed to a Canonry of Canterbury and left Farnham after 15 years; his successor was named as Canon E. M. Girling, vicar of Send, near Woking. There were changes, too, in the council offices, where a new, younger, generation took the reins. Mr. J. W. Wright retired after 43 years' service—18 as Clerk—and Arthur Albert Minns, his assistant, was promoted to Acting Clerk at £500 a year. Dr. Sloman finally went after 50 years, and, on 4 August, he was succeeded as Medical Officer of Health by Dr. Frank Bedo Hobbs, a partner of Doctors Hussey and Roberts, and a finalist for several years in the Brightwells tennis tournaments. Lastly, Mr. Cass retired from active work as Consultant Surveyor.

Fire Chief Chitty reported that the steam hooter attached to the brewery was threatened by the closure of those premises and recommended the installation of an electrically-operated siren at the fire station, costing six guineas.

With a deep sense of nostalgia, the Farnham United Brewery brewed their last drop of ale at the Lion Brewery on Saturday, 30 June, thus ending 68 years of Farnham's biggest industry. In future, Courages would be using part of the premises as a local depot. They were now offering the unwanted Memorial Hall and sports ground free, gratis, and with no strings attached, but again the Council declined. Courages then asked Trimmers Hospital if they would like them, for the hospital had been heard grumbling about inadequate accommodation, but they turned it down, too. It was all most embarrassing. Mr. Mardon remarked that, if rumours about the town were true, it was possible that the Corn Exchange might one day be closed—in which case, the Memorial Hall might become the only available place for public meetings.

Aldershot Borough Council were now trying to muscle in, under the pretext of sewering them, on the Rural Council's villages of Ash, Normandy, Tongham, and part of Wanborough. They were also hinting at an amalgamation with the Farnborough Urban District.

A big welcome was given in July to His Eminence the Cardinal Archbishop of Westminster, when the 8th centenary of the founding of Waverley Abbey was observed. As the founding had taken place before the Reformation, the celebration of it was strictly a matter for Father Robo, as the Catholic priest, to mastermind. An estimated 4,500 people were present, and no fewer than 236 motor cars were counted in the park.

In August, a licence was granted to Sidney Hayter to run two buses between Guildford and Farnham, via the lower road through The Sands, Seale, and Puttenham. This became the Yellow Bus Service and was to function for many years, surprisingly left alone by the Traction Company.

Farnham said goodbye to Canon Crum on Monday, 17 September. He had chosen as his parting gift one of the new 'toys of civilisation', a wireless receiving set. In thanking the parishioners, the Canon mentioned that he could claim a family connection with the science of sound transmission through his Uncle William— Lord Kelvin, 1824–1907—who had laid the first cable across the Atlantic. Privately-owned wireless sets were gradually finding their way into people's homes. Mrs. Philip Snowden of 'Eden Lodge', Tilford, told an audience in October that she looked forward to the time when sets were as common in houses as baths.

The Rotary Club lent its weight to the pressure groups campaigning for the Council's acceptance of the Memorial Hall . . . J. Alfred Eggar, President of the Field Club, recommended 'Vernon House', West Street, as the town's library and museum—it wouldn't cost more than about £18,000 at the most.

In October, it was learnt that the tenants of the Town Hall shops in The Borough had received notice to quit, by March 1929. Speculation was rife that the much-disliked town hall was going to be replaced by a building more in keeping with the Farnham vernacular. Those in the know kept mum; even Mr. Langham did not know—'wait and see', Mr. Borelli told him.

The 1928 Brightwells season was a huge success. Tennis tournaments had attracted 50 entrants, two or three hundred spectators watched the doubles final. An average of some 1,200 people attended each of the eight band concerts. The swimming bath, too, had a bumper season.

Perhaps 'The Grange' at Cobham had proved somewhat ambitious for the Guildford Diocesan Board, for in October a ray of hope was kindled by a recommendation at a Decanal conference that the bishop should take up residence in part of Farnham Castle. The Royal Institute of British Architects had been briefed to prepare a scheme of adaptation. But the Board, when next meeting in November, were solely concerned with where to build the new cathedral—a site on Stag Hill, Guildford, was chosen—and the R.I.B.A.s plans for Farnham Castle were deferred.

One can discern the hand of Chairman Borelli, whose mind dwelt fairly equally on the past, present and future of Farnham, in two quite charming activities that autumn. One ingenious proposal was to restore the ancient machinery at Bourne Mill and harness it to the steam pump at the sewage farm. John Taylor and Sons, engineers, were called in to report on feasibility.

The other project—the revival of the parish church carillon—did materialise. The bells, cast in 1723, were badly in need of restoration and in some cases replacement. The estimate of a church bell foundry in London came to close on £300, so, as this did not rank as an item chargeable to rates, a subscription list was opened. The money was quick to come in. This carillon was one of Farnham's special glories. The chimes rang out every third hour, day and night—at three, six, nine, and 12 o'clock. Lying in bed at night, a few yards from the church, one's pulses would beat time to the ditty, having been awakened at each third hour for this purpose. But they were beautiful—quite beautiful. There were four verses, of which the first is the one generally quoted:

> Life let us cherish
> While yet the taper glows,
> And the fresh flow'ret
> Pluck ere it close;
> Away with every toil and care,
> And cease the rankling thorn to wear,
> With manful hearts life's conflict meet,
> Till Death sounds the retreat.

1929

It's nice to think of Farnham in the days of long ago,
When everything was sleepy, dead and slow;
Before the days of motor cars, hurry, rush and speed,
When everything was tranquil—oh, happy days indeed!

I've often heard dear people with a sigh that's almost pain,
Say how they'd love to have once more those peaceful days again;
And now I come to think of it, I see no reason why
We cannot have them back again. We can at least but try.

We have the men who are in the mood; they have the money too;
So let's sit down and have a try and see what we can do.
A by-pass road we've got to have—I think we should have two—
Then motor traffic goes right round and nothing comes right through.

By 'nothing', I mean motor cars and everything that's new;
Of course we'd have some donkey carts and perhaps a horse or two;
There is Castle Street, for instance, so lovely and so wide,
All talk of 'public places' must be brushed aside.

A row of handsome barricades down the centre there should be,
With ducks and chicken running round, cackl'ing with glee . . .

G.M.F., *Farnham Herald*, 8 June 1929

THE MOTORING AGE brought new problems. Initially, one of these problems was discernible in the town centre. As the years of the 'Roaring '20s' passed, an expanding tide of visitors from outer space roared into Castle Street. They alighted from their private cars or public charabancs with one common thought in mind. When a cursory glance had failed to reveal the magic sign, it would occur to the trippers that Farnham, being a superior sort of place, would naturally wish to remain discreet about such matters. The inviting alley-ways which here and there separated the ancient frontages in Castle Street and The Borough beckoned as places ideally suitable for such an establishment. Detachments would be sent to investigate and report back. The natives selling picture postcards would watch them dart in and out of the passages, and finally leap into their cars and go off to search elsewhere for one without spending a penny in the town.

This was not good for the postcard business. The need for the Council to overcome their reluctance to spend good ratepayers' money on public conveniences became pressing. The locals generally warmed to the idea. Those who did not warm were about 500 people living in the vicinity of Castle Street, and whose eyes had watched the sanitary inspector's every move. He came up with four alternative sites and was told to look further into Scheme A, which entailed the alteration of 2 Park Row, a cottage owned by Miss Margaret Kelly, who lived nearby in Castle Street and was asking £450 for it. When this leaked out, the Council received a petition with 550 signatures suggesting that the site was in no way suitable, and inviting the Council to look elsewhere for some other petition. So they studied Mr. Sargent's other recommendations—at the rear of Nos. 11/12 Castle Street, up the yard by No. 3, and underground in the middle of Castle Street opposite Long Garden Walk. All three were ruled out as impracticable. They looked up the yard by the International Stores. Someone suggested building one on the triangular piece of no-man's land at the bottom of Bear Lane, with the entrance facing north so that clients might approach the door furtively via the park. Mr. Sargent kept up his search.

*   *   *   *   *

At their monthly meeting on 8 January, the councillors recorded the death that morning of Dr. Samuel George Sloman, who had recently retired after 52 years as Farnham's Medical Officer of Health. He lived at 39 West Street. Born in 1847, he was the eldest son of Dr. S. G. Sloman, senior, who had come from Exeter as a young man to marry Catherine Mary Newnham, daughter of Dr. William Newnham of 27 West Street. Dr. Sloman had been in partnership with a brother, Herbert, before taking on Dr. H. F. Ealand as partner. He was a cousin of Edna Lyall, the writer, whose introduction in 1900 to the *Homeland* handbook on Farnham contains nostalgic references to 'the dear old two-storied house' in West Street and 'sweeter far than any foreign carillon, the well-known Farnham chimes'.

The appeal launched in 1928 to raise the £300 asked by Mears and Stainbank to restore these long-silent bells had reached £296 by mid-January, and, on 26 January, the *Herald* announced that the final £4 had been subscribed by 'three old inhabitants of Farnham'. The church clock by which the chimes were regulated also needed repairs, so the carillon did not resume its cheerful jingle until 3 o'clock on Monday afternoon, 29 April.

Dr. W. S. Colman, C.C., phoned through the good news that his Surrey County Council had voted £1,000 towards the purchase of Farnham Park. Another piece of cheer was that the Ecclesiastical Commissioners had reduced their asking price from £500 to £175 for the 3¼ acres of parkland which fronted the Odiham road.

Harry Clist of 'Cranbourne', Alfred Road, had also died over Christmas. He had been active in many spheres, and was on the council from 1918 to 1923. On a lighter note, his colleagues presented Councillor Figg with a canteen of plate to mark his recent marriage.

Elliott Bros. (Bournemouth), Ltd., applied for licences on 25 A.D.C. semi-saloon motor coaches for their proposed route from Bournemouth to London, pausing at Farnham. The Aldershot Traction Co. notified their intention to add to their fleet an improved type of vehicle constructed on a six-wheeled chassis, resulting in a body length of 2½ feet longer than the four-wheeled type. The Traction's fleet now numbered 36 double-deckers, 157 single-deckers, 15 charabancs, and 14 motor coaches. Other operators plying in the area were Sidney Hayter of the Yellow Bus Service, with three single-deckers; Leonard George Hillier of Farnham Coaches, Wrecclesham, with five coaches; and a firm called South London Coaches with four vehicles. In the private hire sector, taxis were run by T. A. W. Mundy, T. W. Shepherd of Station Hill, Basil Giles of Calloways Garage, Shortheath, Edward Lloyd and Son of Frensham, and Jimmy Corpe in Downing Street.

Sixty more council houses were planned under the 1924 Housing Act. If completed by October 1929, these would qualify for Exchequer grants of £7 10s. 0d. per annum per house for 40 years. The latest scheme—Thurbens and Greenfields, Austins Cottages, off West Street, and Coppice and Heath Cottages in Hale—was now nearing completion.

Herbert Mansey of East Street asked permission to place a seat on the pavement at the access from East Street to Stoke Hills as a memorial to the town's much-loved G.P., Dr. 'Paddy' Miles . . . The widening and improvement of Crondall Lane provided work in February for at least 20 hitherto unemployed men . . . There was also a big drive to raise funds for out-of-work miners.

The Stedmans, father and son, submitted their designs for shops and flats to replace the old Assembly Rooms in South Street, and adjoining the *Royal Deer*. Gwendoline Marie Stedman, the daughter, married Councillor Alan Tice on 9 February; they were presented by the councillors with a canteen of plate.

The office cleaner became the proud operator of a Hoover vacuum cleaner, bought from Tilys for £20 . . . Hale councillor J. W. Swansborough resigned because of ill-health . . . The New Year's Honours List included a King's Police Medal for Farnham's Superintendent Lucas . . . The County Council started on a big scheme for the general improvement of East Street; traffic was diverted for the duration, much to the disgust of Swain and Jones, the motor people.

An interesting letter was received in March from Arthur Samuel, M.P., which disclosed that for some years past he had been trying to collect specimens of the 12 known tokens issued by Farnham traders during the years 1648 to 1670. He had only been successful with five; these he now handed over to the Council for safe keeping, perhaps in a museum. The five small copper discs were inscribed:

obverse: IOHN HOLLOWAY—a bunch of candles
reverse: IN FARNHAME 1658—I.H.M.

obverse: AT FARNHAM—I.M.D.
reverse: IN SURRVY a 1658—The Blacksmiths Arms

obverse: IAMES HVNT IN—a castle
reverse: FARNHAM IN SVRREY—I.H. a *Fleur de Lys*

obverse: HENRY MORRIS OF—The Fishmongers Arms
reverse: FARNHAM IN SVRREY—H.E.M.

obverse: IOHN GODDARD
reverse: FARNHAM IN SVRREY

The last three, Mr. Samuel thought, were also dateable to *c.* 1658. He had done some research on James Hunt, who figured in the Hearth Tax books in the reigns of Charles I and II. In 1701, a Thomas Hunt was paid 12s. by the churchwardens of Farnham for ringing the 8 o'clock bell. At a later date, another member of the Hunt family was named as hedgehog catcher to the parish of Farnham. In April, six tokens—another had turned up—were ceremoniously handed over to the Chairman. The sixth was inscribed:

obverse: IN FARNHAM W
reverse: IAMES WRATH 1664

It has been said (*Farnham Buildings and People*, Nigel Temple 1963) that the *Fleur de Lys* was the name of a public house which once existed at 6/7 Castle Street—now Tilys' ironmongery.

Falkner and Aylwin, acting for Courages, submitted plans for the reconstruction of the *Seven Stars* public house in East Street in a pseudo-Tudor style. Several public houses in Farnham were rebuilt about this time . . . Wrecclesham Recreation Ground Management Committee campaigned for a pavilion costing £200, to which the Council contributed £50 . . . Miss Courtauld, who had given £200 towards the Badshot Lea Recreation Ground was invited to open the ground on 18 May . . . The April-September 1929 rate, now one consolidated 'General Rate', was fixed at 6s. in the pound rateable value, with an extra twopence in the area of the Council's water supply.

Councillor Varney chose not to stand for re-election on 25 March. Newcomers to the Chamber were Brigadier-General Leslie Campbell of 'Badshot House', and Arthur Brown of 'Sunnyfield', Rowledge. There was no poll—and little apparent interest. Being a councillor was time-consuming, frequently dull, and mainly unrewarding. When things went wrong, he stood to be pilloried by the electorate; at times of success, there was little appreciation.

The 3rd Farnham Troop, B.P. Scouts—Sir Edward Perceval's Own—were proud of their new headquarters in Long Garden Walk, which was opened on 1 April by Lieutenant-General Sir Edmond Elles, Surrey County Commissioner of Scouts. Farnham scoutmaster, A. T. Daniel, recalled that in 1911, five boys, used to meet at the home of the first scoutmaster, C. E. Mansell, who formed the nucleus of the troop.

Encouraged by their initial success with *The Mikado* in 1928, the Farnham Operatic Society opened at the Church House on 17 April with *Iolanthe*.

The exasperating thing about the river was that, since prehistoric times, the communities upstream had selfishly contrived to harness the flow of life-sustaining water to their best advantage, thus making it difficult for one's own village to do likewise. Apart from its brief incipient journey through Hampshire, the Wey was entirely a Surrey river and the main control of it should have been a duty of the Surrey County Council from the formation of that council in the 1880s. But it was not until April 1929 that a committee composed of seven county councillors and a representative from each district council involved was mooted. An engineer's report, dated 16 April, recommended a joint scheme costing some £240,000, plus about £1,000 a year for maintenance costs, such expenditure to be apportioned between local authorities according to rateable value. The scheme would improve discharge capacity so as to bring down the flood waters from the higher reaches at an increased velocity and greater volume, thereby doubling the existing drainage capacity into the Thames near Weybridge. At Guildford, for instance, the existing discharge, estimated at 1,330,000 tons daily, would be increased to 2,950,000 tons.

The engineer had had many problems to face, for, as everybody knew, riverside dwellers were very sensitive about their rights. Also high on his programme was the need to conserve the many visual amenities along the river, such as the bridges at Tilford—on one of which Conan Doyle had placed his fictional character Nigel Loring, squire of Tilford, to await the arrival of King Edward III and his train on their way from Guildford to Farnham Castle with a view to inducing some of them to 'some small deed of arms against him'. The Farnham Council were delighted that their ancient role as flood-time whipping-boys was seemingly coming to an end. Councillor Figg was nominated as the district's representative on the committee.

Dubbed 'Efforts Week', junketings in aid of local charities opened on Sunday, 5 May, with a united service in Gostrey Meadow, attended by the councillors in full regalia. These frequent festivities were a delightful feature of Farnham life. The streets would be gaily decorated; there would be a fun fair in Broomleaf field; bands would play in Brightwells; livestock might be auctioned in Castle Street; the kids would fight for buns in Gostrey, and the maidens for their honour in the dance halls, or fling caution to the winds at the Grand Carnival Ball at the Corn Exchange on the last night. The climax was always the procession of decorated vehicles through the town, entered by tradesmen and public authorities, or just by individuals. Joyce Robins, dressed as a Russian princess, won a first prize for riding one of her father's horses through the streets. A special prize donated by Mr. Borelli went to Mills and Sons, the builders, for their tableau on wheels, entitled 'Woodman—Spare that Tree!'. Bides were successful with an entry which depicted a baby (played by A. Fry) clasping a gigantic feeding bottle and attended by its nursemaid (Mr. D. R. Evans). Canon Girling wrote to *The Times*:

> The observance in Farnham of a carnival in aid of the funds of our local hospital recalls the fact that on May 10th thirteen years ago, a somewhat similar fete was organized by the Farnham branch of the National Union of Farmers in aid of the Red Cross Fund. During the preparation for this event the objection was raised that a jollification at such a time would be inappropriate and Mr. J. A. Eggar, one of our oldest inhabitants, was much exercised as to the best means of meeting this objection. It occurred to him that a complete silence for two minutes, in remembrance of the fallen, would be the most fitting way, marking our sense of the underlying solemnity of the undertaking. The silence was duly observed, a complete hush falling upon the 2,000 people assembled in the wide Castle Street of this town. This was, so far as I am aware, the first occasion on which the silence was observed and the inhabitants of Farnham are not unnaturally proud of the fact.

Beneath this crust of tomfoolery, the sober side prevailed. There was an urgent S.O.S. from Hale, where the drains were blocked. Poking with rods failed, so the sewer was broken open. The obstruction was found to consist of 10 feet of gravel flints and debris, an iron ball, a polo ball, scrubbing brushes and sacking. Hale people seldom did things by halves. It took four days of 'Efforts Week' to get the sewer working again.

Meanwhile, Mr. Sargent was still prowling around the side alleys looking for somewhere for a public convenience. With the tourist season about to begin, the Council must be seen to be taking the matter seriously. County had vetoed any idea of one on the triangular piece of no-man's land at the bottom of Bear Lane. The yard at 3 Castle Street had a frontage to the pavement 18 feet wide, of which the *Coach and Horses* had right-of-way 8 feet wide; this would leave room for a 10-ft. wide building and cost about £5,000. At 11/12 Castle Street, the toilets could be built at the rear of the shop, in Long Garden Walk. Public Health came up with the obvious theory that the conveniences should be near the parking site for coaches. This was envisaged in Union Road, with the setting back of the Gostrey Meadow boundary fence. This would bring the 'gents' at the Council offices within sprinting distance, and a 'ladies' could be built on to this. It certainly was a problem. In the end, the matter was further adjourned for six months.

Robert Dixon Kingham of 'Summercourt', Tilford Road, died on 5 May, aged seventy-four. He was the second of the 12 children of William Kingham, once of 'Devonshire House' in The Fairfield, founder of the wholesale grocery business. R.D. had been a councillor from 1895 to 1903.

County Cinemas Limited planned a new super cinema on a site in Downing Street. The announcement flourished the superlatives so beloved of the motion picture industry—the building would be 'the finest and most luxurious house of entertainment ever known', with a 'fully equipped stage and commodious balcony'. The proprietors promised to feature only 'talking pictures'. The *Herald,* unconvinced, hoped that the architect would do his best to build in keeping with the character of Farnham, and not 'give us an erection that will be an eyesore to this and succeeding generations'.

On 23 May, the foundation stone of the new St Joan of Arc Catholic church in Tilford Road was laid by the Lord Bishop of Southwark, Dr. Amigo. Over from France for the occasion was a Mademoiselle C. de la Flechere, a descendant of St Joan. The design of this fine church was that of Nicholas and Dixon-Spain; it was built by Mills and Sons.

Then the Farnham Market House and Town Hall Company came up with a truly spectacular project—the replacement of Farnham town hall. Built in 1866, the existing town hall was on Farnham's plum site at the corner of The Borough and Castle Street. A 1912 guidebook said of it 'it is essentially utilitarian and makes no architectural pretensions'. This was not strictly true. Farnham possessed a structural vernacular all its own, which was totally different from that of the town hall. To pull the lot down and start afresh—this time using local talent, such as Harold Falkner—smacked of wild extravagance, until people realised that the prospect was so attractive that the money would be well spent. It was not public money, anyway.

A small point occurred to the Council. Right on the corner, and visually incorporated into the existing Hall, was the old Conduit, a tiny arched recess. This in the dim past had housed the village pump; at some later date, it had served as a shelter for what passed for the town's fire engine; latterly it had become a sort of glory-hole, even being suggested as a site for a public toilet. The Council asked the Town Hall Company if they would like to buy the site for inclusion in their new building for £100—an offer which was accepted.

The year 1929 was noteworthy as the year when a branch of Woolworths came to Farnham. It was rather late in the list—possibly owing to a suspicion that the town's chauffeur-driven shoppers thought in pounds rather than sixpences. At 2 The Borough, the premises of J. Ward, boot repairer, and Miss Tigwell, newsagent, were removed to make room for it. In digging the foundations, a scatter of clay pipes came to light. They were marked with a heart symbol and the initials W.R. It was thought that 'Woolies' would give employment to about thirty Farnham lassies.

As more and more people became car-borne, the cavalcade, especially on Sunday evenings in summer, became almost a spectator attraction. The nose-to-tail procession through the inadequate streets of the town would start soon after teatime, and go on until late at night. This sort of traffic could not wait for the by-pass road that was now being discussed up at Kingston. County urgently undertook the improvement of main streets through Surrey towns. By June, the reconstruction of East Street had been advanced some 1,180 yards along the north side from the hospital to Arnold and Combens. Most of the kinks in Crondall Lane had been straightened out, and the road surface tarmacadamed at a cost of £2,867. The full length of the Ridgway/Shortheath Road–Stickhams Lane thoroughfare was started in July, and plans were in hand for the road from the Ridgway to the Bourne cross-roads. These road works were a heaven-sent answer to the prevailing unemployment problems.

The Labour Party reorganised their local branch in June under the chairmanship of Mr. S. Young, with Mrs. Fry as Hon. Secretary. The *Herald* predicted 'a tough time ahead if they thought to convert Farnham' . . . Under delegated powers, the Council renewed stage-play licences for the Church House and the Bourne and Wrecclesham parish halls. The Church House was now the accepted venue of the Farnham Amateur Dramatic Society . . . Councillor Marsh's wife, Madame Esty, broadcast on the radio. In September, she appeared with her daughter, Hilda Esty, in a show at the Aldershot *Hippodrome* entitled 'The Letter' . . . Ian Forbes Robertson submitted plans for extensions at his house, 'Lanefoot Cottage', Lower Bourne.

Mr. W. Lightbody, the hon. librarian, started a reference book section at his library in the Council offices . . . Mr. Brockhurst lent the museum at the Farnham Institute the horsecloth from the horse of King Charles I. This, trimmed with gold braid and bearing the royal crest, had been left behind at 'Vernon House' in the hurried departure of his captors, who feared a rescue attempt.

A 'notable incident' was enacted on 30 July, when the agreement for the town's purchase of Farnham Park was signed by the respective parties. Councillors Mardon and Borelli were congratulated for the part they had played in this important acquisition.

General Sir Robert Baden-Powell, who lived at Pax Hill, Bentley (and was therefore a 'local'), was also in the news. Scouts at a World Jamboree at Birkenhead had each contributed not more than one penny towards a motor car for B.P. This materialised in the form of a splendid Rolls Royce, nicknamed by its owner as 'Jam Roll'. The chassis was supplied by Swain and Jones of East Street, and the bodywork added by Page and Hunts, of Wrecclesham—who duly received a telegram: 'Congratulate you and your staff on excellent and punctual completion of car, Baden-Powell'.

Having eased the passage of through traffic, the County Council now resolved to carry out big improvements to the bed of the River Wey. These would cost about £240,000 and the work depended upon a contribution from the Unemployment Grants Committee. This committee were also tapped for a grant towards a proposed new swimming bath, adjoining the existing one in Brightwells. This old bath had been built to commemorate the Diamond Jubilee in 1897; it had served its purpose well, but was totally inadequate by 1930 standards. In October, Mr. Sargent produced his plans and specifications for a new pool. Construction costs, he advised, would amount to about £2,500, with filtration plant and machinery a further £600. Spread over 30 years, loan charges should come to £220, against which a government grant of £77 might be expected. Annual running expenses would be some £343, and income about £260—a deficit of £83. A council is not in business to make a profit, and it was resolved to proceed with the new bath. Perhaps of all his indelible marks upon the town, the large swimming bath became Mr. Sargent's greatest memorial. Eighteen tenders were received, the lowest being that of Captain G. F. Marshal of Worksop in the sum of £2,260. Bell Bros., of Manchester, quoted £920 for the filtration plant. The *Herald* recalled the days before 1897, when the town's young men—and sometimes women—used to disport themselves in the mud and water of the river, sheltered by corrugated iron fencing.

Mr. Lightbody reported that, during the year ending 30 September 1929, 11,369 books had been borrowed from the public library. There were now 750 borrowers and the books had been changed three times.

Mr. A. O. King moved his hairdresser's business from The Borough to 'one of the beautiful little shops built on the site of the old Assembly Rooms in South Street' . . . Smyths were extending their premises at 10 East Street . . . Workmen excavating the foundations for a new *Marlborough Head* discovered a 16th-century brick oven five feet down, and under the boards of a first-floor room 26 pennies and ha'pennies dated 1718.

The Right Hon. Philip Snowden, Labour Chancellor of the Exchequer, had come to live at 'Eden Lodge', Tilford. Mr. Langham, taking a deep breath and declaring his newspaper to be uncommitted, commented that Snowden had produced an excellent budget. The *Herald* was on surer ground in reporting that year's Annual Cricket Week. The game against Liphook had been exciting—'the most remarkable game ever played in the Park'. The visitors had declared at 214 (E. C. Loe, 105), leaving Farnham 95 minutes in which to bat. The old Surrey professional, A. Baker, and his nephew, R. F. Baker, scored 122 and 81; the balance of 12 was contributed by two other batsmen. Tennis was quickly becoming Farnham's second love. In the finals of the Brightwells tournaments in September, Miss Godby beat 'Babs' Wiltshire, and Ken Mitchell beat A. G. Cross in the singles. In the mixed doubles, Miss Godby and her father, General Godby, beat B. W. Pyle and Miss Barling.

Flying Officer H. R. D. Waghorn, who had flown at 328 m.p.h. in the Schneider Trophy Air Race in June, was married on 7 September at the Bourne church to Miss Watson of Bourne Ridge.

In the press on 26 October was published a claim which struck at the very roots of Farnham's most cherished sacred cow—the John Henry Knight motor car, universally acknowledged to be the first ever motor car on British roads. The claim was made by L. A. Durant of 'Rustic Walk', Lower Bourne, who, according to the *Daily Sketch*, had given King Edward, when Prince of Wales, his very first car ride in Richmond Park in 1894. Mr. Durant told a *Herald* reporter that his first motor, built in 1894, was powered by a 2½ horse-powered, air-cooled gas engine, with a flat belt drive over wooden pulleys. The chassis was made from 2-in. gas piping, the wheels were those of penny-farthing bicycles, 54-in.

rear and 30-in. front. Durant then made his remarkable assertion that this vehicle was the first car ever to run on English roads. Whilst testing it in Richmond Park, he had been hailed by Lord Knollys, who introduced him to the Prince of Wales. After being given a run in the car, the Prince had pinned a diamond pin in Durant's scarf; this had since remained a cherished possession. Mr. Durant claimed even earlier experiments—in 1888—when he had fitted a side-car to a tandem pedal bicycle. He had also assisted in C. S. Rolls' early experiments in a little workshop in Richmond. Strangely, the matter aroused little excitement locally. With a town now full of the blessed things, perhaps people were disenchanted with motor cars.

At the end of October, the engagement was announced between Miss Molly Ellis and Major Eric W. N. Wade, M.C., East Yorks Regiment, of Bentley. This stirred up recollections of an incident in April 1923 in the North-West Frontier of India. Molly Ellis, then 17, had been kidnapped and taken across the frontier by Afridi tribesmen, whose object was to bargain her release in return for a pardon for their tribe's murder in 1921 of a British officer and his wife. Unable to mount a police operation across the frontier, the British Chief Commissioner had conceived the idea of sending an English woman, preferably one with medical knowledge. Lilian Starr, a nursing sister in a mission hospital was chosen. Disguised as an Afridi woman, and accompanied by trusted men of that tribe, she made her way over the hills into territory in which, apart from an expedition in 1897, no Englishman had ever set foot. At the end of the second day, the party reached a fortified village. Here, the Mullah, who knew the purpose of the visit, and was in sympathy with the kidnappers, conducted the bargaining with a view to lining his own pocket in the process. Molly Ellis was produced. The terms demanded by the Mullah—50,000 rupees and a complete pardon for the 1921 murderers—were unacceptable. The tribesmen held all the trumps; after some hours of wrangling, the meeting adjourned so that each side might withdraw and think over the position privately. During the respite, Molly and her party were violently attacked by a gang with anti-British feelings and this had the effect of softening the Mullah's heart in her favour. The two women left on the morning of the third day, in what was almost a friendly spirit. The incident made front page news at the time in the London dailies. Lilian Starr in due course became the wife of Colonel G. E. Underhill of 'Khyber Cottage', Boundstone. Now Molly Ellis was about to move in next door, so to speak.

The roads in the Bourne were baptised—this having escaped the attention of earlier authorities. There was some bickering over the name 'Bourne Hill' for what the locals had always known as Gravel Hill . . . Fourteen more council houses were planned at Trapes at a cost of £5,691 . . . The fire brigade's old motor tractor and manual engine were finally abandoned. The Chief Officer asked for a high wooden tower in the council yard for the dual purpose of mounting a new electrically-operated hooter, and hanging out the hoses to dry.

Falkner and Alwyn planned additions to the *Railway* hotel, later re-named the *Blue Boy*. The same architects rebuilt the *Alliance,* with a splayed corner to provide a better sight-line from Downing Street into West Street. They offered the Council a site for a public toilet, but this was declined.

On 22 November, the following decisions were taken, by 85 votes to 39, and passed on by the Guildford Diocesan Board of Finance to a Diocesan Conference scheduled for May 1930:

> (a) That in the opinion of this conference it is desirable that the Bishop of the Diocese should reside at Farnham Castle, unless this is found to be impossible on financial grounds.
>
> (b) This conference is of the opinion that the best way to use that part of the Castle not occupied by the Bishop as a residence is to adapt it as a retreat and conference house, unless this is found to be impossible on financial grounds.

At the December council meeting, Councillor Tice observed that Castle Street was now the town's car park, and, in his opinion, always would be. Therefore the public convenience must be in the vicinity. An underground one, say in the cobbled area at the bottom of the street, could be made to look unobtrusive, hardly noticeable in fact, despite all that the outraged residents might say. Councillor Winter grumbled that the Council were too flexible to the will of the public—'We want a little more iron in our blood, and a little less water'.

In December came the glad news that the Minister of Health had sanctioned a loan of £7,750 for the purchase of 298 acres of Farnham Park. Well-wishers and the County Council had between them promised contributions amounting to £1,000.

The downstairs room at the Council offices was now inadequate for the expanding needs of the library, so it was decided to move this to Brightwells House. The old room could then be used by the cashiers for collecting the Council's revenue, thus releasing space in 'Montrose' for the recently-formed Town Planning Department. The Town Planning Act 1925 was a move by government to invite local authorities to enter the 20th century; all the best councils were adopting it. The idea was roughly to pin a large-scale map of the district on the wall and hatch on it zones, according to a pre-arranged code, which denoted types of future development. It was a fine idea—out of it came Farnham's neatly-contrived industrial estate off Guildford Road.

With the coming of the rains in December, the misery of floods returned to the low-lying streets. A great gale on 11 December killed horses in the park and dislodged masonry on the spire of the Congregational church. Detailed readings were taken and sent to County with a covering letter.

1930

'Well, it was like this. My husband and I had just returned from a delightful holiday in Italy. The telephone bell rang and a voice said "Oh, Mrs. Anderson, we are glad you are back—we want you to save the Castle" '.

As related to a *Farnham Herald* reporter by
Mrs. Amy Anderson of Waverley Abbey

THAT VOICE ON THE TELEPHONE signalled no less a dramatic episode in the long history of Farnham Castle than the events so romantically depicted, for example, by the imaginative Neville Lovett some 20 years earlier. In the spring of 1930, the situation regarding the castle was that following a protracted series of embarrassing meetings, the Guildford Diocesan Board of Finance had finally decided that to use the building as a residence for the bishop was just not on. The arguments in support of this decision were many and mostly sound. Ideally, the bishop's residence should be within the curtilage of his future cathedral. Formerly, Farnham had been a central point in the sprawling diocese of the Bishop of Winchester; now it was on the edge of the newly-formed Guildford Diocese. More practically, the old castle was now past it—the abode of bats and owls, rats and mice, as someone put it. The probable cost of renovations and conversions would be prohibitive. Thus, Farnham learnt that, owing to the enormous expense involved—a figure of £17,500 had been mentioned—Farnham Castle would cease forthwith to be the seat of the local bishop.

The question now arose—what was to become of it? As English castles go, it had to be admitted that, even through the rosiest of tinted glasses, it was difficult to foresee it in the years to come as a picturesque ruin of the type favoured by the tour operators. Harold Falkner, writing on 4 January 1932, about the unfortunate necessity to fell the two famous cedars from the Lebanon planted in 1787 by Mrs. Brownlow North, stated that the Norths' reason for planting the trees had been that the building behind them was held in those days to be particularly ugly. Bishop Waynflete had done his best on the front elevation by adding the entrance tower; but generally, the building lacked the castellated charm of, say, Bodiam Castle in Sussex. In these early weeks of 1930, Farnham Castle, like Bunyon's Doubting Castle, seemed to be in the grip of Giant Despair. But not quite; the Diocesan Board had rather under-estimated the natives.

The situation called for the subtle touch of a woman. Mrs. Rupert Anderson of Waverley, who had proved herself during the war years to be a person of infinite capability and resourcefulness, was just the right person to raise £17,500. She attended the Diocesan Conference in May. As the reason for turning down Farnham Castle had been due to the expense involved, would Conference agree to defer their ultimate decision for six months, and, if at the end of that time she could produce the £17,500 required, would they rescind the recommendation of the Finance Board? The meeting agreed to this. The Farnham Castle Fund Committee went into action, with Mrs. Anderson as Chairman, and the Earl of Onslow of Clandon Park, who had given Stag Hill as a site for the new cathedral, as Hon. Treasurer. They started off with promises of contributions amounting to £1,100, and had increased this to £3,028 by the beginning of July. Five hundred pounds each was subscribed by Mrs. Herbert Ryle, in memory of Bishop Ryle (who had once lived in the castle), Richard Combe, the brewer, Miss Lily Antrobus of Charles Hill, and Miss Courtauld of 'Whiteways End'. Sir Lawrence Halsey, Chairman of the Diocesan Board of Finance—bless him!—sent £250. The fund reached £7,014 in mid-July, helped on by £500 from Sir Louis Baron, head of the 'Craven A' cigarette firm. The *Daily News and Chronicle* of 17 July commented:

> A woman's plucky effort at the eleventh hour to save Farnham Castle for the Bishop of Guildford seems likely to succeed. Mrs. Rupert Darnley Anderson, Waverley Abbey, Farnham, appeared on the scene when an important Diocesan Committee had thrown up the sponge and, in eight hours, collected £1,100. This was at the end of May and by this enterprise she encouraged the Diocesan Conference to make another attempt. Since that time a committee has been formed with Mrs. Anderson as Chairman and the Earl of Onslow as Hon. Treasurer and over £6,000 stands now to the credit of the fund.

By the beginning of August, it was up to £9,022; there had been another £500, from Mr. and Mrs. Philip Lyle of Compton. Individual contributions did not rise above that figure, or fall below one shilling. The *Herald* of 27 September reported a total of £13,010; on 11 October, it was £14,014. Courages added 100 guineas; Miss Elinor Murray of Cringletie, who lived at Camberley and was a cousin of Charles Burke, once of 'Wilmer House', sent £500, and Field Marshal Viscount Plumer of 'Firgrove House' gave five guineas. On 8 November—four days from the deadline—the total was £16,530. Mrs. Anderson made a final impassioned plea. On 12 November, she handed over £18,152 0s. 3d. Canon Hunter called her 'the Princess of Beggars', Bishop Greig described her as 'a brilliant first-line skirmisher'.

*   *   *   *

Old Harry Parker of 1 Beech Villas, Park Road, died on 1 January, aged eighty-six. He had distinguished himself in the Zulu war, on 24 January, 1879, when he was one of 80 men of the 24th Regiment who successfully held Rorke's Drift.

Superintendent William Robert Lucas retired in January after over 40 years in the police. Son of a Metropolitan police officer, he had joined the Hampshire Constabulary in 1887, transferring to Surrey two years later. He received the King's police medal from the hands of the Prince of Wales in 1929. He was succeeded by Inspector Stovell from Camberley.

Before the Town Planning Map could be signed and sealed, the Co-op came up with an application for a bakery, dairy and garage right in the middle of an area off Arthur Road which had been coloured in on the map as a residential zone. The Co-op appealed against the refusal, and, at the tribunal on 24 April, the Ministry Inspector took the view that the bakery could be regarded as a domestic undertaking rather than a factory and, with certain modifications, he approved the plan. He pointed to a squalid area a few yards away, used by the railway as a shunting yard.

A degree of unsightliness is inescapable even in the best kept towns. High on the list of visual atrocities were the petrol-filling stations now mushrooming into being. The Council were quick to take whatever action possible under the Petroleum (Consolidation) Act 1928, but, whereas the motor car in its various stages of development had a certain visual appeal, its servicing agencies were generally repellent.

The Premier Omnibus Company of Shepherds Bush applied for licences for 12 coaches on a half-hourly schedule between London and Farnham, but were told that two companies had beaten them to it—the Aldershot Traction Co. and Farnham Coaches.

The library re-opened at Brightwells House, with volunteer Miss Isobel Gravenor handing out the books.

With the signing of the conveyance on 6 February, Farnham Park became the property of the townspeople. It was a solemn occasion. Many good things have been said or written over the years concerning the park. Edna Lyall, remembering her childhood days, wrote in 1900: 'To be sure there were also horned beasts in the park, our favourite playground, but they were amenable creatures intent on eating, and there were so many other delights in the park that we could contrive to forget them. There were hawthorn trees to be climbed —one memorable one very near the castle was large enough to accommodate the whole cousinhood—five Brightonians and seven Farnham cousins. Then there was the great elm avenue with its long, stately, cathedral-like aisle, and, beyond, one could generally catch glimpses of the Bishop's deer with their branching antlers'. George Sturt's *The Wheelwright's Shop* mentions a workman, Johnny Gunner, who lived at Hale: 'In order to get home the more quickly, he used to climb the fence about a furlong away from the shop and strike across the Park. A track through the turf there was pointed out to me as Johnny Gunner's Path'. 'The Park here is delicious', wrote Lord Tennyson in 1853, 'What an air after Twickenham! I walked over to Hale and looked into the old premises'.

More practically, Medical Officer Bedo Hobbs described the park as an 'admirable lung'. A sub-committee of Open Spaces was formed to come to grips with things which demanded immediate attention. Additional access from Adams Park Road was provided. Mr. Pearman, who had been park keeper for some 29 years, lived in the Ranger's House. Because of its size and architectural elegance (especially in the top storey, where it showed from the castle), the Council were of the opinion that the house was perhaps out of keeping for a keeper. So they put his name down for a council house and opened a file 'Ranger's House—and what to do with it?' The Farnham Cricket Club was another fixture to be taken over; the club's tenancy was renewed—a mere formality, for not to renew it would have been civic suicide. The cricketers straightway came up with plans for a new pavilion, and obtained £100 from the Council towards its cost.

Farnham Operatic Society staged their third success at the Church House in February with *The Yeoman of the Guard*. Dr. Ealand took the part of Shadbolt.

Mr. Sargent, ever prospecting for likely sites for public conveniences, reported that to add a 'ladies' to the 'gents' in East Street and South Street would cost about £110. This seemed reasonable, but the councillors still hankered after one in Castle Street. The Sanitary Inspector was instructed to prepare such a scheme, underground if possible, opposite the almshouses in that street. There were snags—others before them had been underground at this spot. A brick barrel-arched culvert took surface water from Castle Hill to the river; there were the roots of the three plane trees, planted to commemorate Queen Victoria's Diamond Jubilee; there was a sewer some eight feet down, and an old tank or well from which the natives once drew water. The owner of 16 Castle Street, however, was willing to sell this house to the Council for conversion to a toilet. With a frontage of 16 feet and a depth of 84 feet, this would serve the purpose well and preliminary details were entered into. In the meantime, it was decided to spend £60 on a 'ladies' extension to the one at 91 East Street.

J. H. Chitty of the fire brigade was due to retire on 30 June, and Major A. G. Wade of 'Ash Cottage', Bentley, was chosen out of five applicants as Chief Officer of the brigade . . . F. H. Newnham arrived from Ventnor to be Deputy Clerk of the Council; the office staff now numbered 24, and was steadily increasing.

If a date can be given to the outbreak of discord between the faction favouring a by-pass road north of the town and those who preferred one on the south, then perhaps 28 March 1930 may be adopted. For, whilst there had been stirrings in the undergrowth for some months past, that was the date on which the town planners brought the matter into the open. A report was published which outlined the relative merits of the two routes—one through the park, the other through the meadows and along Abbey Street and Red Lion Lane. Immediately 462 ratepayers rallied in support of the southern road. To avoid bloodshed, the Council convened a special meeting on 8 April, at which three motions were considered:

> That in the opinion of this Council it is desirable that provision be made in the (Town Planning) Scheme for the construction at some future date of a relief road for through traffic.
>
> That the southern route be provisionally adopted for inclusion in the Council's Town Planning Scheme and that application be made to the Surrey County Council for an indemnity against any compensation that may be payable in respect of the inclusion of this proposal in the Scheme.
>
> That the Council do convene a public meeting in order to ascertain the views of the ratepayers upon the question.

The *Herald* of 19 April noted that 'all Farnham were discussing the by-pass issue'. At least it took their minds off public conveniences.

At the election on 7 April, retiring members Borelli and Mrs. Stroud were challenged by Sidney Alfred Baber, a builder of 23 Sheephouse, and W. R. Lucas, the bowler-hatted police chief of 'Alverstoke', Crondall Lane. Mrs. Stroud came bouncing back with top marks; the big surprise was that Mr. Lucas beat Mr. Borelli by one vote. At a meeting on the following day, Councillor Mardon voiced the sadness of all members that Mr. Borelli should have lost his seat after 24 years as a councillor. General Godby became the next Chairman, with Mr. Sanders as Vice-Chairman.

East Street was re-opened on 11 April, after massive improvements which had taken 12 months, during which traffic and pedestrians alike endured great inconvenience. The 'new street' was finished just in time for the Ascot and Tattoo motor cavalcades. Mr. Starling was warmly congratulated for his part in the works.

The question of district boundary changes, under the Local Government Act 1929, now arose with the County Council inviting the views of local authorities. The availability of Farnham's drainage facilities went a long way to boost the town's bargaining powers. Already, under special arrangements, the sewers had been extended to properties beyond the urban boundary, some even across the county boundary in Hampshire. Therefore Farnham was able to aim high—even with the suggestion that the Surrey–Hants border might be adjusted so that Farnham could take in the rest of Rowledge. Southward, they asked for an extension as far as the Hindhead watershed, to take over the Surrey villages of Elstead, Thursley, and parts of Wanborough and Puttenham. Perhaps it was a little ambitious. The already truncated and economically unviable Farnham Rural District Council stood to be eliminated in the process; also the Urban Council was worried that it would be responsible for an immense area that was unlikely ever to be developed, and which, although one of the country's beauty spots, held little promise of financial return.

There was talk in May of the coming of another bank—Barclays—in the place of Ransom's Tearooms at 22 The Borough, on the corner of South Street. Arthur Ransom, son of the George who had started the restaurant, had recently retired for health reasons.

A scheme was approved whereby residents would be invited to plant trees in the avenue through the park in memory of dead relatives, as replacements for those trees which had fallen by the wayside. Mr. W. J. Baker, who rented grazing rights in the park, had his tenancy renewed at £125 a year.

Work commenced on the new swimming bath on 2 May. Captain Marshal's quotation had been raised to £2,325, but was still the lowest. The work qualified for a subsidy from the Unemployment Grants Committee amounting to 100 per cent. of the interest on a loan of £3,400 over the first seven years, and 50 per cent. over the next eight years, provided the job was completed within four months of 2 June 1930.

Baron Davidson of Lambeth died on 25 May; he was remembered as the Bishop of Winchester at Farnham Castle from 1895 to 1903. Another death mourned in the Council Chamber was that of Councillor Mrs. Stroud's son, Flying Officer R. W. A. Stroud, who was killed on active service on 17 May.

The days when the Chief Officers on the Council staff—being the only officers —had to type the letters and lick the stamps were numbered. With Farnham's burgeoning profile, more and more responsibility had been thrust upon Mr. Sargent. Now he was expected to keep an eye on the building of the new swimming bath—thus saving the expense of a clerk of works. A junior in the person of Peter Meddows Taylor was taken on. He was a son of the East Street schoolmaster.

A route plan of the proposed southern by-pass road was sent to County. The Chamber of Commerce produced their idea for a through-route—branching off East Street by Trimmers Hospital, through Stoke Hills into Wykeham Road and via High Park Road and Park Row into Castle Street. This was, rightly, considered impracticable, though another suggestion of the Chamber's, for a central car park on the east side of Bear Lane, was filed for future reference. It had not yet occurred to anyone in Farnham that traffic demands in the years ahead would become insatiable—that a by-pass road should be sited where there was room for a likely doubling of its width, and that car parks would proliferate until most of the back areas of the town were taken into use. However, they were learning. The Town Planning Committee completed their Map 1. On it were some zones coloured dark green, denoting open spaces; purple for industrial areas, near the sewage farm and in Hookstile Lane; light green for agricultural land, or private open spaces, and (importantly) for a belt of open land forming a 'lung' between Farnham and Aldershot; yellow and Vandyke brown for houses not exceeding, respectively, six and two to the acre; uncoloured for development up to 10 houses per acre.

A lay-out plan for a new estate at Brookley Park, Runfold, was submitted by Mr. T. Allen . . . Canon Girling recommended a civic reception for His Beatitude

Meletios, Pope of Alexandria, and other delegates from the Eastern Orthodox Church at the Lambeth Conference, who would be visiting Farnham on 12 July.

The church was pleased with the windfall of £445 18s. 7d., towards the repair of church fabric and other essential work, raised by a pageant in the forecourt of Farnham Castle. The scenario was by the Rev. Neville Lovett, once Farnham's dynamic rector and now Bishop of Portsmouth; it was produced by Mrs. Bernard Limpus with the help of Dr. Ealand and Edward Leroy. In 10 episodes, the pageant depicted the highly fanciful history of the castle—the original building; King John's visit; a royal baby's visit in 1486; blind Bishop Fox shooting a line to local children in 1527; Cardinal Wolsey's visit, 1530; Queen Elizabeth's in 1588; the Roundheads' takeover, 1648; May Day, 1670; Farnham folk in the Georgian age, 1774; and Bishop Sumner's arrival in 1828. It was vintage Lovett, and the audiences loved it greatly.

The fine new church of St Joan of Arc between the Tilford and Waverley roads was consecrated by the Bishop of Southwark on 1 June . . . Close by, Broomleaf field, the arena for many years of open-air festivities, was bought by E. C. Sayers, who was soon to build himself a house therein (which later, for a time, became the home of the present chronicler), and in due course to develop the Broomleaf estate.

There was a minor sensation in June when it was learnt that Mr. G. E. Aldridge of Watney's brewery, Castle Street, had drawn the favourite, Diolite, in the Calcutta sweepstake. The whole town was in a ferment of excitement during the run-up to the Derby. The lucky holder had bought ticket No. F 3,000. He had sold half to Charlie Clark of the Farnham Motor Co., who had re-sold a quarter (i.e., one-eighth of the whole) to Fred Brockhurst, caretaker at the Institute, and a third of what was left to someone else—well, anyway, Mr. Clark had ended up with a 5/24th share. People manned their wireless sets. Diolite led the field. Then it was overtaken by two other horses. The Aga Khan's Blenheim won; Diolite came in third.

Herbert Edward Bide died on 13 June, at the early age of 57 . . . Improvements on the Ridgway–Shortheath roads were finished in July, and this through route was adopted by the County Council . . . Mr. H. C. Patrick, the undertaker, came into prominence as a marksman. The *Herald* of 26 July reported that he had set a record at a recent Bisley meeting by gaining a prize in all competitions except one.

At the conclusion of the July Council meeting, the fire brigade entered the Chamber in force. The retiring Chief Officer, Mr. J. Chitty, was formally presented with an inscribed watch and a cheque, and his wife with a gold brooch. Second Officer 'Berry' Elderfield presented him with a case of pipes on behalf of the firemen. Chitty had been with the brigade since 1896; he retired as Honorary Captain.

Two-thirds of the front page of the *Herald* dated 2 August were taken up by an advertisement for the new super cimema at Aldershot—the *Empire,* opened on the day before. This was the first luxury cinema purpose-built for the 'talkies' within visiting distance of Farnham. 'Alf's Button' was the main feature film—'an all talking, singing and colour production, packed with oriental splendour and hundreds of dancing girls—the Sound Sensation of the Year!'. The *Empire's* café was to mature, unexpectedly, into a pleasant, well-mannered place in which to spend an hour or so with one's friends over cups of coffee.

Aldershot had a flamboyant way of projecting their image. They showed their hand in the prevailing controversy over the break-up of the Farnham Rural District by voicing a drainage project estimated at around £122,484. This smacked of an attempt to shift the Hants–Surrey county boundary.

In August, the local soccer clubs booked their pitches for the winter—the post office, gas company, Old Farnhamians, the schools, and the Church Army sanitorium to play in the park, and the various village teams on their local recreation grounds. Football in Farnham had never attracted the same enthusiasm as cricket, bowls or golf. The Ladies' Hockey Club was given leave to use the hockey pitch in the park. Farnham Cricket Club's new pavilion was ready for use on 4 August. In the Brightwells tennis finals, Nancy Ball beat Miss H. Wells, 6–3, 6–1.

Twenty-five pounds had been spent in the cleaning up of the Rangers House in the park, and it was now in agents' hands . . . A stern letter from Hollest, Mason and Nash, acting for a client, effectively put paid to any idea of turning 16 Castle street into a public convenience. Again, they looked up and down Castle Street, telling Mr. Sargent to report on one site—'near the lampost'.

August's plans included one from Mr. Mardon for the replacement of the old *Cricketer's* inn at 35/36 Downing Street, on the corner of Ivy Lane. This was to become Mr. Goodridge's attractive outfitters' shop. Mr. A. J. Stedman's design for Barclays Bank at Ransoms corner was also considered that month. They tried to persuade the bank to cede a splayed corner sightline, but without success, for the area was already on the small side for a bank.

Renovations at 99 East Street for Mr. E. T. March brought to light a cupboard beneath the plaster. Inside was found a man's coat of a long-past cut reaching to the knees; there was also a dressing-gown. They were thought to have belonged to Henry Poppleton who had a school there half a century earlier. Formerly a pupil at Mr. Poppleton's school, Frank Sturt of 'Newnhams', West End Grove, died on 29 September, aged seventy-one. He was a brother of the local historian and had once been in business as a bookseller at 41/42 The Borough, and a partner of Martin and Sturt, the printers. He had been a close friend of Arnold Bennett, the writer.

A miniature rifle range was opened at Broomleaf by Miss M. E. Foster, the markswoman who won the King's Cup at Bisley in 1930 . . . A new swimming pool was opened in the Manor Park, Aldershot, and was highly acclaimed. The mayor was heard to acknowledge during the ceremony that Aldershot was not up to 'Farnham's aesthetic advantages', but his borough was trying hard . . .

Miss Joan Coxon, the singer, and daughter of Lieutenant-Colonel A. W. Coxon of Hale, was now broadcasting regularly . . . By the will of Miss Ethelred Laura Seawell of 'The Welches', Bentley, the Council acquired a dolls' house for exhibition in the Farnham museum when it came.

By a substantial majority, the Guildford Diocesan Conference at the Borough Hall, Guildford, on 13 November, confirmed that Dr. Greig would reside in part of Farnham Castle . . . Big alterations to the *Bush* hotel, to the design of Falkner and Alwyn, were planned. Rumour had it that the hotel was soon to change hands.

Clay Hill and Ford Lane at Wrecclesham were given the treatment at a cost of £2,471 and £1,756 respectively. They were now starting on the Boundstone Road. Roads in that part of the area were also named. The road from The Square, Rowledge, to Manley Bridge Road was christened Bird Lane; from Swans' shop to Manley Bridge Road, Pontypool Road; and the road from the Shortheath bus stop to Wrecclesham, St Peter's Hill.

Gordon Grey Tompsett of 'Stafford House', Firgrove Hill, now 83, and not far off death, reminisced about his long career as a local builder, first with F. C. Birch and later forming his own firm. He recalled the decision to raise the height of the church tower because of its unfinished appearance. On the top of the existing tower was a small bell. This had been rung for five minutes after the peal of the main bells before church services. This small bell was removed to St James's church in East Street. The architect for the tower alterations was an aptly-named E. Christian of London. Materials, quarried in Dippenhall, Binstead, Selbourne, and Headley, were hauled to the top of the tower in barrow-loads by horse-drawn pulley. At one juncture, two men working on the top had thrown their coats to the ground below and someone had dashed round to the yard and told Birch that two of his men had fallen off the tower. After the job was completed, it had been Tompsett's duty to place the weather-vane on top. Mr. Tompsett had also helped in the demolition of the old Market House and the building of the town hall which replaced the *Goat's Head*. He had taken part in the building of Shaw's Bank in Castle Street and the London and County Bank at 38 The Borough. Following the Crimean War, 500 men employed by Frank Birch had travelled to Aldershot each day to build the camp.

The Rev. Owen C. S. Lang, one-time rector of Bentley, was quoted in the *Herald* of 15 November as saying that Sir Walter Scott (1771–1832) had been a close friend of his grandfather, Mr. Robert Lang of Moor Park, and that during visits, Scott would most certainly have been a visitor to Waverley Abbey. Hence the title *Waverley Novels*.

First Engineer A. H. Bailey resigned after 34 years in the fire brigade. He was warmly thanked and given a gratuity of £10. Major Wade's quarterly report stressed Farnham's greatest fire hazard—countless acres of tinder-dry heath between here and Hindhead. The brigade feared a hot summer as residents in the low-lying parts of the town feared a wet winter—fire and floods, Farnham had them both to endure.

The Council were slow to emerge from the era of horse-drawn dustcarts, but now they agreed to a demonstration by Messrs. Shelvoke and Drewry of that firm's seven-cubic-yard capacity S. D. freighter. One big reason against mechanisation was the expense. Horse-drawn vehicles cost about 1s. 9d. an hour to hire, whereas motor lorries cost 3s. to 3s. 6d., for 30–40-cwt. trucks, and as much as 7s. for a five-ton truck. Moreover, motors were soulless beasts; horses were human —well, practically so. For instance, one of the Council's horses, named 'Sampson', on returning to the Council yard at the end of a working day, would find its way unaccompanied across the yard to its stable door. When they became due for retirement, these faithful servants were usually given light duties on the sewage farm or somewhere.

Drawings for a new town hall were on the table at the November meeting. Writing for *Bumbledom* in 1961, Harold Falkner recalled that—

> Charles Borelli, who over the years had acquired a majority of the Town Hall Company's run-down shares, had always agreed that I should do the design. But other directors pressed for an outside brain and T. W. Benslyn, architect to the Birmingham Educational Authority, and a friend of mine, was brought in. In all respects, however, the design was mine—Benslyn's role being to eat the directors' dinners and soften them up.

Initially, the company opposed Falkner's ideas of a colonnade along the frontage in The Borough. Fortunately, the Inland Revenue offered an attractive rent for the upper storey provided they had more floor space than was possible within the area available, and the only way of enlarging this space was to build out above the pavement. A problem arose at the east end of The Borough frontage in restoring the old Bailiffs' Hall, the front of which had long since disappeared. No illustration of the ancient building could be traced, so it was left to Mr. Falkner's imagination. When a drawing did afterwards come to light, he had not departed far from the original. Above was left a flat open space, with access from a recessed first storey; this was intended at the time to provide an open-air café. Falkner topped his masterpiece with a model, six feet tall and the same in width, of Drake's 16th-century *Golden Hind*, based on contemporary drawings of the ship made by Thomas Elsley of Great Titchfield Street, London. Of beaten copper, gilded over, the vane was made to turn on an agate bearing on a steel spindle. Its mounting was heralded with much comment, both admiring and otherwise; it was quite impossible to ignore it. To his lasting shame, the writer joined the ranks of the jeerers—but not for long.

Bourne Mill—that splendid monument to the past in Guildford Road—had been acquired by the Council for two reasons. It had outlived its original purpose, and it might come in handy for pulling down for road-widening purposes. The land on the north, now let out in allotments, was later used as a site for council houses, but, meanwhile, what could be done with the decrepit old house, its cottage and the mill? Restore them, of course—so Mr. H. Y. Margary, the architect who lived close by, was called in to examine the possibilities.

Trimmers Hospital in East Street, presented to the town in 1895 by George Trimmer, the brewer, was in dire need of additional accommodation. Adjacent land at Stoke Hills had been acquired for an extension, and the builders were ready to move in. But wait! All the other bodies in Farnham were building themselves brand new premises—so why not the town's hospital? With all due respect to the late George Trimmer, his 'cottage hospital' did look like a cottage-type property. When it came to raising funds for hospital purposes, people were always eager to put their hands into their pockets. So a good site was acquired to the south of the town in Waverley Lane. The next step was a public meeting on 11 December to form a committee to launch an appeal.

PRICE 2d.

The ..
Pageant of
Farnham Castle

Author: The Lord Bishop of Portsmouth.

PRESENTED AT FARNHAM CASTLE

JULY 3RD, 4TH, 5TH, 7TH, 8TH, 9TH, 1930

Prologue spoken by the Spirit of the Castle.

I.   The Building of Farnham Castle.—A.D. 1147.
II.   King John visits Bishop Peter des Roches.—A.D. 1215.
III.   The Royal Baby at the Castle.—A.D. 1486.
IV.   The Blind Bishop and the Farnham Children.—A.D. 1527.
V.   Cardinal Wolsey comes and goes.—A.D. 1530.
VI.   Queen Elizabeth at the Castle.—A.D. 1588.
VII.   The Castle held by the Roundheads.—A.D. 1648.
VIII.   May Day at Farnham Castle.—A.D. 1670.
IX.   Farnham Folk in the Georgian Age.—A.D. 1774.
X.   Bishop Sumner comes to the Castle.—A.D. 1828.

FINAL TABLEAU.

For Characters and Impersonators see
Book of Words on sale.   Price 6d.

P.T.O.

Cover of the programme for the 1930 Farnham Pageant.

1931

'When we builds—we builds'

Attributed to John Knight—or it may have been James Knight—Farnham banker (to customers eyeing the extravagant grandeur of the new Knight's Bank in 1869)

NOW, IF YOU PLEASE, Lloyds Bank were going to scrap 75 Castle Street and replace it with a building that looked like a bank and less like some Elizabethan cloud-capped tower with knobs on. People could hardly believe their ears—surely they could not destroy Farnham's pride and joy! How Richard Norman Shaw (1831–1912) should have come to design the bold Knights Bank was, conceivably, due to a recommendation by Richard Combe of Watney Combe Reid and Co., who was justly pleased with the young architect's work in 1866 on 'Pierrepont', a residence which befitted the lord of the manor at Frensham. Shaw's two early works at Farnham helped to make his name. He was responsible for the New Scotland Yard building in 1890; he was admitted to the Royal Academy in 1877, and died rich and famous in 1912. In 1931, he turned over in his grave; so did John and James Knight. Lloyds had moved out of 75 Castle Street, and Mardon, Ball and Co. had moved in. 'When we pulls 'em down', Lloyds seemed to say, 'we pulls 'em down'. The demolition ranks as Farnham's one excursion into the undoing, in George V's reign, of an Elizabethan property built in Victoria's reign. As with Lutyens' less remarkable Liberal Club in South Street, it was the architect who mattered, not his canvas. Harold Falkner urged that, before the bank's removal, steps should be taken to document it fully for future generations. He said, 'the building is the work of an artist and gentleman, a record of a period when this country was optimistic and prosperous and the inhabitants of this town at least ambitious'.

Was it fortuitous that, concurrently, the three front-ranking buildings in the town centre—the castle, Lloyds Bank, and the town hall—should come into the hands of builders? It was tempting to imagine that up there somewhere was a guardian angel who watched over the destinies of Castle Street. This, of course, was so. The good fairy had not always been reliable. In 1866, for instance, she had condoned the sweeping away of the ancient market house and allowed the building of the absurd-looking town hall. The present joint holders of the office,

Charles Borelli and Harold Falkner, were, in the early 1930s, endeavouring to repair the ravages.

*   *   *   *   *

In January came the disappointing news that Farnham Urban was unlikely to benefit much from the carve-up of the Farnham Rural District. Because of the wish of the County Council to preserve the rustic aspect of this glorious slice of Surrey, it became more and more certain that the Rural District Councils of Hambledon and Guildford would be given the largest helpings of the cake, and that Farnham Urban would be fobbed off with a few crumbs just south of the existing boundary.

The 280 portfolios submitted by leading architects of the day for the building of the new cathedral on Stag Hill, Guildford, had been whittled down to a short list of thirty. These were exhibited at the Trinity Hall, Guildford, and included an entry from Harold Falkner; this was marked '10th'. The one finally chosen was that of Edward Maufe.

George Cecil Whiteley, K.C., of Compton Hill, was appointed Chairman of the City of London Sessions in succession to Sir Robert Wallace, at a salary of £2,500. During the goodbye session at Farnham Police Court on 1 January, Edgar Kempson remarked that Mr. Cecil Whiteley's success could be traced back to the famous case of Rex v. Howard and others, in the Farnham Court, on which the present licensing laws of the country had been subsequently based. In that case, he, Mr. Kempson, had unsuccessfully appeared for the defence.

Post office engineers were installing telephone kiosks at salient points in the district . . . Hodgson's Kingston brewery rebuilt that little bridge which spans the tiny stream to give access to the *Spotted Cow* in the Bourne . . . The Amateur Operatic Society decided on a dual fixture for the 1931 season, with *Trial by Jury* and *The Pirates of Penzance*.

The staff of Lloyds Bank moved on 21 February into temporary accommodation in the Corn Exchange. The *Herald* was disappointed not to see 'smart clerks, escorted by burly policemen, staggering down the street under bars of gold'.

Gales blew down more trees in Farnham Park—as many as fifty-seven. These were sold to a timber merchant, who sawed them up on the spot. The stumps posed problems. A Mr. Jones offered to grub them out and bury them in a nearby chalkpit for £142 10s. 0d. Councillor Ewart suggested that the roots might be demolished by explosives, and this was carried out by the 38th (Field) Company R.E. at a charge of 30s. each. To fill some of the gaps, Mr. G. Murraille of 'Woodville', Old Church Lane, kindly offered 15 walnut trees.

Nos. 12 and 13 Downing Street, owned by Mr. B. C. N. Giles, were declared no longer fit for human habitation and were in due course replaced by a modern building containing two shops . . . Falkner and Aylwin submitted plans for the rebuilding of the *Waverley Arms* public house, and Courages ceded an 8-ft. wide strip of frontage on the Waverley Lane side, which led in 1932 to that road being transformed from a narrow country lane without footpaths into a 40-ft. wide thoroughfare with all modern conveniences.

In the election of 30 March, Mr. Borelli regained his seat by defeating Miss Rosa Wells by four votes in the Waverley Ward. He was given a hearty welcome on his return to the fold. He told colleagues that, on severing his connection with the Council in 1930, the rooks had departed from the trees on Station Hill, but now they were back there again, building their nests. Mr. Sanders became Chairman for 1931/2, with General Godby as Vice-Chairman.

A Vickers–Virginia bomber of the R.A.F. force-landed in Old Park, without injury to the crew. Civil aircraft were taking people up and down at Green Lane Farm, Badshot Lea.

Albert Winslade of East Street, retired after 44 years in the Farnham branch of the St John Ambulance Association. He had joined when the branch was first formed in 1882, becoming Hon. Secretary in 1889. Dedication such as this merited recognition. An informal committee of the Council launched a testimonial fund, and, in August, this shy man was ceremoniously presented by Mr. Sanders, at a public meeting in Brightwells, with a cheque for £100 and a copy of *The Knights of St John.*

The fire brigade were campaigning for an escape apparatus of the type on sale at a price ranging from £875 to £1,900. The Council naturally cast their eyes on the lowest figure, but, surprisingly, the Minister approved the £1,900 job. Such a public outcry arose that they finally settled for a second-hand Morris Commercial vehicle costing £70, with which to tow a 60-ft. telescopic ladder. Heath and Wiltshires reconditioned these and painted them red for £69 15s. 0d. The Minister of Health also approved the transfer of 416 square feet of Gostrey Meadow, at a nominal price of £10 to the Emmanuel church to make possible an extension of the church buildings.

The Minister, currently the Right Hon. Arthur Greenwood, M.P., thirdly agreed to come down to Farnham on 23 May in order to preside at the opening ceremony of the new swimming bath. This was Mr. Sargent's great day; the new bath had been his baby from drawing-board to diving-board. He received much praise. It measured 100 feet by 35 feet, and sloped in depth from three feet to nine feet. The filtration plant renewed the water completely in 4¼ hours. There were 100 dressing-boxes, 50 for each sex. It had cost some £3,500 to build. The opening was a splendid occasion. Translucent, greenish-blue water, reflected the gleaming white paintwork of the diving tower and balcony rails. A Union Jack, lent by Mr. A. A. Wilcox, fluttered bravely. Mr. A. Bullen of Heath End, appointed baths attendant at £3 a week, was resplendent in his unsoiled fatigue suit, with Mr. J. C. Greenwood (no relation of the Minister) as second in command. Master I. O. Newton had been inducted as cashier, and Mr. R. W. Kirk of the Ridgway Stores had won the refreshment rights. Mr. Borelli had presented the clock. In this idyllic setting, the distinguished company on the gentlemen's balcony watched Farnham's more accomplished swimmers compete for prizes donated by Councillors Sanders and Avery. Minister Greenwood was heard to remark what a beautiful place he thought Farnham was. Patronage of the new bath initially exceeded all expectations despite inclement weather. That summer, 19,838 people paid to come in. Four galas were held during the summer, two in July and two in August. The number of non-swimmers in Farnham fell dramatically. The nicest time was during the lunch break, when there were no noisy children to mar the enjoyment.

People were deeply shocked on 5 May to hear of the death of Flight-Lieutenant Henry Richard Danvers Waghorn, the 1929 Schneider Trophy winner. 'Dick' Waghorn, aged 26, died when his bomber crashed at Farnborough. He was buried in the old Bourne churchyard—that neglected, yet beautiful, sacred precinct which encircles the site of the first Bourne church.

The *Herald* on 16 May reported that Mr. Falkner's new Morris car had caught fire at Dippenhall and that he had extinguished the flames with his hat. This, the paper was sad to relate, had been hopelessly burnt, and readers would miss 'a very old friend'. 'By the way', Mr. Langham added, 'there is a rummage sale at St James' Schoolroom tomorrow, with old hats at a penny each'. Men like Harold Falkner were expected to have their little foibles. It was a commonly held belief in the town that, whenever Mr. Falkner decided on having a new hat, he would go along to Sammy Bates at Silvers, fling his old hat into a corner, take a new one at random, throw it on the floor and stamp on it, then pull it over his ears, pay and depart.

George Heath died on 23 May, aged eighty-seven. He had started business in Alton as a coach builder and later taken over the works of Charles Keen in East Street, Farnham. In 1905, he entered into partnership with W. C. Wiltshire. A son, also George, managed the firm's branch in Cairo.

The service at the parish church on 7 June was broadcast by the B.B.C. . . . The Rev. F. J. Layton, pastor at the Congregational church for 14 years, moved to Uckfield . . . On 8 June, the Guildford Diocesan Board passed Walter Tapper's plans for the conversion of Farnham Castle into a bishop's residence and a conference house, subject to the approval of the Ecclesiastical Commissioners. The work was expected to take about a year, and a Farnham firm of builders would be engaged.

At 1.26 a.m. on Sunday, 7 June, the effects of an earthquake, which shook a wide area of the country, were felt in Farnham . . . Plans were drawn up in June for the rebuilding of the *Jolly Farmer* public house at Runfold . . . The Council placed an order for two seven cubic-yard F.M. patent refuse collection bodies, fitted with dustless automatic, foot-operated covers, each mounted on Thorney-croft type A forward chassis, with pneumatic tyres. They cost £640 each.

The press reported that Major Rupert Anderson had put Waverley Abbey on the market . . . J. Alfred Eggar—that 'grand old townsman'—retired after 64 years in business. Born in 1849, he had established his estate agency in Bentley in 1867 and opened his Farnham branch at 74 Castle Street in 1870. His son, J. Graham Eggar, would continue to run it.

There was also mention of George Conway Brown, once a pupil at Farnham Grammar School, and brother of Mrs. Frank Sturt. He was now in Burnaby, Vancouver, B.C., where he was President of the local Board of Trade, Chairman of the Public Library Board, and Town Planning Commissioner. He also owned and edited the local newspaper, and was closely involved in the provision of public parks in the Burnaby area. His latest venture was to be named Farnham Park.

Besides the three major properties in Castle Street, the *Bush* hotel was undergoing big-scale alterations, designed by its new owners, George Whitehead and Co., to bring it into the 20th-century whilst retaining its Dickensian flavour. When stripping the north wall of the old coffee room, workmen had brought to light mural paintings, adjudged to be 16th century, and, here and there, in reasonably good condition. One panel was of a classical subject, with two female figures and a man on one knee. A river or lake formed the centre background, with a mountain beyond, and on the right was a house or cabin with a window. Two other panels depicted cupids.

There was further conjecture concerning Sir Walter Scott's choice of the name 'Waverley'. Sir James Douglas of Folkestone, in a letter to *The Times* in July, seconded Mr. Owen Lang's suggestion. He, Douglas, had often heard his mother speak of Scott visiting her father, Robert Lang, at Moor Park. In another letter to *The Times,* Henry G. L. King, 15 Cavendish Mansions, West Hampstead, referred to a correspondent, James Dundas White, who had quoted Lord Rosebery as saying that Scott might have visited Waverley Abbey whilst gathering material for his *Life of Swift*. This, thought Mr. King, would hardly do, for the book was not published until 1814, whereas the first seven chapters of *Waverley* had been written, and the name chosen, by 1805. Lockhart, on the other hand, did mention that Scott was researching on Swift as early as 1808. It was possible that Scott had been taken to see Waverley Abbey by George Ellis, whom he had visited at Sunninghill in 1802. The historical promise of the Abbey certainly would not have been lost on the author.

Mr. H. C. Patrick and his son, Eric, were both through the first round for the King's Prize at Bisley. Back in East Street, they were at work on the latest order from the Graves Commission. This was a Portland stone plaque commemorating the men who gave their lives at the mole at Zeebrugge on St George's Day 1918, thus blocking the harbour used by the German U-boats. The four men were Wing-Commander F. M. Brock, O.B.E., Lieutenant-Commander A. L. Harrison, V.C., Lieutenant C. E. V. Hawkings, and Mechanic Second-Class J. Rouse.

They were still looking for a spot for a public toilet. Nos 124/5 East Street currently for sale, would have been a good site, but Courages wanted £3,500, and the Council refused to go over £3,000. This was where the old 'Fourteen Penny' House had once been.

In July, an extension of service was allowed in the case of Second Engineer A. Budd, who had reached the age limit of 60 after 37 years in the fire brigade. He died three months later and his place was taken by Third Engineer A. Collins, with Senior Fireman Barnett moving up to No. 3. Mr. Norman Goolding of Compton was taken on as supernumerary fireman pending a vacancy. The brigade was still a family affair.

The wholesale development in the domestic field, which was ultimately to lift the population of Farnham from the 20 to the 30 thousand mark, had begun. Housing estates everywhere mushroomed into being. The Council's commitments widened, and, progressively, the cost of local government soared. The half-yearly rates—at about 5s. in the pound on, by modern standards, ridiculously low assessments—began to rise, and this bothered councillors and ratepayers alike. Charlie Binfield, a member for Hale, called for a comparison between 1914 and 1931 levels of expenditure, staff salaries, etc. He was told that expenses were £16,092 and £139,920 respectively, and that salaries had risen from £800 to £6,023. If anything, added the Clerk, the percentage paid in salaries was slightly lower.

On 20 July, the County Council made known the disposal of the dying Farnham Rural District Council's assets. The 21,026 acres were distributed between:

Farnham Urban District	3,053 acres
Haslemere Urban District	2,645 acres
Guildford Rural District	9,318 acres
Hambledon Rural District	6,010 acres

Thus the Farnham Urban area would be increased from 11,390 acres to 14,443, and the population from 20,481 to 21,962. The nearest villages—Frensham, Churt and Dockenfield—would in future be governed from offices in Guildford.

The Brightwells season was now in full swing. Councillor Marsh suggested a balcony built on to the wall of the new swimming bath from which spectators might watch the highly popular tennis tournaments. Bands played on Wednesdays on the lawn in front of the library, with dance music later in the evening. Or there was bowls to watch, or one could buy ice-creams or hot drinks from Mr. Kirk's kiosk.

A traffic island was tried out experimentally at the junction of Downing Street and Longbridge, and further white lines appeared at other corners. There was even talk of replacing the policeman who waved to motorists from the top of South Street with lights. But Farnham's real answer to the traffic problem lay in having a by-pass road. Currently, the scheme still favoured was a southern route from Coxbridge to the *Albion,* passing through Red Lion Lane, Bridge Square and Darvills Lane. Its estimated cost was £87,845. Oddly, there was no murmur of outrage at the threat to the antique Bridge Square.

On Tuesday afternoon, 18 August, people in the streets gazed upwards at that most most majestic of aeronautical sights, an airship gliding overhead. The

Graf Zeppelin, out of Friedrichshafen with 44 crew, commanded by Dr. Eckener and with 24 passengers, one of whom was Mr. Oliver K. Whiting of 'Combe Orchard', Farnham. On the way over, Mr. Whiting had asked Dr. Eckener if he had any objection to flying over Farnham. 'Certainly—show me on the map where it is', was the answer. Invited into the steering-room, Mr. Whiting pointed out Lord Tennyson's house, 'Aldworth'—the skipper was an admirer of his poetry. Lloyd George's house at Churt brought the ship's officers to the windows with field-glasses. Frensham Ponds were clearly visible. Soon, Mr. Whiting was able to point out his own house. Then the great aircraft floated over the town, serene and beautiful.

In the autumn, the hoardings and scaffolding were removed. First, the new town hall. This aroused much praise for Falkner and Alwyn, and for J. Mills and Sons, who built it. The *Herald* hoped that the arcade beneath the arches would be lit at nights, 'otherwise it may prove to be a convenient place for a temporary . . . (unspecified)'. The National Provincial Bank moved in on the ground floor on 17 September, under the managership of Mr. C. T. Butler. Then Lloyds Bank at 75 Castle Street opened. This evoked less enthusiasm when it was revealed on 26 November. 'It will do', the *Herald* grudgingly admitted, and went on to confess that the new building suited Castle Street much better than its predecessor had. The altered *Bush* hotel delighted everyone, with its fine shops along The Borough and its plushy interior.

The castle was still in throes of extensive alterations. Mardons were hard at work on the conversion to the Residence and Theological College (or Retreat House, or whatever might be decided upon), with the Great Hall between the two, and common to both users. Several ancient features had been uncovered, such as the missing oratory or chancel.

Minor works elsewhere in the town were being carried out. Walker Stores, Ltd., were rebuilding 39/40 Downing Street; Mr. Langham had plans in for 114/5 West Street, and Timothy Whites for 48/9 The Borough.

The new *Bush* hotel was the venue of the Venison Dinner on 3 December. The guest of honour was J. Chuter Ede, Vice-Chairman of the Surrey County Council. He was not, he admitted, a son of Farnham, but a grandson. His great grandfather had been born in Abbey Street in 1822 and had been present at the churchyard when Cobbett was buried. He had seen Daniel O'Connell at the graveside.

1932

What's in a name? That which we call a rose
By any other name would smell as sweet
Shakespeare: *Romeo and Juliet*

IN THE ADMINISTRATION of their local government district, a wise council had above all to exercise diplomacy. Opposition could come from alert bodies such as the Chamber of Commerce, or the still powerful religious sects in the town, down to loosely knit retired colonels who aired their views in the local paper. In the *Farnham Herald*, Mr. E. W. Langham also found it expedient to adopt a policy of strict neutrality, for he was obliged for business reasons to please both sides in any dispute; his impartial coverage of any controversy was a model for provincial journalism anywhere. On the odd occasion when he was personally involved in the dispute, his moderation was truly remarkable.

The fields on the north side of the Waverley Abbey estate had been sold by Major Rupert Anderson in the late 1920s, and resold in building plots to prospective residents whose villas were encroaching up the broad slope of the hill between Tilford Road and Waverley Lane. On and over the crest of the hill, houses on a grander scale were on the drawing-boards, for this delectable spot close to Compton was earmarked as a rival to the Great Austins Estate further to the west. The lanes which had for time out of memory divided the fields of the estate would be given the treatment as and when development took place. One of these bore the name of Brown's Lane. Mr. Langham was one of the discerning persons with enough wealth—through having been good friends with all his readers—to buy a plot which fronted on Brown's Lane.

When it came to naming streets in their area, the local council exercised absolute control. That is to say, it did not involve parliamentary legislation or even the authority of the County Council. They usually chose the existing name, if there was one, which at least had stood the test of time. The Council fastened on to 'Brown's Lane' as the official address of the palatial residences that were about to grace this sought-after environment. Letters from prospective residents began to appear in the *Herald*. Provided these were signed by the correspondents, no-one could accuse the editor of taking sides.

'Brown's Lane', said one, 'had a historical connotation'. According to a 90-year-old villager of Compton, Bishop Edward Harold Browne, who was at

155

Farnham Castle from 1873 to 1891, married the daughter of the owner of 'Culverlands', Compton, and used to do his courting in the lane. Over the years, the final 'e' had been dropped from the name. This fascinating vista, said another, was open to doubt. Bishop Browne had been a middle-aged family man when he arrived in Farnham. It was true, however, that one of his sons, afterwards a vicar of Tilford, had courted and wed a lady living somewhere hereabouts. After much further controversy, Major Rupert Anderson came up with the most likely explanation. In the 1860s, a William Brown had rented part of the Waverley estate and farmed 31 acres, one of his fields, known as Brown's Field, abutting on the lane in question. William Brown of Broomleaf Farm was an elected member of the Board of Surveyors in 1850, and the Local Board when it was formed in 1866. He was one of the early grumblers about the railway level-crossing gates, which were then kept closed across the highway and operated only when road traffic approached. Eventually the name 'Brown's Lane' was discontinued, and the road was christened 'Old Compton Lane'.

*   *   *   *   *

One of the two fine cedars at the castle, planted in 1787, had been felled during Christmas because it was found to be rotten and unsafe. The second tree was also doomed.

The Operatic Society's choice for 1932 was *The Gondoliers,* produced by Madam Alice Esty, who took the part of the Duchess of Plaza-Toro.

At their meeting on 2 February, the Council approved, by 15 votes to 4, plans for a super cinema in East Street, on a site recently vacated by Heath and Wiltshires and Robins and Sons. This opened up all sorts of possibilities. The 50-car capacity park at the rear of the proposed cinema would require access over the Council's right of way to Brightwells, so a deal was done for the public's use of the park outside cinema hours. John Harrison of the *Marlborough Head* next door must have jumped for joy at the prospect of cinema audiences popping in for a quick one. On the debit side, there was the spectre of some huge, obtrusive, stuccoed building flaunting its garish purpose upon the quiet Farnham street scene. Guardian angel Charles Borelli went into action. He met the promoters, Regal (Farnham), Ltd., in London, and told them that Farnham was a brick town and that a fall in standards was unacceptable. It cost the company a lot more, but the *Regal* was eventually built in bricks. The golden age of the 'super cinema', a status symbol in all towns of any size, lasted until the advent of television. The initial response in Farnham was one of delight. 'If another cinema will add to the well-being of Farnham, then . . .', commented the *Herald,* thus expressing both sides of the argument.

Councillor Figg was invited by the County Council to inspect the now completed first phase of the works undertaken to improve the flow of the River Wey. He returned jubilant with the news that the level had been lowered by nine or 10 inches and that, when the scheme was finished, flooding in Farnham should be eliminated.

The Hoverplane Company, Ltd., registered in February, with D. Martin, J. R. Sturge Whiting, Oliver K. Whiting, and R. H. Hackett on the board of directors, set out to exploit world rights in two aircraft inventions, primarily those of Sturge Whiting. One, a hovercraft built jointly by E. D. Abbott and Heath and Wiltshires, was tested at the old brewery and later developed at A. V. Roe's works at Hamble. The other was a static flight-tuition craft, fixed some 35 feet above ground level, in which trainees could go through all the motions of handling a plane without fear of accident.

Mr. A. Julius Stevens, in a talk to the Chamber of Commerce, told of his great-grandfather, James Stevens—'Farnham's first banker'. As a hop-grower, James had sold his produce at Weyhill Fair, returning home with a full purse. To thwart muggers on the way, he had travelled with an armed servant, and other growers had come to make use of this arrangement. Later, James Stevens adopted a system of paper money, i.e., cheques, and this eventually led to his establishment of Stevens Bank in Farnham, which afterwards passed to the Knights.

Bishop Theodore Woods, lately at Farnham Castle, died in March. He was succeeded as Bishop of Winchester by the Rt. Rev. Cyril Forster Garbett, Lord Bishop of Southwark. Aged 57, the new bishop was a son of the Rev. C. Garbett, one-time vicar of Tongham. In 1885, he had joined the third form at Farnham Grammar School, before transferring to the Grammar School at Portsmouth under the headship of J. C. Nicol, M.A., who was likewise from Farnham.

The venerable group of buildings at Bourne Mill found sympathetic tenants in the persons of Mr. and Mrs. Grace, who planned to use the mill part as tea-rooms and the house as a guest house. The old machinery had to be removed and minor repairs carried out at a cost of £325 10s. 0d.

During alterations for Timothy Whites at 49 The Borough, the old trade name 'Higgins, Chemist' was revealed above the shop window. William Higgins had been the pharmacist here some fifty years previously. He was the father of Air-Vice-Marshal Sir J. F. A. Higgins.

The Rev. J. Penry-Davey, ex-army chaplain and a man of outstanding personality, arrived in March to take the place of Mr. Layton at the Congregational church . . . Eille Norwood of 'Top-o'-the-hill', Lower Bourne, staged an amateur play at the Church House called *Daphne Grows Down,* with parts taken by Dr. Ealand, Edward Leroy, H. C. Patrick, Eileen George, and other Farnham operatic types. Norwood was a British film star, known for his role as Sherlock Holmes.

There was little excitement at the election on 4 April. Those elected or re-elected were Dr. Archibald Graydon, 'St Cross Cottage', Thorold Road (Bourne); Herbert Rothwell, 'Glenhurst', Beaufort Road (Waverley); and Sidney Alfred Baber, 'Mendip', Firgrove Hill (Castle). Councillors Borelli and Sanders had been present at all 22 council and committee meetings during 1931/2. At the Annual Meeting, it was suggested that perhaps the silver-headed mace, given by the late Bishop Woods and adorning the overmantle in the Council Chamber, might in future be placed on the table during sittings, but this was defeated by eight votes to nine.

It was announced that the non-residential part of the castle would be opened in July 1933 as a theological college . . . Sewage Works Committee reported that some 266,329 gallons of effluent passed daily through the pipes . . . 40 tree roots in the park had been exploded out of the ground . . . Sherfield Bros. planned 16 houses in Waverley Lane . . . Every room in every house was being measured up one by one in preparation of the second valuation list under the Rating and Valuation Act 1925.

One pleasing item in otherwise routine business was the report of Councillor Winter's Fire Brigade Committee, which listed the recent recipients of long-service medals. Second Officer F. Elderfield had 35 years; Third Officer E. F. Brooker, 32; ex-First Engineer J. Cole, 30; First Engineer A. Collins, 32; Second Engineer F. Barnett, 20; Fireman F. Baker, 19; First Motor Engineer H. Greentree, 14; Second Motor Engineer N. Avenell, 11; Third Engineer J. E. White, 12; Fireman J. H. Edwards, 12; Fireman J. W. Sawkins, 11.

The Council had lodged an objection against the County Council's reorganisation of the Rural District. Farnham was particularly sad about not being given the village of Tilford, especially as prior to 1866 the village had formed part of the old parish of Farnham. The Minister of Health was fair—he put the matter to the Tilford villagers direct. At a meeting held at the Tilford Institute on 24 May, chaired by Canon Martin S. Ware, it was resolved that the village should remain a rural area and not be included in the Urban District of Farnham. And so this lovely village—'the most beautiful village in this part of England', said one —went instead to the Hambledon Rural District Council. Aldershot Borough had unsuccessfully made a bid for Ash and Tongham, which would have entailed an alteration in the county boundary.

A plan in June for a new shop front at 43 The Borough for Silvers, the tailors, was put forward. The 'guardian angel' had a big say in this one, and it was modelled on Fribourg and Treyers shop in the Haymarket, with entirely happy results.

A sub-committee was formed to take firm action for the provision of a public car park and toilets. 'I hope', remarked Councillor Winter, 'that this will not be thought a convenient way of shelving it'. The Chamber of Commerce took up arms; their ultimatum to the Council read:

(1) It is eminently desirable in every town that there should be one place of resort for all motor vehicles carrying passengers.
(2) That this provision will have to be made in every town of any size within a comparatively short period of years from today.
(3) That the longer the initial step is delayed the more difficult it will become to find any really suitable place for the purpose, regard being had that

the preliminary consideration is to give ready access of car and bus users to
the business part of the town.

(4) That, taking a long view of the matter, the facilities asked for should be
provided free of charge to the users.

(5) That any scheme suggested should be complete with lavatories and waiting rooms.

The Chamber went on to suggest a few suitable sites' The Hart, South Street
meadows; the Council yard; the market place in South Street; or the cobbled
area in Castle Street. But the Council had not themselves been idle; they had no
less than six likely sites for a public convenience in mind: 1 Park Row (which
Courages were willing to sell); land at the Hart owned by Kinghams (unwilling);
and four spots in Long Garden Walk (two of which they could have). They
favoured the one in Park Row, 40 feet or so in from Archie Harrison's *Nelson
Arms*—a tourist attraction itself. The cottage had a frontage of 24 feet and
contained a living-room, small sitting-room, scullery, and four bedrooms. Downstairs could be converted into a 'ladies' and 'gents', and upstairs into a flat for a
caretaker, for about £200. Courages could be offered, say, £300. The flat did
not materialise. In due course, No. 1 Park Row came to vie with the castle as
Farnham's most important tourist attraction.

About this time, the G.P.O. at 107 West Street was given the treatment, with a
new counter, a *Kassac* floor, and the replacement of 'the old sloping desks' formerly
used by customers. There was also a new telephone exchange for the 11 operators
who manually dealt with a daily average of between four and five thousand calls.

The post office had replaced 'Leigh House' in 1910. General Herbert Plumer
had occupied this house at the turn of the century. On 16 July 1932, as Field-
Marshal Viscount Plumer of Messines, he died at the age of seventy-five. His
daughter, the Hon. Eleanor, had at some function spoken with affection of her
family's stay in Farnham. She recalled being with her father at his triumphant
homecoming at the end of the South African War, when he was conveyed from
the station to 'Leigh House' in an open carriage drawn by the townspeople.

On 13 July, Eric Patrick, doubtless spurred on by hearing that morning that
he had passed the final of the Chartered Accountants Examination, scored 100
in the first leg of the King's Cup Prize event at Bisley. His father and grandfather
also shot their way into the King's 300 with 98 each.

The *Herald* of 13 August carried a letter from 'A New Resident' who, seeing
the way Castle Street seemed to be going, wrote of the 'change in one of the
most beautiful streets in England into a garage. Why not complete the job?
I suggest that the street be roofed over and that American firms be invited to
tender for petrol stations, that mechanics should be available, and that a junk
heap for scrapped cars be established'. He also suggested having a snack bar and
fried fish and winkle stalls.

A lengthy article on Farnham in *The Architect and Building News,* dated
12 August, paid tribute to the successful endeavours of Charles Borelli and his

architect, Harold Falkner. The *Herald* referred to Mr. Borelli as 'Farnham's Amenity Man'— much the same as 'guardian angel'.

County planners and Transport Ministry engineers were now engaged on plotting Farnham's by-pass road. They wanted more details concerning the proposed southern route and wanted to know why no route north of the town had been put forward. In reply, the Council denied having eschewed a northern route, and submitted two alternatives, namely:

> *Route 1.*—Coxbridge, north of Coxbridge Farm and Chantreys Kilns and south of the Trapes housing estate to Crondall lane, which the proposed road crossed at a circus (roundabout); then north of the Beavers estate to Castle Street, with a circus and a link road from Folly Hill; thence through Farnham Park parallel with its southern boundary and joining the Hale Road at the *Six Bells* public house (circus); and a continuation via Water Lane to connect with the Guildford Road at Sandrock Cottage. The road would be 2¼ miles long and was estimated to cost in the region of £83,513 (including the demolition of properties, £11,020).

> *Route 2.*—Coxbridge, north of Coxbridge Farm, to Crondall Lane at Three Stiles (circus); east through the Rawleys estate and across Knowles Lane (circus); through Farnham Park, 400 feet north of and parallel with the avenue; across Hale Road at the *Six Bells* (circus) and on to the Guildford Road by Sandrock Cottage. This covered 2½ miles and was estimated at £85,169, with only £2,480 spent on demolitions.

Route 2 was favoured because of the need for fewer demolitions and its greater remoteness from the town. But it did seem a pity to desecrate the park.

Finding a tenant for the Ranger's House in the park was an even bigger problem than Bourne Mill had been. This 200-year-old property was of over-generous proportions for a council workman. The house had been thoroughly neglected for ages past and this, together with its isolated situation far from the haunts of mankind, made of it an elephant whiter than white. They tested it on the market, offering a seven-year lease, with grazing rights for 30 animals, but the two bids that came in were subsequently withdrawn. A fresh advertisement attracted Mr. J. H. Hewes, licensee of the *Coach and Horses,* who bid £200 a year provided that certain repairs were first carried out by the Council. New drainage was installed; electricity and the telephone laid on; a new bathroom with running hot water and linen cupboard added; the kitchen was fitted with a Triplex range, and the floor covered with quarry tiles; old two-inch bricks found on the premises were used to build fireplaces in the bedrooms; many old features of the house were exposed and restored, and the old orchard was fenced in. Mr. Hewes's horses became a familiar sight in the park for the next seven years. It was not until the Second World War, during which the house was used as an air-raid report centre, was over that a sympathetic tenant transformed the Ranger's house into a charming residence.

The locally-based Hoverplane Company were away to a good start, with rooftop demonstrations at Selfridges, the Galeries Lafayette in Paris, and a store in Brussels . . . Farnham Blue Coaches won first prize at a *Concours d'Élégance* held in Eastbourne for one of their fleet, built by E. D. Abbott, Ltd., of Wrecclesham . . . The local branch of the League of Nations debated 'Germany's Demand to Arm' . . . The Hambledon cricket club, commented the *Herald,* had not been the only club to pioneer the game in the 18th century. For, according to Dr. W. G. Grace, they had had strong rivals in a club called the Three Parishes Club, which consisted of players from Farnham, Godalming and Hartley Row.

In September, the Committee of Management of Trimmers Cottage Hospital leaked that they had resolved to extend their existing building at a cost of between two and three thousand pounds, rather than build a new hospital in Waverley Lane. The *Herald* went to extraordinary lengths in deprecating this economy—which might have been the object of the exercise. The old hospital was in a busy, noisy street, and in every way unsuitable for a town such as Farnham. George Trimmer, if he were alive in 1932, would undoubtedly cry from the rooftops—'Build a New Hospital on a New Site!' The management committee gracefully bowed to public opinion. At a further meeting on 20 December, a motion to build anew in Waverley Lane was carried *nem con.*

Major Rupert Anderson retired as Chairman of the Farnham Bench after 10 years. Edgar Kempson, who had been a familiar figure in the courtroom for the past 45 years, suitably spoke from the floor. Captain E. E. Craig became the next Chairman.

Plans in October included alterations at 18/19 The Borough for Sainsbury's, and next door at 20/21 for Mr. Wyles's corner drapery shop.

The 10 November was the day the whole town had been waiting for, when Bishop Greig arrived to take up residence in part of the castle. He was subjected to the awesome ritual of a public welcome in the Institute from 6 to 7.15 p.m., then whisked along to the *Bush* hotel to be wined and dined at the 1932 Venison Dinner. The effort by Mrs. Anderson had saved the castle, at all events for the time being. As a finishing touch, when Bishop Woods had moved to Winchester, the portraits of 24 past bishops residing in Farnham since 1367 had been removed and Mrs. Anderson had arranged for copies of these to be made, by various copyists under the direction of Bertram Priestland, R.A., and these were now on the walls of Farnham Castle.

At speech day at the Girls' Grammar School, Canon Girling voiced the general feeling that the girls could no longer be expected to make do with the boys' cast-off premises in West Street, and that what they needed was a brand new school of their own.

When the 1.26 p.m. down train arrived at Farnham station on 8 November, the mutilated body of a man was found on the roof of one of the coaches. He was identified as Richard Francis Kindersley, 27, a son of Sir Robert Kindersley, director of the Bank of England, and President of the National Savings Committee. It was assumed at the inquest that, for some private reason, he had climbed on top of the coach and had been struck as the train passed under a bridge.

William Welsby Williams died on 12 November. Born in 1849, son of Anthony Williams, he had inherited the family business which was founded in 1780. This was the wine merchants at 122 West Street; it was Farnham's oldest business still remaining in the same family.

The unemployment problem was so serious that in November a public appeal was launched for funds, aimed at a figure of about £3,000, with which to finance a job-creation scheme. Works were put in hand such as land drainage in the park, improvements to the Bourne recreation ground, forming a new recreation ground in Morley Road, making up driftways and widening Crondall Lane. These jobs provided work for about 112 men for two weeks at a wage of 10d an hour.

The Council opposed an attempt by the Traction Company to cut down on bus services, halving the Rowledge schedule from half-hourly to hourly. This was more serious than at first glance, for many London commuters relied on these buses to get them to the station. Armed with a petition signed by 800 residents, the Clerk and Councillor Avery attended a public enquiry on 13 December. They won the day with the Rowledge service, but made minor concessions in others. Season tickets between Aldershot and Shortheath went up to £2 12s. 6d. a quarter.

1933

Attended by a Maid Servant I surveyed every part of the Palace; my first enquiry was after the Old Kitchen and the famous Cooking Utensils I had heard of there; the Kitchen still remains but with very little shew of Hospitality, or Good Living; One of the great Fire Places is closed up; Old Hospitality is Lick'd out of Doors; and made to give way to Taste; a Bishop's lady now vies in dress and Gaiety with a Duchess and has as many public Balls etc. and as gaudy an Equipage. Charity at the Gate and Religion in the Mansion are rarely known. The House is sadly run to ruin and the present Bishop is suing the Heir of his Predecessor for dilapidation; in the meantime the House will fall to pieces. The Hall is very large, the Chapel neat, and some of the Lodging Rooms commodious; the Long Gallery is furnished with modern frippery, as Tambour Frames, etc. (proving that the Petticoat rules the Cassock) and with a long low Couch, meant, I suppose, for Devotion; on which the Bishop may be often on his knees.

Extract from the Journal of John Byng, later the 5th Lord Torrington, concerning Farnham Castle which he visited during a tour of England on horseback in the latter years of the 18th century. Reprinted in *The Church Times,* August 1933.

THE FIRST WORLD WAR had set in slow motion a transformation in almost every sphere of human activity. The next war would accelerate this process. But just now, between the wars, mankind was in transit between the ancient and modern. Nowhere would the change be more revolutionary than in the field of office work, though, as things were in the early 1930s, there was still some way to go before 'desk jockeys' would cease to resemble something out of Dickens by Phiz. The desks and other furniture in the Rating Department of the Council in 'Montrose', South Street, belonged personally to Alf Thorp, who had been made Rating Officer in 1890. It was almost certain that he had inherited them from his father, John Thorp, a pharmacist from Thame who had drifted into the rating business sometime back in the mid-1850s. Therefore, this furniture was contemporary with Dickens.

There was a typewriter, of the type found nowadays on display in museums. This, of course, could not take thick bound volumes; loose-leaf systems being mistrusted by the Auditor, ledgers were still kept by hand. Somewhere down the years, the Thorps had given up using a feather, and a pen was now the

163

accepted equipment. A pen was a slim cylinder about six inches long, with a steel nib at the sharp end; the blunt end was for chewing. The nib would be dipped into a blue-black fluid called ink. A second inkwell, with a separate pen, would be used for such purposes as underlining headings and adding a touch of colour to one's fingers. Perfectionists used usually red ink for this purpose; occasionally one found a third colour, often green. Lying within instant reach would be a sheet of absorbent material called blotting-paper; this was used to mop up spilt ink. In the darkening shadows of a winter's afternoon, when the soft radiance from the candle fell across the pages of one's ledger, and the muted sounds were those only of scratchy nibs and the occasional aborted snore, the whole cosy setting might well have modelled for Hablot K. Browne. A competitive spirit, ranging from friendly rivalry to pure bitchiness, existed between the junior pen-pushers and found expression in informal contests to become the Most Immaculate Ledger Keeper of the Year (MILKY). Points would be awarded for neat handwriting, accuracy of figure-work, absence of blots, and getting through to Mr. Thorp, who was stone deaf.

Outside in the Council yard, a few feet from 'Montrose', was the timber-built tower used by the firemen. On top of this was mounted the siren which summoned the brigade from their places of work throughout the town. So loud and strident was the siren's wail that it was said to be audible in far-off Frensham. From a few feet away the effect was shattering. That was when the blotting-paper came in handy; nibs could always be replaced, and the inkwells refilled; one could, if it came to that, take a new ledger and start all over again. Mr. Thorp, dozing at his desk with one eye on the torpid street-scene outside, was unaffected; he was stone deaf.

*　　*　　*　　*　　*

The unemployment relief fund had reached £2,480, and some 92 men had been given temporary work. People were urged to find odd jobs about the house, like washing the car, cleaning boots, carrying coal, sawing logs, beating carpets, cleaning windows, tidying-up the garden—anything that would keep a man busy for an hour or two, at 10d. an hour.

Ten manufacturers of automatic traffic light systems sent tenders, nine for 'Fixed Time Cycle Installations' and one for 'Vehicle Actuated Traffic Control Signals'. The latter type was chosen for the South Street junction and ordered from the Automatic Electric Company, Ltd., at a cost of £397 10s. 0d. The days of the copper on point duty, with his semaphoric arms and suspicious glares, were numbered.

Bides asked 7s. 6d. each for 60 elms, with iron guards at 5s. each, for planting in the gaps in the avenue in the park, which was, alas!, no longer Edna Lyall's 'long, stately, cathedral-like aisle'.

Four hundred pounds was voted towards the provision of a public mortuary, at the rear of the Council depot. This to consist of a post mortem room, operating room with swivel tables, three cubicles for corpses, waiting-room, and lavatory accommodation. So far, the Council had had an arrangement with Patricks in Royal Oak yard, but this was due to expire shortly. The Council preferred to be masters in their own house, but, on this occasion, they were talked out of it.

The *Herald* of 14 January had some notes on Moor Park which had the rare distinction of not once mentioning Swift and Stella. The first recorded possessor of Compton Hill, as the estate was then called, was Sir Thomas Clarke; on his death in 1633, it passed to his son, Sir John Clarke. Sir William Temple bought it in 1682 and devised on his death in 1699 to two grand-daughters, Dorothy and Elizabeth. Dorothy married Nicholas Bacon of Shrubland Hall, Suffolk, and Elizabeth married a cousin, John Temple. Elizabeth died childless, and the whole estate passed to her nephew, Basil Bacon, who carried out extensive alterations, including a new south front. The house later fell into decay; in 1796, a London merchant named Tenison, who leased the estate, laid out formal gardens. Owner-ship passed from Basil Bacon to a younger brother and then through various descendants to Charles Williams, who changed his name to Bacon. In 1933, Moor Park was still in the ownership of the Bacon family, and Bacon of Hale Lodge was able to trace back to Nicholas Bacon who had married Sir William Temple's grand-daughter.

Dr. W. S. Colman presented a facsimile of Rocque's Map of Surrey, 1762, which was framed and hung in the Council offices . . . 3.96 acres of land adjoining Coppice Cottages, Upper Weybourne Lane, were bought, of which part was used for road widening, part resold in building plots, and the rest made into a recreation ground . . . Bridgefield received its name-place, though it was not considered necessary to indicate its position through the Fairfield . . . Liptons submitted plans for a shop at 117 West Street . . . There were more floods—so bad that the laundry undertook to dry out people's carpets free of charge, and the fire brigade pumped the water out of their houses.

The Council contributed £20 towards the publication by the Chamber of Commerce of a second edition of *The Book of Farnham*; containing little factual information, the format was of a superior kind designed to attract only the right sort of strangers to the town.

Phase 2 of the new town hall was started in January—the main office section and three shops. The Inland Revenue hoped to move in during August. Mills' workmen had discovered a 16th-century kitchen midden some seven or eight feet down, which contained sherds of green pottery of a once local vintage, and animal remains like deer antlers, oyster shells, and bones. An old well, probably that of the *Goat's Head* inn, was also found.

The ancient name of Snailslynch was retained, to please Mr. Borelli, by dropping the snails and applying the name 'Lynch' to one of the new roads off Waverley Lane.

At the Brewster Sessions in February, the Justices objected to the renewal of licences in respect of a further nine public houses. Edgar Kempson for Courages pointed out that since the famous case of 1902, half of Farnham's 51 pubs had been closed. This fresh onslaught was really too bad. The Bench relented; only one case was referred to Surrey Quarter Sessions in June. This was the *Rose and Thistle* at 47 West Street; it was said in Court that it was reputed to be the smallest licensed house in the county.

With effect from 1 April 1933, the Farnham Rural District Council passed into history; their sole claim to distinction, perhaps, being that for a few years they had admistered a glorious slice of countryside. At a meeting on 2 February at Millmead House, Guildford, the liquidated Council's assets and liabilities, its ratepayers and staff were shared out among the absorbing authorities.

The opening of the *Regal* cinema on Friday, 31 March 1933, had good cause to be considered unique in the annals of cinema opening. For, whereas this ceremony was one which was normally performed by some exotic film star, Farnham's cinema was declared operative by no less a person than His Grace the Lord Bishop of Guildford. This unlikely mixture of the sacred and profane was an astute move on the part of the directors, acting in the belief that since Farnham was the seat of the bishop, and the faithful were seen to flock to the many local places of worship, albeit in diminishing numbers, the town was under the yoke of the Church. The move paid off; that dispenser of balanced opinion, the *Farnham Herald,* commenting that this must be the first occasion of a bishop being associated with a cinema, was moved to exclaim that the incident could be looked upon as a sign of the growing good feeling between the Church and the cinema. All 1,280 seats were sold out. The audience included the councillors and representatives of other public bodies in the town. From 7.15 to 8 p.m. there was a programme of music, played by the band of the 7th (Queen's Own) Hussars. As the bishop and his lady, accompanied by the rector, Canon Girling, and other members of the opposition, entered, six trumpeters sounded a fanfare; this was followed by a rendering of the National Anthem sung by Marjorie Hodge. Then a voice intoned 'Pray Silence for the Right Reverend the Lord Bishop of Guildford'. The bishop replied, 'I would rather you did not keep silence for the Bishop of Guildford because for once in his life he feels himself entirely at sea'. He then proceeded to declare the cinema open with a few well chosen words.

After the speeches there was a silly symphony cartoon in colour, entitled 'Babes in the Wood'. Donald Calthrop, the well-known film star, appeared in person to entertain the company. There followed an auction of two antique chairs, given by Canon Girling, an antique silver and cut glass decanter, given by Mr. Borelli, and a wireless set, given by Major J. T. Wallace of Shortheath, and other goodies. The main feature film was J. B. Priestley's 'The Good Companions', starring Jessie Matthews and Edmund Gwenn. Without any deductions for expenses, the evening's takings were donated to the funds of the Farnham Social Service Committee. The evening was a huge success. Directors C. J. Donada and W. J. May were showered with compliments. The *Regal,* said Councillor Borelli in the Council Chamber, blended in beautifully with the surrounding town. It had originally been intended to build in white stone, or imitation stone, but, on being told that the local format was red bricks and tiles, the directors had at once agreed to adopt this style at a much increased cost. Stanley E. Perkins, from the *Manor Park Pavilion*, Aldershot, was promoted to manage the *Regal*; he had a staff of twenty. The old picture palace, the town's second cinema, opened in 1913, closed its doors on 25 March. It was rebuilt some years later as the *County* cinema.

Farnham had a happy knack of moulding foreigners to its own intrinsic character. The proprietors of the *Regal* cinema were men who were orientated more or less wholeheartedly on Aldershot, yet in this extension of their empire in Farnham they readily and quickly were absorbed into the local pattern. They allowed a mission service to be held in the *Regal* on Good Friday evening, at which the bishop was again present. On being touched for a sub towards Red Cross funds, they generously donated the proceeds from the second house performance on 12 May. They were also co-operative about car parking facilities at the back of the cinema, collaborating with the Council over rights of access and the purchase of a piece of land for an extension of the 50-slot park.

Mr. H. Cox, the builder, developed the south side of Ridgway Road with six shops and flats, as well as three houses fronting Edward Road . . . Mr. A. R. Bide was allowed to plant a weeping copper beech tree on the lawn in front of Brightwells House as a memorial to his brother . . . It was decided to build more public conveniences between 65 and 66 East Street at a cost of £740.

There was greater interest in the election on 3 April that year, except in the Castle Ward, where Councillors Lucas and Mrs. Stroud were returned unopposed. In Waverley (one vacancy), Frederick Lawson, surgical footwear dealer in South Street, beat Colonel Martyn Rogers Strover of 'Eachway', Lodge Hill Road, by 296 votes to 229. A year or so earlier, Colonel Strover and his wife had established the highly successful 'Woodlarks Camp' for cripples in woodland opposite their home.

In Hale (two vacancies), Charlie Binfield (213 votes) and James Chuter (117) easily defeated H. G. Hale (60) of 'Hambledon Cottage', Lower Bourne—whose name may have prompted him to stand for the Hale Ward. In the Bourne (one vacancy), Councillor Greenway (206 votes) lost his seat to Samuel Lathey (276) of 'Brackendene', Dene Lane; and in Wrecclesham (one vacancy), Arthur Brown (192 votes), lost his to Colonel G. E. C. Underhill (214) of 'Khyber Cottage', Boundstone, husband of Lilian Starr, who had made front-page news on the north-west frontier in 1923.

William Willett (1856–1915), born in Waggon Yard, Farnham, instigator of the Daylight Saving scheme, featured briefly in the *Herald* on 15 April. Little known, perhaps, was the fact that Willett's recommendation was that clocks should be altered in separate moves, each of 20 minutes. This was considered by the government to be too complicated.

Edgar Kempson died in an Eastbourne nursing home on 28 April. Born in Worcestershire in 1861 and educated at Bedford Grammar School, he had been with two firms of solicitors before coming to Farnham as a partner in Knight, Saunders and Kempson. He was later the sole partner, until joined in 1919 by G. F. Wright. He had acted for the brewers in Rex v. Farnham J.J., 1902, and since pleaded for the public houses, right up to the last court in February 1933.

The hard tennis courts in Brightwells were re-surfaced in red instead of the familiar green dressing. In the kiosk, Mrs. Dale won the catering rights with a bid of £10; her toasted buns were much sought after by the lunchtime swimming set. The lawn at the diving-board end of the bath was fenced in as a sunbathing area. On hot nights, the baths were floodlit and opened from 9 to 11 p.m.

The Operatic Society staged *The Mikado,* with H. R. James in the title role . . . A dark brown gelding on the Council's strength sank to its thighs in a hole at the Guildford Road pumping station in which a fire was smouldering and was so badly burnt that it had to be destroyed . . . More and more, criticism of Adolf Hitler's Nazi Party appeared in the local paper . . . Also in the *Herald* were weekly lists of new telephone subscribers and their numbers.

The 19 May was a big day in Farnham Red Cross circles, with a tableau at the *Regal* cinema. Joyce Robins took the part of 'The Lady of the Lamp'—so close to Brightwells House, where, it was believed, Florence Nightingale spent her last night in England before leaving for Scutari.

Miss D. M. Drought was leaving the Girls' Grammar School to become headmistress at Altrincham County High School. Her successor was Miss E. D. M. Winters, M.A., senior history mistress at the County High School, Colchester.

Among the five passengers killed when a Farnham-bound train hit a derailed steam train near Wimbledon on 25 May were Colonel H. H. and Mrs. Norman of 'Fernlea', Old Frensham Road, Lower Bourne. They had been up to the Chelsea Flower Show. Dr. Hussey had a narrow escape; he was buried in the debris.

All this time, the by-pass road portfolio had been doing the rounds at high government levels. The southern route, it was observed, would entail the widening of Red Lion Lane and Abbey Street, and could hardly be regarded as a by-pass road, for it would pass through the town's built-up area. Further, there would be no provision for traffic approaching from the north. True—but there was more of a traffic problem from the south; however, the Council agreed to submit particulars of a northern road, and perhaps put the question of whether to have a north or south route to the ratepayers.

Mr. Alfred Ross Patrick died on 29 June, aged seventy-four. Born at 22 East Street, a son of Henry Patrick, the Farnham builder, and educated at Mr. Poppleton's school, he later became Sanitary Inspector to the Farnham Rural District Council for over 46 years. He was a first-class shot, having reached the King's 300 at Bisley on 12 occasions, and the 100 three times. In 1932, he had won a King's Badge with a score of 271.

Mr. L. A. Durant, digging a pit in his garden at 'Rustic Walk', Lower Bourne, unearthed two Roman vases. Shaking out the sand, out fell Roman coins bearing the head of Antoninus Pius, A.D. 86–161.

Thirty-two council houses were being built at Trapes, Crondall Lane. On completion of the first block at the end of July, Chairman Sanders blessed the estate from a platform erected by house No. 1, and Councillor Figg ceremoniously unlocked the front door.

The summer of 1933 was a hot one. The town's alternative to floods in the winter was heath fires in the dry summers. One fire, on Tilford Common, from 8 to 12 September, was four and a half miles in circumference. Major Wade listed no fewer than 13 calls; he was full of praise for the brigade, but there was little the men could do apart from protecting properties threatened by the flames.

The Co-op were busy extending their empire in Union Road with a confectionery shop, a grocery dispatch room, and butcher's shop. The local authority was closely involved with the butchers' trade. The Slaughter of Animals Act 1933 imposed certain conditions on slaughtermen. They now had to be licensed, and at least 18 years of age. Animals had to be stunned by a mechanically-operated instrument before being killed, though this provision did not apply to sheep unless the Council so willed. Twenty-four licences were issued in Farnham.

Work on the castle was now finished. The original purpose of the non-residential part had been that of a theological college, but the financial crisis which had bedevilled the country since 1930 rendered it unwise to proceed with this project for the time being. In the meantime, it was decided to use the accommodation as a Retreat House and Conference venue. Canon Girling explained that many people regarded a Retreat House as some sort of glorified almshouse for aged clergy. That was not so. A 'Retreat' was formed by a number of people, clerical or lay, who felt the need to escape the tensions of modern life for a few days and 'be alone with God'. They would be in the charge of a 'Conductor', usually a priest, who would give addresses and recommend subjects for meditation. A rule of silence would be kept. In Farnham Castle, services would be held in the old Norman chapel, and meals would be taken in the refectory, originally the Great Kitchen. A Miss How had been installed as Lady Warden, and the first Retreat, the Mothers' Union, had been arranged for four days commencing 9 October. A party of Sunday school teachers was coming in November. A Service of Benediction on 18 October, strongly attended by the top brass of both Guildford and Winchester Dioceses, launched the scheme. All were charmed with the excellent work of renovation. Seven of the 26 rooms were already furnished, at a cost of £40 a room, donated by persons in memory of loved ones.

At the other end of the street, a lay party, on 27 September, had acclaimed the completion of Phase 2 of the new town hall building—the National Provincial Bank premises, the Inland Revenue office above, and the shops in the colonnade facing The Borough. People's enthusiasm for Falkner's most outstanding masterpiece was tempered somewhat by a disappointment that it contained no hall which might be hired for public functions, unlike the old building, with its huge Corn Exchange, the venue of most public functions. But the rents had proved too great a lure for the Town Hall Company. As one councillor remarked—now that Farnham has no public hall, should the Council not consider building one?

The next step in the building programme was the eastern section, with the continuation of the colonnade, with more shops, and Mr. Falkner's dream—a replica of the old Bailiff's Hall, the bedraggled remains of which had been cleared away in 1866. The architect was casting around for evidence of the original on which to base his design.

Trimmer's Trustees were now giving attention to raising money for their proposed new hospital in Waverley Lane. Collecting for hospital purposes usually had the sympathy of the public, and no great problem was envisaged. The Trust persuaded the Council without much difficulty to agree to underwrite any possible annual deficiency up to a ceiling of £500.

Disappointingly, the County Council did not support the local Council's decision to spend £13,174 on modernising and widening Waverley Lane to 50 feet, despite the fact that it was now a busy residential road. On the other hand, County gave their full support to a renewed application for a Charter of Incorporation.

Open Spaces Committee observed that there was no cup for the Ladies' Diving Event at the annual swimming sports; all the other events had one, they said—looking hard at Mr. Borelli . . . Sir Edward Perceval suggested a nine-hole golf course in the park; this was met with enthusiasm—the park would be an ideal setting, and its natural undulations would lend themselves to the game; though there might be a danger to children.

Diocesan Conference finally decided to build the new cathedral on Stag Hill, Guildford, but prudently resolved to collect a minimum of £50,000, towards the total estimated cost of £250,000, before commencing the work . . . Aldershot Council invited Farnham to share a joint project for an aerodrome on the lines of a report written three years previously by Sir Alan Cobham . . . 106–108 East Street were replaced by new shops—destined for a short life before being bulldozed out of the way for the Woolmead development later in the century . . . The *Plough* inn, 74 West Street, was also given a facelift.

The run-up to Christmas was marred by what may be described as Farnham's most sensational murder. 'Sunnyhurst', one of the four Zingari Terrace houses at the end of East Street, was a boarding-house kept by Mrs. Florence Jane Wilson and her daughter, Florence Doreen Wilson. One of the boarders, who lived in a loft over the garage, was a Dutch geologist, Dr. Gysbert Herman Bakker. He was an odd, screwball type, frequently at loggerheads with his landlady. At about 6.30 a.m. on the morning of 15 December, Bakker entered the bedroom where Mrs. Wilson and her daughter slept and killed them with a shotgun. He also tried to disfigure the daughter by pouring hot wax on her. He then returned to the garage and shot himself. A letter found on Bakker's person stated, 'I have the pleasure to inform you that tomorrow morning at 6.30 I shall shoot Mrs. F. J. Wilson . . . I will hang myself on the doorway of the garage . . . I may also disfigure the daughter . . .'. He was buried in unconsecrated ground.

1934

Wherever God erects a house of prayer,
The Devil always builds a chapel there;
And 'twill be found, upon examination,
The latter has the largest congregation.

Daniel Defoe: *The True-born Englishman*

YOU CANNOT PROVIDE THE MASSES with motor-cars and wireless sets, and one day off a week—and expect them to spend that day in church. The '20s and '30s were notable for the breaking away by the people from a conventional observance of the Sabbath. In increasing numbers, they stayed away from church to drive to the sea for the day, or to sit at home with ears glued to loud-speakers. When it became clear that, despite all that the prophets had threatened in the past, hell-fire and damnation did not descend upon their shoulders, the word of the neo-pagans spread, and more and more families opted out. The hold which the clergy had had over the community for so many generations was finally and irrevocably broken.

Those rebels who did not join the Sunday motorcades to and from the seaside stayed at home and listened-in. Observing the growing trend, the B.B.C. introduced religious programmes on Sundays so that listeners might salve what remained of their consciences without having to dress up and go to church. It had become the tendency to acclaim the stars rather than their performances on the cinema screen; now this nonsense was applied to radio personalities. Dick Sheppard, broadcaster of many of the religious services, became an idolised, though unseen, figure. Thus when the Very Reverend H. R. L. Sheppard, C.H., D.D., who lived at 'Shoelands', Seale, and thus had a relationship with Farnham, preached at the Parish church on Sunday 31 December 1933, the rebels packed the church to the gunnels simply to see what their idol looked like in the flesh.

Between the wars, films—the profane sort—were immensely popular. Going to the 'flicks' vied with pub-crawling as the main item on one's weekend agenda. In places where men talked among themselves, it was generally conceded that there couldn't be enough of either. Such an attitude inspired Mr. E. E. Boniface, an assistant in Kings' hairdressing salon in South Street, to organise a petition in favour of the *Regal* cinema opening on Sunday evenings. By May 1934, some

171

700 customers had affirmatively appended their names to the question: 'Are you in favour of Sunday performances? Help to brighten the town, provide recreation for the young folk and keep the money circulating in the town where it was earned'. Mr. Boniface was a brave man. He aimed at a thousand signatures; by the end of June, he had collected one thousand two hundred. Then he handed the prayer to Mr. Perkins, the *Regal* manager, who forwarded it to his head office in London. Over the ensuing weeks, the inhabitants of Farnham split into two sharply opposing camps—the Local Sunday Defence Committee, chaired by the rector, and the Farnham Sunday Films Association. The Council acted as referees. It could not be said, however, that they were strictly unbiassed, for, whilst they were expected to lead their constituents in prayer, they themselves chose, rather tactlessly, to permit the playing of bowls and tennis in Brightwells on Sundays between 2 p.m. and 6.30 p.m., with effect from 5 August.

The provisions of the Sunday Entertainments Act 1932 were complex. The local authority had first to pass a resolution to make application to parliament for powers to enable the County Council, as licensing authority under the Cinematograph Act of 1909, to allow cinema entertainments on Sundays, subject to conditions required by law and such other conditions as the licensing authority might think fit to impose. This first hurdle was cleared by 12 votes to six, but, before an approach was made to the Secretary of State, a public meeting of local government electors was held at the Church House on 30 November, whereat a show of hands revealed 117 persons in favour of proceeding further, and 104 against. A formal poll of the electorate was then the next step. This was fixed for Saturday, 15 December.

In their pre-election campaign, the antis darkly warned about 'threats to workers' interests' from powerful trade organisations in the form of Cinema Combines and Syndicates; that the much vaunted charity aspect of Sunday opening was 'known to be a myth'—in Portsmouth and Southampton, an average of only 2s. 7d. each week was contributed to deserving causes; that the weekday offered to cinema staff in lieu was 'no fair equivalent for a Sunday'. In their reply, the F.S.F.A. quoted—rather meanly—a recent comment by the rector: 'I don't think it's any use for us in these days to adopt the sabbatarian attitude—the time for that has gone by'. They touched briefly on 'fair play for the cinema staff', also that the Surrey County Council were stipulating that 1s. 9d. 'in the pound on gross takings should be devoted to local charities'. Most neighbouring towns already had Sunday opening, with 'beneficial results'. It 'reduced loitering in the streets' and the young had somewhere warm and comfortable to go. Above all, they stressed that voters should 'respect the liberties of others'; those who voted against would be under no compulsion whatever to go to the cinema themselves on Sundays.

On 17 December, the Returning Officer published the following Declaration of Poll:

Urban District of Farnham
Sunday Entertainments Act 1932
Cinematograph Entertainments on Sundays

Whereas a Poll of the local government electors of the above mentioned Urban District was taken on the Fifteenth day of December 1934 with reference to the proposal put to the Public Meeting held on the Thirtieth day of November 1934 that application should be made to Parliament for powers enabling the appropriate Licensing Authority under the Cinematograph Act 1909 to allow Cinematograph Entertainments in the said Urban Districts on Sundays, subject to the conditions required by Law and to such other conditions as the Licensing Authority might think fit to impose.

I, the undersigned, being the Returning Officer at the said Poll, do hereby declare the number of votes recorded thereat is as follows:

In favour of the Proposal	2,803 votes
Against the Proposal	1,139 votes
Majority in favour of the Proposal	1,664 votes

Dated this 17th day of December 1934

A. A. Minns

*   *   *   *   *

The Countryman for January–March and July–September 1934 contained hitherto unpublished letters of George Sturt. Like all his writings, they were nicely-phrased outpourings in praise of the working classes, whilst pointing to his own superior status. In January, Cambridge University Press reprinted his *The Wheelwright's Shop,* first published in 1923.

Trimmer's Hospital Trustees got away to a fine start in their fund-raising activities, with advance bookings with the Council for such events as a band concert, gymkhana and American tennis tournament in Brightwells on 12 May; a rendering of *Midsummer Night's Dream* in July, and a flag-day on Buttercup Day, 28 July. A Grand Farnham Hospital Carnival Week was scheduled for 6 to 12 May. Local builders had volunteered to bear the expense of erecting a giant barometer on the corner of the new town hall which would indicate the rising total as donations flowed in.

An Alton lady, Mrs. de Renzy-Martin, noting the charm of Farnham's town centre, sought out Mr. Borelli for his advice on how to preserve the old buildings in her own town. The 'guardian angel' arranged a sight-seeing tour of Farnham for a party of representatives of the Hampshire County Council, Alton and Farnham Councils, and Mrs. de Renzy-Martin. In his fight against vandalism, Mr. Borelli came in for a lot of chaff from his fellow townsmen. The *Herald* never missed a chance for good-humoured banter whenever some tree had to be felled or an old building was threatened. On the other hand, the paper was fulsome in its praise of the undoubted successes of this preservationist policy.

At the January meeting, Councillor Borelli put his cards on the table with a formal motion 'that the Council take such steps as may be necessary to control the elevation of houses or premises within the Urban District about to be built or reconditioned'. He felt that the Council should regard themselves as the trustees of the beautiful buildings left by their ancestors, and should prevent atrocities being erected in their place. A member demanded to know what was wrong with modern buildings—some of them were quite attractive, as well as being better suited to their up-to-date purpose. It was found that the Ministry of Health had had similar ideas and had appointed panels of architects up and down the country for the express purpose of advising local authorities on private developments. A Mr. R. Goulburn Lovell, A.R.I.B.A., A.T.P.I., was Hon. Secretary of the south-eastern Society of Architects; he was invited to Farnham in April, and, as a result, Mr. Borelli's motion was passed by 14 votes to one.

Farnham's architectural gems are possibly the better framed by the meaningless hodge-podge which surrounds them, for a townscape which is all nice tends to be confusing to the eye and individual buildings are robbed of the onlooker's concentrated attention. Farnham, though, could do with a lot more of them. Nowhere is the Victorians' lack of interest in town planning more in evidence than in South Street, even though that street contains a Lutyens building. The Local Board of the 1870s were exclusively concerned with the provision of an access road from the town centre to the railway station; the thought did not appear to cross their minds that here was a splendid opportunity to dictate the design of an entire street on virgin soil; they even gave it an unimaginative name.

P. J. Bartlett, A.R.I.B.A., the architect of Boots the Chemists, co-operated with Farnham's new code in converting 41/42 The Borough into a fitting neighbour to the Spinning Wheel at No. 40.

R. W. Mason retired after serving for 23 years as Clerk of the Magistrates, a post which his father had held for 30 years before that. Police Superintendent James Stovell also retired; he was replaced in February by Inspector Thomas J. Runnegar from Weybridge, who had risen from a constable in the space of four years.

Bishop Talbot died on 30 January in his 90th year. He had been active up to the end, last re-visiting Farnham Castle at the opening of the Retreat House in October.

Every now and again, the by-pass road controversy had a way of bubbling up and spilling over. As in another civil war in America, when northerners confronted southerners across the Appalachian Mountains in 1861, the Council-led southern routers glared across at the County Council-led northern advocators. At some point in the proceedings, a practical joker must have turned the compass round, for now the County appeared to favour the southern route, and the locals the northern. The 'S' route was costed at £115,000 (which included a link road to

Firgrove Hill), and the 'N' route £135,000 (including £53,000 for a link from the south of the town). The Articulated Road Sub-Committee of the County Council emphasised that, in an important matter such as this, money was of no account, but went on to protest against dis-parking some 4½ acres of Farnham Park.

The locals stated their case at an interview with County on 7 March:

> *Southern Route.*—This would entail two crossings of the river and the construction of the road on land liable to flooding. By interfering with the flow of the river, this would tend to increase flooding. The road would be a relief road rather than a by-pass; e.g. it would pass within 150 yards of the main approach to Farnham station and level-crossing. The active development now taking place in the Waverley and Tilford Roads will increase traffic and it was not possible to synchronise the level-crossing with traffic signals at the new road. It would impede the flow of local traffic from the town to the south. A danger point would be created at Hickleys corner, where five roads would converge. Development at the sides of the road, though possibly undesirable, would be in any case difficult on land liable to floods. Cost of widening the A31 and A235 would also be added to the cost. It would be detrimental to Farnham as the road would encourage traffic to avoid the town.

> *Northern Route.*—The road would open up potential building land north-west of Farnham. There would be minimal demolition and compensation. Minimum engineering difficulties. It would provide direct communication between military camps at Aldershot, Ewshot, Bordon and Blackdown, and stop heavy military traffic passing through the town, and relieve traffic to the Aldershot Tattoo and Horse Show. The suggestion that the road might destroy the amenities of the Park was neutralized by the unspoiled Windsor and Richmond Parks, through which roads had been made. The road would attract visitors to the Park. Gradients on the route were negligible.

On 17 January a letter came from the Clerk of the Privy Council, on behalf of the Lords of the Council, with the information that Their Lordships were not prepared to consider a Petition for Incorporation unless the population of the town at the 1931 census exceeded 20,000. Farnham's ancient borough status never was restored. It really was tough; there was Godalming, with a 10,400 population in 1931, and Basingstoke, with 13,862, not to mention Aldershot, a perimeter village of 660 inhabitants about a hundred years ago, and now a borough with 34,281. Yet Farnham, with 18,294 at the 1931 census was not good enough for Their Lordships.

Portsmouth fire brigade was buying a new turntable escape ladder and offered Farnham its old one for £50. A little money spent on it and a lick of paint would make it look quite smart. A new one would cost up to £3,500. In no time at all, it was in the Council yard, and the question arose of where to house it. Someone suggested the steam-roller kennel just inside the entrance; others thought why not a little house of its own next to the hose-drying tower.

Father Christmas, sponsored in January in aid of the Hospital Building Fund brought in £70. Donations, many three-figured, were pouring in. The Amateur

Orchestral Society made its bow to the public at the *Regal* cinema on 11 February and sent up the barometer on the town hall to over four figures. There was plenty of money in the town.

On 19 February they had a sharp reminder that their fellow men in other places did not have enough. Fifty hunger-marchers came down Castle Street, carrying banners and singing the *Internationale*. They marched through Downing Street into Union Road, where they were given a free meal at the Co-op. Then they marched to Aldershot. These unemployed men were between 25 and 35 years old, except for one old man playing a concertina. Their passing brought a whiff of poverty to affluent, élitist Farnham.

Major Wade resigned from the fire brigade as at 31 March, his reason being pressure of other commitments. Certainly membership of the brigade was time-consuming, with heath fires in summer and floods in winter, in addition to the town's quota of property fires, not to mention routine drills and the civic ceremonies. And the Major certainly had other commitments. He was Baden-Powell's right-hand man and, as we have seen, an ardent archaeologist. It was a golden rule that the chief officer of the fire brigade should be an officer and a gentleman. Farnham was abundantly provided with such material. But strangely no-one wanted to boss the fire brigade. As far as we're concerned, the retired military seemed to say, Farnham can burn. So the Council took the unusual step of promoting a ranker. He was Second Officer F. Elderfield. 'Berry'—Elderfield, Elderberry, Berry—had joined as one of the lads and worked his way up the brigade's ladder. He ran the upholsterer's business just across the road from the fire station and so was well placed to beat his colleagues to it when the siren went, which gave him time to crank up the engine and open wide the station doors, and put the kettle on.

Mr. Mardon did not seek re-election that year. Only the Waverley Ward was contested, with Mr. A. O. King, the hairdresser, standing against the two retiring members, Councillors Borelli and Sanders. In reporting the result, the *Herald* seemed surprised that Mr. Borelli should top the poll with 528 votes ('a vote of confidence in his policy of preserving the amenities of the neighbourhood') and that Mr. King should beat Mr. Sanders, who lost his seat.

The *Regal* cinema repeated their Good Friday gesture with a showing of the film 'Sign of the Cross', together with a service conducted by Bishop Greig. The audience contributed £23 towards the Hospital Building Fund. This now totalled £1,487.

Southampton, Bournemouth and Farnham were the test areas chosen by the Post Office for the transportation of mail by scheduled bus service. This made more possible the delivery of letters on day of posting, but the surcharge, sixpence a mile, was high by current standards.

Dr. Charles Tanner of 'Tancred's Ford', Tilford, died on 12 April, aged seventy-four. Medical Officer for the former Farnham Rural Council, he had taken an active part in local affairs. It was due to him that Farnham got a swimming pool in 1897—many years before most other towns; Guildford, for instance, did not get theirs until 1933.

A small congregation of councillors and public gathered at the top of South Street at 11 o'clock on Monday, 23 April. They were led in the Lord's Prayer by the Rev. A. J. Dance, who then pronounced a blessing on the newly-installed traffic lights. Councillor Alan Tice switched them on, and the people watched in amazement as they changed colour from red to amber, from amber to green, then back again. The *Herald* ran short courses on how the lights should be used, for some motorists, unused to such refinements, made a botch of it and were fined 40s. in the magistrates court. Pedestrians, too, were a little bothered, but generally the reaction was one of enthusiasm, and a similar system was ordered for the Hale crossroads. On 2 May, the lights were out of action for half an hour after being hit by an engine towing trailers to the hospital site in Waverley Lane, which was being used as a fairground in the carnival week.

The public petitioned for a one-way traffic route through the town centre, until such time as a by-pass road would relieve congestion. The Council did not consider the time was ripe for this, but they did authorise 'avenues' or crossing places for pedestrians at seven busy street junctions, as well as official stopping places for buses.

Mills and Sons undertook alterations and additions in April to a house in Lower Bourne. This became 'Al Aman', the English residence of Sir Sidiq Mohammad Abasi, H.H. Nawab of Bahawalpur, whose son was at Frensham Heights School. One of the ruler's hobbies was model railways, for which he built a special outhouse. He also bought the land opposite, so that his privacy would not be disturbed. He was to stay for several years.

Carnival week was a great success. On the procession day, Wednesday, 9 May, a mile-long train of gaily decorated vehicles wound its way through the streets of the town. On the Thursday there was an old-fashioned fair in Castle Street, with a roundabout outside the *Nelson Arms,* 'the like of which had not been seen since this ancient feature had been abandoned in 1874'. The fund for the hospital soared towards the £5,000 deadline needed to start the building off. Designed by H. Y. Margary, L.R.I.B.A., the hospital had 24 beds—10 each for men and women, and four for children. Tenders had been received from seven Farnham building firms which ranged from £10,798 to £12,185. The second lowest, that of Mardon, Ball and Co., in the sum of £10,825, was selected. This caused some surprise among those who had donated money to the venture, and an embarrassing situation for the lowest tenderer, Crosby and Co., who publicly announced that the Hospital Committee had done their firm a great injustice. Mrs. Rupert Anderson laid the foundation stone on 27 June.

Sid Varney, son of a Hale councillor, came on the staff as telephone operator and tea-boy. Of his wide repertoire, two come to mind. Being in the centre of the telephone network, he was well informed on prevailing inter-staff squabbles and gained much amusement from dialogue which ensued when he rang two officers he knew to be at loggerheads and plugged them through to each other. The other—when collecting up empty tea cups, he was wont to conceal about his person two small metal plates which, when dropped, produced the sound of breaking crockery.

Farnham was stirred in July by the news that Bishop Greig intended to retire soon because of heart trouble. He was 69 . . . The Council welcomed a County Council 'Good Rule' bye-law designed to stop people creating a noise with wireless sets, loud-speakers, and gramophones . . . There was further talk about having a local museum for the town's many archaeological artefacts.

Big alterations were planned for Sainsburys at 18/19 The Borough. The firm was advertising English sirloin beef at 1s. 4d. a pound, and eggs at 1s. a dozen. Nearby at No. 14, W. H. Smith and Son submitted designs for a new shop. The time seemed ripe for the widening of the town's bottleneck. The new town hall had been arcaded on The Borough frontage partly in anticipation of this, and Mr. Wyles at the Bear Lane end had purpose-built expendable display spaces in front of his new shop. But the prospect of a by-pass road in the near future put the brake on further consideration of the scheme.

The Rotary Club voted for a southern by-pass. In June, the Minister of Health also favoured this route. Any objection in favour of a road through the park could be thrashed out in the Appeal Court.

Another pleasant opening ceremony took place, this time in the park, where Sir Edward Perceval's golfing vision had materialised with the minimum of fuss— the undulating landscape lending itself admirably to the purpose. It had been suggested that the first tee should be close to the Ranger's House so that Captain Hewes might sell waiting golfers refreshments. Chairman Alan Tice drove the first ball; then two professionals from local clubs played two rounds—that is, 18 holes. Experienced players were soon to comment that anyone with a low score in the park could play well anywhere.

And yet another opening ceremony—to commemorate the restoration of Farnham Castle. On 1 August, H.R.H. the Duke of Connaught motored over from Bagshot Park to lunch at Waverley Abbey. In the afternoon, His Highness and his hosts proceeded to the castle, where the duke unveiled a plaque in the Great Hall, inscribed:

> This tablet was unveiled on August 1st 1934 by H.R.H. the Duke of Connaught and Strathearn, K.G., K.P. K.T., to commemorate the restoration during the years 1931–1933 of Farnham Castle and of its ancient Chapel in part as a residence of the Bishops of Guildford and in part as a theological college or retreat and conference house, or for other purposes of the Church of England.
>
> The funds required for that purpose were provided by donors within and without the diocese, and were raised through the enterprise of Mrs. Rupert Anderson, O.B.E., of Waverley Abbey, supplemented by a donation from the Ecclesiastical Commissioners.

A Mr. H. Cossins submitted plans for a block development at Heath End of 194 houses; this was approved subject to the provision of a shopping area. In the fulness of time, these new roads were, unimaginatively, named after the four points of the compass.

Mr. W. H. Hadfield arrived in October as Clerk of the Justices in place of Mr. Mason; he had held a similar office at Stockport since 1916 . . . Jack Hobbs batted for Surrey Club and Ground during Farnham Cricket Week in the park . . . Cubitt and West, estate agents, with branches in Dorking, Effingham and London, took over the agency of R. C. S. Evennett, who had died on 24 August. The Hon. C. G. Cubitt was a son of Lord Ashcombe, Lord Lieutenant of Surrey.

In October it was learnt that Dr. Greig's successor as Bishop of Guildford was to be Dr. John Victor Macmillan, O.B.E., Lord Bishop Suffragan of Dover, Canon of Canterbury, and Archdeacon of Maidstone. He would be no stranger to Farnham, for some thirty years previously he had studied at the Bishops' Hostel at 27 West Street and had been a curate under the Rev. Thory Gage Gardiner, lodging at 78 West Street. Aged 57, he was a son of Alexander Macmillan, founder of the publishing firm. In reporting the event, the *Morning Post* caused much indignation locally by describing the town as 'the village of Farnham'.

George Hawkins, butcher at 5 East Street for some forty years, retired and handed over to John Smith of Aldershot . . . A serious fire broke out which gutted the store at the rear of Kimber's greengrocery at 3 Castle Street . . . Film star Eille Norwood and his actress wife moved from Farnham to resume professional work in London.

Sunday Cinemas

★ ★

To the Local Government Electors
  of Farnham.

On Saturday you are asked to vote on the question of the opening of your Cinema on Sunday evenings and we ask you to vote in favour.

Most of the young people, including those in lodgings, domestic service, &c., &c., have no vote, BUT YOU HAVE, and for this reason an appeal is made to you to record your vote IN FAVOUR even though you may not desire personally to visit the Cinema on Sundays.

In view of statements which have been made, it is desirable to emphasize that no member of the Regal Cinema staff can be permitted to work 7 days a week. The Act of Parliament provides very clearly for this and IT CANNOT BE EVADED. The whole of the staff of the Regal Cinema desire Sunday performances. None would be compelled to work on Sundays and those who did would work 5½ days a week instead of 6 as hitherto.

SUNDAY CINEMAS

A Statement

and an Appeal

to Electors

in the Urban District of

FARNHAM

from the Local

Sunday Defence

Committee

Pamphlets produced by the rival parties in the great Sunday cinema debate.

1935

A communication from the English Speaking Union draws attention to
the recent formation of the Namesake Towns Association, whose object is
to promote friendship links between towns in the United Kingdom and
those with similar names in the Dominions. It is pointed out that Farnham
has a namesake in Quebec, Canada. The Council have agreed to join the
Association.

News item: *Farnham Herald,* 5 October 1935

FARNHAM, QUEBEC, 'is a military and industrial centre at an important railway
junction some forty miles from Montreal, first settled in about 1800 by British
stragglers across the 49th parallel, following their defeat in the War of Independence. It was incorporated as a village in 1862, as a town in 1876, and as a city
in 1956. By the mid-1950s, the population had grown to 6,000, of whom 87 per
cent. were French-speaking', according to the gazetteers. Colonel Vandeleur of
'The Sands' sent the *Herald* a cutting from the *Norfolk Observer,* Ontario, which
said that the name adopted by the pioneers in 1799 came from a town in Surrey,
England, where a certain Mgr. de Saint-Valliern had once spent two years in
captivity. Recently published information in the Farnham and District Museum
Society's *Newsletter* relates that a 'de Sainte-Vallier, Bishop of Quebec' was
captured by the British aboard *La Seine* in 1704 and incarcerated in the Market
House, Farnham, until ransomed by the French in 1713. It is tempting to connect
the two incidents, but, as the bishop, who was born in Quebec in 1653, would
presumably have died *c.* 1725, he would not have been around when the Canadian
township received its name in 1800.

Some years ago, a determined effort was made by the author to discover who
it was that passed on the name of his home town in Surrey to the settlement in
Canada. Monsieur J. B. Luneau, Secretary-Treasurer of Farnham, Quebec, was
unable to be of assistance. 'I would like to furnish you more informations,
characteristics etc., but I am lacking time right now', he wrote. He did send a
guidebook of the place; it looked rather nice. Later on, a further attempt was
made. The *Montreal Star* confirmed that the township was named after
Farnham in Surrey. The McLennan Reference Library of McGill University said
they were working on it. The Public Archives of Canada in Ottawa undertook
a search of indices and logical sources. McGill did send a copy of relevant

extracts from an M.A. thesis submitted by Bruce Dudley Walker in 1974 on *The County of Missisquoi in the Eastern Townships of the Province of Quebec.* This revealed that the eastern half of the township of Farnham was granted to Samuel Gale and his 22 associates in October 1798. Grants were not made in the western half until 1805, though a few adventurers had settled in the area in the late 1790s without title. One of these was Joseph Higgins, who later played a prominent role in the early development of the town. Others included Isaac Gibbs and Artemus Welsh. By 1809, the west part was almost entirely owned by George Allsopp, who obtained the grant for service to the British government. Other colonists had followed Higgins—a William Cook in 1817, John and James McCorkill in 1822, John Bowker, who built the first sawmill, in 1827, and, also in 1827, John Frier Whitfield, who built the first store. The French-Canadians began to infiltrate in growing numbers in the 1820s, despite discouragement from the British.

If the name 'Farnham' had been established before settlers came in force, then the field is narrowed, say, to Samuel Gale, Joseph Higgins, Isaac Gibbs and Artemus Welsh. Higgins had been a private variously in the 60th Regiment, raised in North America in 1756, the 6th and the 41st. Gale, who arrived in 1798—a Samuel Gale was a King's Bench judge from 1834 to 1848—is a more likely choice. There were Gales in Farnham, Surrey; three of them were married in the parish church between 1768 and 1789.

In the scatter of correspondence which took place in 1935 on the letters page of the *Farnham Herald,* letters were published from a Bert Gillett of Crystal City, Manitoba, regarding a Church of England missionary named John West of Farnham, Surrey, who had sailed to Canada in 1820 as a chaplain in the Hudson Bay Company. The *Winnipeg Free Press* recalled that West's work was mainly with the settlers brought to Canada by Lord Selkirk, on the banks of the Red River, north of the present city of Winnipeg. His mission had proved something of a failure since, as an Anglican clergyman, he was of little use to Selkirk's Gaelic-speaking Church of Scotland settlers. Dr. Archibald Lang Fleming mentioned that John West had travelled north and fallen in with the English explorer, John Franklin, who had inspired him to take the gospel to the Eskimo tribes. This John West was almost certainly the Rev. John West (1778–1845), son of William West, hop-planter of 70 Castle Street. The timing could be right, but there is no evidence that West visited the Quebec Province, some 1,200 miles east of his known territory.

*   *   *   *   *

The long unsolved problem of Farnham's by-pass road became ever more pressing. Increasingly, motorists were passing through the town at excessive speeds. Committed to a northern road, the Council had earmarked a broad strip of privately-owned land, through the fields west of the park on the north-west of the town. However, Miss C. M. Hazell, the owner, now submitted an outline application for the development of the whole of this area. As the matter was currently *sub judice,* the Council turned it down. Miss H. promptly appealed. A suggestion that the strip might be left clear for the road fell on deaf ears. They were not protected by an insertion of a northern by-pass clause in their Town Planning Scheme, for there was none. They briefed an expert to represent them at the appeal enquiry, and the Minister was persuaded to adjourn the application *sine die,* pending the outcome of the road controversy.

The rebuilding of 125 East Street at the bottom of Bear Lane—once the *Queen Street Tavern*—resulted in a most attractive shop for A. W. Chennells, the men's outfitters. Unfortunately, it was swept away for Woolmead.

Frank Moulding, who ran a sports equipment business at 29 The Borough, exploited Farnham's love affair with cricket by opening, on 5 January, the Farnham School of Cricket in a building behind East Street in St Cross. Before an assemblage of top-ranking enthusiasts, the school was declared in play by H. D. G. Leveson-Gower, president of the Surrey County Cricket Club, and an exhibition was given by A. Sandham and A. Gover, Surrey's opening batsman and fast bowler.

An appeal was launched for the repair of the stonework of the parish church tower. They had £100 in hand and needed £500 more. By the end of the year, the fund was struggling through the £700s; it seemed a pity to stop it.

The final phase of the town hall building, the replica of the Bailiff's Hall— Falkner's signature—was finished and ready for occupation. Stuart Lawrence leased it as an exclusive hairdressing establishment; he had learnt his trade at Lionel Smith's.

The Soames' occupation of Moor Park House was over. Major Mervyn Soames had sold the 200-acre estate, except for 'Stella's Cottage', to Dick Martin, a partner in the firm of Quinette Crushes, Ltd., who made soft drinks in Castle Street. The object was development, as befell most great estates, however long and enchanting their history. But Moor Park was not doomed to the jerry-builder, for Martin was a man of understanding and restraint. He had developed land at 'The Sands' and at Pilcot Village, Dogmersfield. Only houses of a superior type and density would be built, and the amenities of Moor Park would be safeguarded. The surplus contents of the house were auctioned by John D. Wood and Co. on 11/12 March.

In the past, Farnham Park had always been grazed by a herd of deer, but for economic reasons this had been discontinued. The Council, full of ambition to restore the gracious amenities of the park were tempted to reintroduce these fine animals—say, 18 or 20 for a start. But deer were expensive to keep, and the idea was reluctantly abandoned. Another plan for an aviary in Gostrey Meadow also came to naught.

Madam Alice Esty, wife of the councillor when they lived in 'The Jungle', Abbey Street, died on 1 February. Born in Boston, U.S.A., she had gained a considerable reputation as a singer and was at one time with the Carl Rosa Opera Company.

Major Wade, the archaeologist, dug up the remains of a giant mammoth during sewer laying operations near the isolation hospital in Weydon Lane. The pieces consisted of a tusk, a large shoulder bone, and a molar nearly two feet long.

A 30 m.p.h. limit for traffic was imposed within the area lit by street-lamps, with effect from 18 March. Driving tests under the Road Traffic Act 1934 also came into force for learner drivers with licences dated after 1 April 1934. White lines painted on each side of the roadway were proposed for a distance of 30 feet from The Borough to indicate 'No Parking'. The existing unilateral parking in certain side-streets was no longer adequate, and the prospect of spending large sums of money on central car parks loomed nearer. The motor car had taken over the town; its appetite for space was insatiable, and as more was given to it, so its need increased.

Two new faces appeared in the Council Chamber as a result of the election on 1 April: those belonged to Charles Ernest Clark of 'Kevington', High Park Road, and G. E. Aldridge, Watneys' manager, who had once been a councillor from 1908 to 1920.

The County Council's flood prevention works on the River Wey reached upstream to Farnham in March. The engineer in charge, Mr. G. T. Griffiths, brought woeful news. A 250-yard stretch of the river bed between Hatch Mill and Longbridge would be deepened and widened and the kinks straightened out; the weir in Gostrey Meadow would have to go, and—Heaven forbid!—the lovely willows which lined the river bank must be felled. If you don't want floods in Farnham to continue, then the proposed works will have to be carried out, was County's reply to Farnham's protest. Under the heading 'Lament for Weeping Willows', the *Herald* of 13 April reported that so far some 13 willows had been removed, revealing a dreadfully depressing view of the backs of houses in Abbey Street. But Mr. Griffiths was humane; he left a dummy weir in the river in Gostrey.

In February, Admiral Molteno, who now lived at 'The Chestnuts', in East Street, decided to move. Living in the shadow of a mighty super-cinema must have been overpowering. This time, the Council's opportunity to acquire this property could not be ignored. The house would lend itself to all manners of useful purposes—a library, perhaps, or a museum—whilst the long garden at the back could be merged into Brightwells Garden—or even as a site for new Council offices. Cubitt and West were asking £2,550; the Council got it for £2,500, with completion on 25 April. In the opinion of many, it is questionable whether the best civic use has since been made of this excellent site. The house, which would have made an ideal library or museum right in the town centre became instead the offices of the local employment exchange. Apart from a narrow opening, a brick wall continued to sever 'The Chestnuts' and Brightwells gardens. A grass tennis court was not a success. It proved a useful site for a Health Centre; on the other hand, a large part of the garden was wasted for a pair of service houses for Council employees.

A storm broke out in April when it was learnt that the *Regal* cinema would in future run two performances on Sunday evenings, with doors opening at 5.30 p.m. instead of 7.45 p.m. as originally agreed. In support of this earlier opening, they flourished an Order approved by the House of Commons on 1 March and a Resolution of the House of Lords dated 5 March. The County Council regulations on Sunday opening also allowed for performances between 5.30 and 11 p.m. The Cinema Company agreed that their original intention had been for one showing only, as in their other cinemas in the Aldershot area, but this concession had been made on the assumption that there would be no organised opposition from the local churches. As it was, the churches had blown the whole thing up to the extent of having a public referendum, and the Company felt so strongly about it, that they had decided to take full advantage of the position. Headlines like 'Company's Breach of Good Faith' and 'Council's Strong Protest' appeared in the *Herald*. The paper accused the Company of money-grabbing, but had the decency to retract this in a following issue, together with the comment that anyone who objected to Sunday performances was himself under no compulsion to go to the pictures.

They made big improvements to Crondall Lane costing £1,329, and rounded off the corner by the Temple Lounge . . . Mr. Borelli recommended taking photographic records of any local buildings of historic interest due for demolition or alteration . . . Farnham Cricket Club won £72 towards the £80 they needed for replacing the thatched roof of the pavilion in the park with pantiles . . . The Rev. Arthur Edge, brother of the late Rev. W. H. F. Edge of Tilford, handed over his brother's collection of Neolithic flints, all found within a mile of Tilford church . . . Counsel's opinion regarding the by-pass road question was that the Ministries of Transport and Health should be asked to receive deputations from the urban and county councils.

Alf Thorp, the Rating Officer, was now sixty-nine. He had remained in office in order to improve his pension entitlement, but now, after 38 years in service, he was put out to grass with effect from 30 June 1935. His senior assistant, Frederic Aubrey Holloway was a product of Farnham Grammar School, that is to say in the old boy network. Broadly, there were four groups in Farnham— the 'pukka sahibs' in the big houses; the 'old boy network'; the impoverished natives; and the influx of strangers from outer space who never really made it. Traditionally, the plum jobs went to the old boy network. In the mid-30s, the younger generation, who had followed their fathers through the Grammar School, were grooming themselves to take over, and, in the meantime, pack-hunting in second-hand cars the good pubs and bad women. It accomplished little to remind them that one's own Grammar School had doubtless beaten theirs on the cricket field. Holloway got the job. He was to die before his time as Chief Valuation Officer for Sevenoaks.

R. T. Cosgrove was imported from Brighton as Baths Superintendent. He was a very fine swimmer . . . J. H. Chitty died on 2 May. He had lived in the town for 54 years, first as a carpenter at Goddards, then as a newsagent and off-licence keeper at 62 East Street. He had been Chief Officer of the fire brigade until 1930 and his funeral was led by the two fire engines, 'Princess Mary' and 'Margaret Joan'.

The 6 May was the King's Silver Jubilee Day. A telegram to Buckingham Palace read:

> The inhabitants of the ancient town of Farnham in Surrey pray leave to approach Your Majesty and offer to you and the Queen their heartfelt congratulations upon the twenty-fifth anniversary of Your Majesty's accession to the Throne.
>
> They beg also to send you their sincere thanks for the inspiring example you have so consistently set of an unswerving pursuit of duty and an unfaltering love of our dear land and Empire.
>
> To your person and family they proffer their loyal devotion. May God bless and keep Your Majesty, our Queen, and all your family.
>
> Alan P. Tice, Chairman, Farnham Urban District Council

There was bunting in the streets; the bands played and the church bells rang out. A thanksgiving service was held in Gostrey Meadow, followed by a service from St Paul's Cathedral relayed over the wireless by Hales. English oak trees were planted in the park and elsewhere, and the old folk were treated to dinner in the community halls. There was a Jubilee Cricket Week, and a fair and entertainments for the children, with a firework display by the scouts. Amateur movie-camera enthusiasts made a film of the week's celebrations that was screened in the old picture palace on 10 June. Mr. Philipson-Stow asked whether there was any truth in the rumour that, because of his many appearances in the film, Chairman Alan Tice had been offered a contract from Hollywood.

The *Herald* held its own *post mortem* on the past 25 years. In 1910 the population had been about 7,300; now it was close to 20,000. The town had been mostly confined between the station, the *Albion* hotel, Mount Pleasant, and the castle; it had grown from a small country market town into the shopping and civic centre of a large residential district. In 1910 a local firm, the Pilgrim Motor Company, had produced the Pilgrim car, skid-proof because of a front-wheel drive. The first plane to land in Farnham, on 13 May, 1913, was a Bleriot two-seater biplane, piloted by Major Higgins, a native of Farnham. He had been on his way to Farnborough, but was forced down by a broken petrol pipe. Just missing Achille Serre's shop in South Street, he had broken various telephone wires before landing in meadows adjoining Darvills Lane.

George Murrell of 'Stella', Crondall Lane, died on 5 June. He had been born in Farnham in 1849. After a few years in the office of Hollest, Mason and Nash, he had been appointed Relieving Officer and Registrar of Births and Deaths for

Frensham, then from 1881 to 1914 in the same capacity for Farnham. He was a councillor from 1914 to 1926, and in the Chair 1921/2.

On 18 June, the centenary of his death, a wreath was laid on the tomb of William Cobbett in the parish churchyard. It bore a green and yellow ribbon—the green representing the hop vine, and yellow the golden hops, the growing of which was once Farnham's staple industry. At his death *The Times* commented 'take this self taught peasant for all in all, he was, in some respects, a more extraordinary Englishman than any other of his time'. Cobbett left clear instructions for his funeral. A local plumber, Mr. Edwards, was to make the leaden coffin and Mr. Johnson was to conduct the funeral. The tomb would be provided by Cobbett's son, James, a barrister, who gave the work to Mr. Milne, an artist of Judd Street. The monument was to be in the style of Saxon-Gothic, the first of its kind in England. Seventy-eight-year-old Mrs. Trusler of 31 Church Lane had an old panelled dower chest about four feet long, on the front of which was a nail-studded signature G 1734 C—assumed to be that of George Cobbett, grandfather of William, who had died in 1760. Mrs. Trusler told a *Herald* reporter that, over a century ago, an illegitimate child was born in Farnham, of which the father was said to be a Cobbett, probably one of William's brothers. The infant was handed to a Mrs. Budd, the grandmother of her husband, John Trusler. The child grew up in the name of Budd, and was known in later life as 'Uncle Billy Budd'. The chest contained the baby's clothes; it had a panelled front and two drawers at the bottom.

During the summer, a series of talks took place between the Council and Eggar and Co., who were acting for Jac Martans, Limited, the name of Dick Martin's development company proposing to build in Moor Park. One hundred and seventy acres of parkland were planned at a density of two acres to each house, and the 50-ft. wide roads, together with access roads presented the Council with a good deal of extra mileage to maintain. The opportunity was taken to ensure the preservation of the sites of St Mary's Well (Mother Ludlam's Cave) and Foote's Cave, by specifically listing them in the Council's town planning scheme.

Woolworths extended their premises in July by taking in 3 The Borough; this had been Frank Shaw's drapery. There was another plan to convert the old kiln at the rear; this became the Old Kiln Studio. Other applications included alterations for Chilcott, Ltd., at 8 West Street, and the rebuilding of the *Spotted Cow* public house in the Bourne.

A somewhat blood-chilling communication arrived at the end of July from the Home Office, giving preliminary notice of the need for local authorities to formulate measures for the safeguarding of civilians against the effects of air attacks by an enemy. Later in the summer, a conference of Surrey district councils was convened to agree on an outline scheme for Air Raid Precautions. This new dimension made sluggish progress. There were more important things to think about, anyway. That summer, the Council decided in principle to build themselves new offices, to the design of the winner in an open competition, in accordance with the rules of the Royal Institute of British Architects. The R.I.B.A. stipulated that the competition should be conducted their way, under their conditions; they would appoint an assessor and stage-manage the whole thing. Events moved quickly—a Mr. E. Vincent Harris, O.B.E., F.R.I.B.A., of 29 St James Square, London, consented to act as assessor, and the competition was advertised. Three awards were offered: first prize, £150; second, £100; and third, £50.

The new Trimmers Hospital in Menin Way was opened on 31 July by H.R.H. Lady Patricia Ramsay, daughter of the Duke of Connaught. Mr. Margary's design was greatly admired, though some wondered why the roof was flat. The photograph of George Trimmer, who had bequeathed £15,000 in 1863 for the building of the cottage hospital in East Street, had been re-hung in the new building. Subsequent legacies from the Trimmer family had totalled £8,100. Miss Catherine Elizabeth Price had left £6,750 to the fund. The total cost of the new hospital was £16,500. The Isolation Hospital at Weydon now decided on enlargements costing £9,290 and called for the Council's share of this. The Hale Road Institution, too, was in process of additions.

Life that summer was spiced with conjectures about 'The Man with the Glaring Eyes', who had made several attacks on women in the district. Then a man arrested for a murder was identified by a victim in Aldershot on 26 August as the person who had attacked her: he was Arthur Charles Mortimer. He was sentenced to be hanged, but was reprieved on mental grounds.

Aldershot Military got a severe reprimand when their tanks returning from manoeuvres thundered through Farnham at about 30 miles an hour, shaking the buildings as they passed . . . County were pressed for the adoption of a bye-law prohibiting the cycling on footpaths. Legend had it that one Farnham councillor, whilst speaking out against this objectionable practice, had a summons in his pocket for the very same offence in Great Austins.

All this time, W. H. Smiths had been waiting to move from their shop in South Street to their new premises in The Borough. But, all this time, the County Council had been wondering whether or not to widen The Borough. Now Dewhursts, the butchers, submitted plans for a new shop-front at 16 The Borough. In 1934, Boots had moved from 14 The Borough to Sturts' rebuilt premises at 41/42, and had assigned their lease on No. 14 to Smiths, who negotiated with Lintern and Peters of No. 13 for a mutual exchange of tenancies. Smiths thereupon submitted an application for the rebuilding of No. 13. At a subsequent juncture, Smiths' deal with Lintern and Peters had fallen through. Smiths thereupon submitted an application for the rebuilding of No. 14. County had got as far as acquiring a strip of land at the rear of the shops along this side of the street with a view to compensating tenants for frontages taken for widening the street. Now the local council were amazed to find that County had lost interest in the whole thing because the coming by-pass road would ease traffic in the bottleneck. From now on, anything to do with The Borough was the locals' responsibility.

They all sat round a table—Smiths, Dewhursts, the local and County councils, the Ministries of Health and Transport, and the Metropolitan Real and General Property Trust, Ltd. (the owners of the block). To widen the street might cost some £13,000 alone in compensations for disturbance of business; this was the deciding factor in cancelling the whole project. But Smiths did build their new shop with the front section open to the pavement for quick sales to passersby.

At the General Election on 14 November, Sir Arthur Samuel romped home in the Farnham constituency, as everyone had expected. Councillor Lawson was congratulated by his colleagues on having won the East Leicestershire Division.

A fund was opened to pay for a memorial to George Sturt . . . The Railway Company received the go-ahead for the electrification of further sections of their line, including the Woking-Alton stretch . . . 'Elmer House', 41 West Street, was converted into a hall for the First Church of Christ, Scientist . . . Father Robo's learned work, *Medieval Farnham,* was published at 10s. 6d. a copy . . . Courages were given permission to build a row of shops and flats in South Street, adjoining the *Royal Deer.*

They decided on yet another go at borough status. The petition of 1919 had failed because it had lacked the support of the County Council; population had then been 13,000. The Royal Commission on local government had set a minimum of 20,000; Farnham's was now up to 19,850, but in very special circumstances a town slightly below 20,000 stood a chance.

A few minutes after 6 a.m. on 30 December, the fire brigade was called to E. D. Abbott's motor works at Wrecclesham. The body-building workshops were completely destroyed, together with nearly forty cars, including two Rolls Royces, a Daimler, and a staff-owned Vauxhall worth £700, which had caused a sensation at the Motor Show. The damage was put at between £18,000 and £20,000. Abbotts were currently engaged on big contracts for bodyworks on Talbot and Fraser-Nash cars, and several of these, too, were burnt out.

These premises had been built by 'Sailor' Knight of St John's Road. They had been Warren's Coach-building Works before passing to Page and Hunt. Abbotts had been there five years, during which time they had constructed the 'Flying Flea', which had been hailed by aeronautical experts as a landmark in light aircraft construction.

1936

In affectionate memory of our Well-Beloved Sovereign King George V, and with respectful homage from the people of Farnham, Surrey. 28 January 1936.

Inscription on silver plate sent with wreath to Windsor Castle

THE *REGAL* CINEMA was a very pleasant place in which to while away a couple of hours or so. The seats still retained the feel and smell of newness; the semi-darkness and ankle-touching nearness of one's loved one combined to play upon the senses. One could even—though this was not obligatory—focus one eye on the screen in front and watch the unfolding of some mighty epic of strong human drama. On the screen, Claude Rains, in the role of Maximus, was being indoctrinated by Jane Baxter, who played the part of a medium, into developing strange prophetic powers which would enable him to prophesy the future with uncanny accuracy, whilst his wife, played by Fay Wray, stood by to see that his immediate prognostication would not materialise. The title of the film was 'The Clairvoyant'; the time—Monday evening, 20 January 1936. At Sandringham, in Norfolk, King George lay dying. Stanley Perkins, the *Regal's* manager, invited patrons to remain in their seats after the programme if they wished in order to listen to the bulletins which were being broadcast every quarter of an hour. Those who stayed shared an unforgettable experience. A solemn hush, like that in a church, filled the theatre as the news items were relayed. Then, five minutes before midnight, the voice announced the end. Silently, the people made their way to the exits.

George V had been a good king. The extravagant terms of endearment conventionally lavished upon a monarch seemed in his case to come straight from the heart. Like Mr. Perkins, the clergy opened their doors. At the Church House, people sang 'O God of Bethel' and heard the Council Chairman move, 'that the inhabitants of the Town and District of Farnham do place on record their heartfelt sorrow at the death of His Most Gracious Majesty King George V; also their profound grief at the sad loss which has befallen the Nation and Empire, and do respectfully offer to His Majesty King Edward, Her Majesty Queen Mary, and the members of the Royal Family their sincere sympathy and assure them of their loyal devotion to His Majesty King Edward VIII and the Royal House'.

* * * * *

189

Air Marshal Sir John Higgins was appointed Chairman of British Marine Aircraft, Limited . . . Dr. H. F. Ealand retired, and into his partnership came Dr. Peverley and Dr. P. Bardsley . . . Father Robo's *Medieval Farnham* was selling well; it had excellent reviews in the *Times Literary Supplement,* the *Church Times,* from Hilaire Belloc in *The Universe,* and Professor Saltmarsh of Cambridge in the *Economic History,* Vol. 111. A second edition was planned by Mr. Langham.

The recessed frontage of 'The Chestnuts', East Street, left a vacuum, a feature of abhorrence to the Council. It would do fine for a bus shelter, for buses would persist in stopping all along the street to put customers down at their front doors. But before the Council could act, a Mr. C. D. Strologo of Shamley Green came forward with an offer to present a shelter to Farnham as his private memorial to the King's Jubilee.

The Farnham Park Golf Club was in the red to the tune of £73 8s. 11d. This was owing to a wet season; the club was still very popular, with 77 members and an estimated 5,700 non-member users. The Council agreed to underwrite losses up to £75 for the next two years; they might even take the club over.

Charles Edward Nicholas Charrington died on 7 January. He had lived at 'Frensham Hill' (later 'Frensham Heights'), which he had bought in 1901 from Mrs. Taylor and completely rebuilt into one of the largest properties in the district. In his garden, he maintained a sportsground for the villagers, and he had his own private cricket team. And it all came from beer.

Ian Forbes-Robertson died, too, on 11 January at his little house in Bourne Grove, Lower Bourne. He was 78; he had come to The Bourne in 1904 after a long and successful stage career in Britain and America. He was a brother of the even more successful Sir Johnston Forbes-Robertson, and his daughter, Dorothy, was also on the stage.

Mr. Vincent Harris came down on 10 January to view the locus of the new Council offices. He advised that the chosen site in Brightwells would require improved road access from East and South Streets. He also suggested having a public hall. The offices would be three storeys high, with a basement.

The committee responsible for car parks—or lack thereof—did not relax their quest for suitable sites. There was plenty of unproductive backland behind the shops in the town, but the cost of acquisition and conversion was prohibitive. They fancied a site in The Hart, but Kinghams' new warehouses scotched that, and they looked at possible areas behind the west face of Downing Street. And so, in increasing numbers, motor cars continued to block Castle Street.

The allotment ground at the corner of Bear Lane and High Park Road came on the market; there was a restrictive covenant which prohibited the building of houses, but nothing to exclude a car park. The asking price was £200; the Council offered £150, but came up to £170, then dropped the idea. Later in November, County thought they might use this site, together with land on the other side of Bear Lane, for an art school. In due course, the corner site became the green of the Farnham Bowling Club, perhaps more fitting neighbours than art students.

The County Highways and Bridges Committee had their arms twisted over the delay in making up Waverley Lane. This road was by now almost fully developed as well as the side roads leading off, but was still served by the narrow country lane without footpaths which had formerly coped with the minimal traffic to Godalming. County obliged—some 817 yards from the station to Old Compton Lane were given the works; it cost £10,155, split between the County Council, £5,594, and the Ministry of Transport, £4,561. The rats moved out of the hedgerows and took refuge beneath the sheds in people's gardens.

The Hospital Trustees thanked the Council for nominating them as a worthy cause to receive the rake-off from the *Regal* cinema's Sunday takings. Up to 31 December 1935, they had received £147 18s. 4d. in this way. Other recipients were the St John Ambulance Brigade and the Curative Post.

Mr. F. A. Morgan—'Moggie' to generations of Grammar School scholars—was Chairman of the Library Committee. He sought an increase in the number of books and an extension of the opening hours, which were two hours one evening a week. The Council were surprised—the library already cost a farthing rate— and wanted to see what would happen when the new offices were built. Another sub-committee was formed to try and get a museum started. There was no shortage of dedicated antiquarians in Farnham—men like Charles Borelli, W. F. Rankine, Major Wade, and William Stroud could always be relied upon to give their time for nothing.

Alf Gover, the Surrey bowler who had performed at the opening of Frank Moulding's cricket school, was taken on as professional. It was recalled that Gover had been twelfth man for England in the 1934 Test, and, during the past three seasons, had taken over 100 wickets for Surrey, including four for four balls against Worcestershire.

On 10 February, the Chairman, Councillor Figg, the Clerk and Town Planning Officer were interviewed by J. Rowland Hill of the Ministry of Transport in connection with the route of the proposed by-pass road. This gentleman stated that, earlier, his thoughts in the matter had been influenced to a large extent by the need for wholesale demolition, and the expense thereof, in the case of a road to the south of the town centre. But this no longer applied, for the southern route had been modified so as to skirt Red Lion Lane, Bridge Square, and Abbey Street. Including a feed-in from Firgrove Hill, the road would only cost about £116,500. If the northern route was adopted, a link road would be needed between the *Albion* hotel and Firgrove Hill, and the job would work out at about £135,000. The southern route was shorter anyway, and had lower gradients. The visitors put their case in vain. A southern road would not by-pass the town; it would intersect it in a dangerous and incommodious manner; it would cut across an existing busy thoroughfare used by local people between the main shopping area and expanding residential localities in the south; also the road would come within 150 yards of the railway level-crossing gates, causing traffic chaos down Station Hill, if not on the by-pass itself. Furthermore, a danger spot would be created at Hickleys Corner. But Mr. Rowland Hill anticipated no such difficulties. There would be a traffic circus at Hickleys, and, as for the level-crossing, this could be eliminated with the railway's co-operation.

The triumphant County Council wrote two days later requesting them to record the southern route in their town planning scheme, and adding that instructions had been given for the work to be commenced towards the end of 1936. The local Council were careful to write in their Minute book that, in their opinion, the northern route would have been the wiser course. This observation, and the care with which they communicated the Ministry's ruling to the people of Farnham, suggests that, by some prescience, they foresaw the fatalities that would follow at Hickleys Corner, and wished to absolve themselves from any blame for them. The *Herald* commented that a road through the park would have proved an asset—look at Windsor Park, for instance. Apart from cricket and golf, Farnham Park had disappointingly failed to attract the public in any numbers; it needed something like a road through it to open the place up.

Madam Emily Chilcott opened her new gown shop at 8 West Street. The non-reflecting glass in the windows was a novelty in the town and attracted much interest . . . Some 457 swimmers petitioned for the heating of the small bath so that it might be used during the winter, but this would cost £1,675 . . . Jac Martans, Ltd., were granted permission to turn Moor Park House into a residential club, to be called Swift's Club . . . On Rowland Hill's advice, they sounded out the railway company about doing away with the level-crossing, but without much hope.

Aldershot still entertained hopes of having an aerodrome at Badshot Lea . . . there was talk of having electric lighting in council houses, but only 58 per cent. of the tenants were in favour . . . 62 more houses were planned at Wrecclesham . . . a site for a public mortuary was found in Victoria Road at the back of the *Hop Bag* . . . Major Wade agreed to attend the government's anti-gas school so that he would be qualified to instruct A.R.P. recruits.

They revived the idea of a public gallery on the flanking wall of the swimming bath for spectators at the tennis tournaments. The Surveyor suggested removing the top tier of men's dressing boxes and forming a wide platform with rows of seats facing both ways. Costing about £500, this would hold about 300 onlookers, and a small charge might be made. Nothing came of it—perhaps it might have been disappointing to the tennis stars to see their fans twisting in their seats to watch the bathing beauties instead.

In March, approval was given to plans for a new Girls' Grammar School in Menin Way. Work on the new cathedral at Guildford was about to start; some £42,000 had already been contributed. The first section would take about three years to complete, at a cost of £94,000. The laying of the foundation stone by the Archbishop of Canterbury was fixed in advance.

Mr. A. L. Addy, who was in the auctioneers' business of his uncle, Mr. S. H. German, was married on 1 April to Miss Doris May Ayling, daughter of Mr. William Ayling of 120 East Street. The *Herald,* in reporting the event, gave more emphasis to the bridegroom's prowess on the cricket field. He excelled, the paper said, as a bowler, and, in 1934, he had had the distinction of taking the wicket of Jack Hobbs. The Farnham Cricket Club presented Mr. Addy with a silver inkstand—though this was because of his wedding.

Two new faces appeared in the Chamber at the election on 6 April. These belonged to Frederick Guy Stevens, solicitor of 62 Castle Street, and Albert James Cherryman of Park Farm, Badshot Lane, who ousted James Chuter in the Hale Ward. Councillor Edwin Winter replaced Alan Tice as Chairman, with Mr. Figg as Vice-Chairman.

It soon became abundantly clear why Mr. F. G. Stevens had contested a seat on the council. It was not necessary actually to live in Castle Street to feel aggrieved about the motor cars which deface the beauty of the street, for Castle Street is a legacy that is shared by all the townspeople. But those who live elsewhere can go home and take it out on the cat. Castle Street residents cannot; their senses are constantly offended by lines of leering radiators.

Mr. Stevens planned his attack with legal precision. He tabled a motion for the setting up of a special committee of not less than three or more than four councillors to enquire into and report within six weeks on the following matters:

(a) the number of motor vehicles for which it desirable that new parking accommodation should be provided within a convenient distance of the shops;

(b) the area of open space necessary to provide a car park or parks to accommodate such a number;

(c) any site or sites suitable as parks;

(d) approximate market value:

(e) approximate cost of preparing site or sites, including access road or roads;

(f) estimated cost of maintenance;

(g) charge or charges for use of park or parks by occasional or habitual users and estimated revenue:

(h) whether acquisition of site or sites would be by negotiation or the exercise of statutory powers;

(i) what measures are reasonable or necessary to prohibit, restrict or regulate the parking of motor vehicles in any, and which, of the streets of the town;

(j) recommendations for the parking of omnibuses of the Aldershot and District Traction Company, or other public motor omnibus company licensed to ply in the town.

Such committee should possess powers to co-opt representatives of the police and Chamber of Commerce, limited to one person from each body.

For years the councillors had been reconnoitering in a desultory fashion the likely sites enclosed by rows of shops—the back gardens of the shopkeepers in the old days when they had lived on the premises. Now at last they had a leader. In July they came up with answers to at least some of Mr. Stevens' questions. According to current requirements, space for about 100 cars would be needed, but the way cars were increasing perhaps it would be better to allow for, say, 250 vehicles. They favoured a central site at the western end of Victoria Road, flanked by the rear of properties in Downing Street and The Borough. Certain existing occupations would be disturbed, namely that of Mr. J. Freeland of the Victoria Transport Co., the Farnham Tennis Club's court, owned by Mr. Borelli, and part of the *Bush* hotel kitchen garden. Access from Downing Street would entail the demolition of one property; there would also be footpath access from The Borough.

It was an ambitious scheme, costing some £9,800 for compensations, £3,343 for constructional works, £350, say, for legal expenses—a total of £13,493. There would be a yearly outgoing of about £600 for loan charges, plus £400 for maintenance. On the credit side, reasonable parking fees could be fixed, and there would be the rent from Merton House. The committee also expressed interest in sites in the South Street market and The Hart.

It was easy to dub the Council, in the words of the Rev. Neville Lovett, as 'a miserable supine body of men'. But they stood to saddle the ratepayers with a debt of 13½ thousand pounds for the sake of car owners, a great many of whom were from outside Farnham. The motion was defeated by six votes to 12 (Councillor Stevens abstaining). Meanwhile, the cars continued to desecrate Castle Street.

There were 35 applications from charitable associations to hold flag-days in Farnham in 1936. The Council had set a limit of 10, but County granted them all . . . a united service was held on Good Friday in the *Regal* cinema, with the showing of the film 'The Holy Land'; perhaps a sign that all was forgiven for opening on Sundays . . . news was received that the Rev. Neville Lovett, Bishop of Portsmouth was to be enthroned on 16 May as Bishop of Salisbury in place of Dr. St Clair Donaldson . . . Major and Mrs. Anderson of Waverley were passengers in the Paris–Rome express train which was derailed in France in May, but, fortunately, they suffered little injury.

June's plans contained one for the rebuilding by James Chuter of the old *Palace* cinema, East Street. This was opened on 19 December with a film featuring Jack Buchanan called 'This'll Make You Whistle'. Now re-named the *County* cinema, it was a nicely-appointed one-storeyed theatre, and it provided a choice of programme. Many years later, it was pulled down to provide spaces for parking cars.

By the end of June, some 35 architects had exhibited an interest in the competition for the new Council offices. The building would contain—

Council Chamber	1,200 to 1,300 square feet
Chairman's private room	288 square feet
Members' room	288 square feet
Lady members' room	288 square feet

Committee rooms (two)	720 square feet
Clerk's department	1,440 square feet (total)
Accounts department	2,016 square feet
Engineer and Surveyor	2,160 square feet
Medical Officer and Sanitary department	1,152 square feet
General enquiry office, etc.	144 square feet
Caretaker's quarters	650 square feet

Four-person capacity lift.

In due course, 79 drawings were submitted. Mr. Vincent Harris hired a room at the Council's expense at the Royal Institute of British Architects, and later they were also on display at 'The Chestnuts', Farnham. The winning design was judged to be that of Cordingley and McIntyre of The College, Dublin, who were awarded the first prize of £250. The second and third prizes both went to Lionel U. Grace of 3/4 Wardrobe Place, Doctors Commons, London. The chosen design was for a building of imposing elevation, a fitting companion to the nearby *Regal* cinema—though Councillor Aldridge remarked that it looked more like a factory building. But whereas the film fans accepted with nothing but enthusiasm their entitlement to a magnificent palace, the rate-payers tended to question the right of the Council to squander £23,000 upwards on new offices. At a special meeting on 19 December, one councillor asked the unlooked-for question—had, in fact, a formal resolution been taken at any time by the Council to build new offices? Well, actually, no—it has only been decided in principle. So the motion was put; it was passed. Having already spent good money on the preliminaries, the project might as well go through. It didn't—the war stopped it.

On 25 July, a cricket match between Tilford and the Bourne was broadcast from Tilford. Commander T. Woodroofe, the commentator, remarked from his perch on top of the *Barley Mow* that he would rather be where he was than at the Test Match in Manchester. He had much to tell his listeners regarding local cricket. The legendary William 'Silver Billy' Beldham had oftimes played on this green. Born at Wrecclesham in 1768, he and his brother, George, had learnt their cricket from Henry Hall. George had played for Hambledon, and William for England. 'Silver Billy' had 35 seasons without a break, and at the age of 68 had still been a first-class bat. A picture of him in a tall hat and pleated smock hung above the south door of the long room at Lords.

The County Council were having a tough time trying to conjure up interest in the government's Air-Raid Precautions Scheme. At a conference at Kingston on 21 July, a local management committee was set up in each district. Colonel Underhill was Chairman of the Farnham contingent, with Councillors Aldridge and Winter as members, with representatives from the police, St John Ambulance and other less disinterested bodies. Their meeting place was in 'The Chestnuts'. There was far more interest in the Coronation Festivities, due to be held in May 1937. A sum of £350 was voted towards expenses.

'Berry' Elderfield retired from the fire brigade after 40 years' service. No obvious successor was in sight, and, in the end, Major Wade consented to come back as Chief for a period of three years, with Major R. E. A. Bridge of Shortheath as Second-Officer. Berry had been one of the lads; any lad calling him 'Sir' would probably have got his bottom kicked. Filling the Third-Officer's vacancy proved more difficult. Mr. A. O. Snell, the Council's lamplighter, was not of the retired army officer type; he was, on the other hand, a man of infinite common sense and ability. So he was recommended for a commission in the brigade. This so displeased the rank and file that the appointment was rescinded and Jimmy Edwards, who had been through the ranks of the brigade, was promoted to No. 3 instead. Mr. Snell's love affair with street lamps was conducted in a workshop at the rear of 'Montrose'. As part of the procedure, it was necessary for him to emerge at intervals with an armful of glass panes which had outlived their usefulness and dispose of them by smashing them with force into a particularly resonant wastebin. Whether he enjoyed doing this was conjectural—there was none of the obvious relish associated with Sid Varney of the metal plates. But there was no question about the effects on the nerves of all within earshot.

The *Regal* cinema was certainly back in favour. On 14 August, a distinguished company which included H.R.H. Lady Patricia Ramsay, General Sir Cecil Romer and the Waverley Andersons were invited by Mr. C. J. Donada, the Cinema Company's Chairman, to a gala performance of 'Show Boat'. The entire proceeds were presented to the Red Cross.

Mr. and Mrs. H. G. Hale of 'Hambledon Cottage', returning from a holiday in Gibraltar, got mixed up in a naval battle in the start of the Spanish Civil War. Increasingly, space in the *Herald* was given to comment on the rise of communism, fascism, Nazi-ism, and all the other isms that were set on polluting the world.

W. F. Rankine discovered a Neolithic site at Badshot Farm. At about this time 'Vernon House', West Street, fell empty, and Mr. Borelli asked his usual question about acquisition by the Council for a library and museum. To his surprise, he was given leave to head a committee to study ways and means. As Councillor Winter remarked, Mr. Borelli's face had a look of triumph.

Mrs. Mary Ann Eade and her husband, Charles, of 'Tilford Cottage', Upper Bourne, celebrated their golden wedding on 29 October. Mrs. Eade was a daughter of David Parratt, who had lived all his life at 'Vine Cottage', Boundstone. He had been a charcoal burner, following the trade of his ancestors over many centuries. It was said that one of them, Eli Parratt, was the charcoal burner who had found the body of William Rufus in the New Forest in the year 1100 and conveyed it on his cart to Winchester Cathedral.

On Tuesday, 1 December, at 10.55 a.m., the first electrically-driven train glided quietly into the station. A second train, at 2.42 p.m., was greeted with cheers from a party of Grammar School boys who were on the platform. The station had been given the treatment for the occasion, with the platforms lengthened to 520 feet, the waiting-rooms improved, and electric lighting substituted for gas. 'Its pale gas lighting has given it a cheerless and dreary look for too long', commented the *Herald*.

Another innovation which attracted onlookers was the television set on display at the West End Radio in West Street. The B.B.C. did not guarantee clear reception beyond a range of 25 miles from Alexandra Palace, and Farnham was 40 miles away. Yet the picture was very satisfactory, considering the many causes of interference.

News of the abdication of Edward VIII came by wireless on 10 December. The *Herald* stuck by its loyalty to the King, but had little good to say about Mrs. Simpson. The Coronation Committee, well advanced in their arrangements for celebrating Edward's accession, switched their allegiance to King George VI.

THE FARNHAM PLAYHOUSE

Licensees -	ENGLISH CLASSICAL PLAYERS LTD.
Directors - -	LAURENCE RAY, STEPHANIE RAY
General Manager and Secretary - -	LEWIS FOWLE
TELEPHONE AND TELEGRAMS - - -	FARNHAM 6511

TUESDAY, DECEMBER 5th, AND WEEK

LAURENCE RAY

presents his company in

YOU NEVER
CAN TELL

By BERNARD SHAW

Play produced by NORMAN BUCKLE

CHARACTERS IN ORDER OF THEIR APPEARANCE.

DOLLY	STEPHANIE RAY
VALENTINE	RICHARD WAUGH
PHILIP	RICHIE GATEHOUSE
Mrs. CLANDON	DIANA VERNON
GLORIA	LORNA VENNING
CRAMPTON	WILLIAM AVENELL
WILLIAM	NORMAN BUCKLE
FINCH M'COMAS	JOHN MARTIN
BOHUN	GORDON WHITING

Play produced by NORMAN BUCKLE

NO SMOKING IN THE AUDITORIUM.

LADIES ARE REQUESTED TO REMOVE THEIR HATS.

A playbill from the Farnham Playhouse, 1930s.

1937

And be it so enacted that it shall be lawful for the said Company to carry the said Railway across and on the level of the several public Roads numbered respectively on the plan deposited as aforesaid, 60 and 123 in the Parish of Farnham in the said County of Surrey.

Section 7: London and South Western, Farnham and Alton Branch, Act 1846

MUCH HAS BEEN PRINTED in local archives during the past 130 years concerning the railway level-crossing on Station Hill (No. 60 referred to in the aforesaid Act). Much more has been said which would have proved interesting reading had it not been for the fact that it was mostly unprintable. Many suggestions have been made for the abolition of this abomination—ranging from the sublime: in 1892, an offer by the Railway Company to construct a loop road through the Fairfield, up and over a bridge to Broomleaf, to the ridiculous: that the Farnham, Bentley and Alton stations be moved to the other side of Station Hill, so that trains would not have to cross the road in order to get to them. In 1937, a re-hash of the 1892 project was served up, with this time the whole expense falling on the public. In that year, it was calculated that, of each 18-hour working day, the gates were closed to road-users for a total of five hours.

Admittedly, there have been minor improvements. In the first years, the authorised shut position was across the road, the gates being operated only to allow the occasional horse and cart to pass through. As road traffic increased it was conceded that it was more realistic to keep the gates closed against the railway and open them each time a train was due. Latterly, light-weight gates have been introduced, controlled by some remote and unseen agency, which make life easier for all concerned. Between the wars, the gates were manipulated by a servant of the railway from a signal-box, which then stood on the up-side of the crossing, in full view of the world at large. The crew were hand-picked for their unenviable task of halting, every 10 minutes or so, the human tide in the road below. They were tough and uncompromising, these men; more than one, it was said, had served at Waterloo. From long practice, they were able to detect and interpret at a glance the merest innuendo of a personal nature directed at them by a movement of the lips or the raising of an eyebrow from the throngs milling at the gates.

Over the years a sort of deaf and dumb language had evolved between the superman in the box and the hapless public at his feet, a means of communication by which, once having mastered the grammar and syntax, the parties were able to converse with some fluency, ultimately without recourse to the phrase book. In these exchanges, such niceties as the definite and indefinite articles would be dispensed with and greater emphasis placed on the adjectives. The frequent dialogues tended to follow the same pattern. A train just pulling out of Aldershot or Bentley station would be the signal for the superman to lay aside his paperback and wind the handle which closed the gates. Observing this, pedestrians approaching from north or south would break into a canter. The leaders, with a series of zig-zag shuffles might succeed in getting through to south or north; the less nimble would arrive in time to have the gates slammed in their faces. Catching the speaker's eye, the signalman would press his face against the window of his box and mouth back some suitable remark from his wide vocabulary—like 'rhubarb!', or 'yours, too, mate!' As the trains took several minutes before passing by, there was always ample time for a full and frank exchange of views, to the accompaniment of massed motor horns. The signalmen in their box have been swept away. With their passing, a bit of old Farnham departed, never to return.

*   *   *   *   *

Albert Winslade of the Farnham Division of the St John Ambulance Association—or Brigade, as it was now called—waxed nostalgic about its long local presence. He had every right to be sentimental, for he had belonged to it for 55 years. St John's had first been established in this country in 1877, and, four years later, training classes had begun at Sister Bessie's house in Castle Street, where Bodkins came later, in 1881—thus Farnham could be regarded as a pioneer unit. Bishop Browne and J. W. Burningham had been the first President and Hon. Secretary. Albert Winslade had won his certificate in 1883 and taken over the secretaryship in 1889. Patients were manhandled on stretchers—in one instance, he recollected, all the way from East Street to Lower Bourne. George Trimmer had given an Ashford litter; in 1912, the unit acquired their first motor ambulance.

The by-pass road, said the County, was to be the most up-to-date in the country—and probably the most expensive. It would be 2.7 miles long; the overall width of 120 feet included dual 20-ft. wide carriageways (capable of being widened to 30 feet), two cycle tracks nine feet wide, and two eight-foot footpaths. It would have three roundabouts, would be spanned by three bridges and pass over three bridges.

Mr. T. E. Mack, the postmaster, retired after six years in the Farnham office, and was replaced by Mr. G. H. Clegg from Petersfield . . . Hales were now advertising television sets which, though Farnham was beyond the 25-mile guaranteed reception range, were quite satisfactory if put in open positions and connected to efficient aerial systems . . . motorists were informed that arrangements had been made with Mr. A. V. Lee, who would receive 50 per cent. of the takings, for the use of the market in South Street as a public car park; the fee would be sixpence a day between 10 a.m. and 7 p.m.

Moor Estate (Farnham), Limited, as Dick Martin's company was now called, were given leave to name the estate roads Compton Way, Monks' Well, Temple's Close, Swift's Close, and Cobbett's Ridge. One of the houses at least bore the signature of Harold Falkner; it was that of Mr. Hadfield, solicitor and magistrates' clerk.

Much local interest was taken in the marriage, at Farnham parish church on 9 February, of Miss Viola Molteno, daughter of Vice-Admiral V. B. Molteno of Goldhill, to Peter Hugh Macmillan, son of the Bishop of Guildford and holder of a commission in the 34th Field Battery R.A.

Mr. Borelli was congratulated on being admitted to the Freedom and Livery of the Worshipful Company of Clockmakers. Even more excitement was caused by the news of the elevation to the peerage of Sir Arthur Michael Samuel, Bt., who became Lord Mancroft, for this would necessitate a by-election in the Farnham constituency. Sir Arthur was reported as saying that, after 19 years as its member, he was sad at having to sever connections with 'my beloved Farnham'. Election fever gripped the people during the run-up to polling day on 23 March. The Labour party, whose eve of poll preachings were concentrated more in the eastern half of the constituency—the Woking class area, so to speak—selected as their candidate Peter Pain of Frimley. This pleasant young man of 23, a barrister in Lincoln's Inn Fields, was a product of Westminster school and Christ Church, Oxford. He was, among other things, a nephew of Captain William Wedgewood Benn, one-time Secretary of State for India, and of Sir Ernest Benn, the political writer; and a grandson of A. C. Pain, first Chairman of Frimley and Camberley U.D.C., and alderman of the Surrey County Council. The Tories narrowed their choice to three candidates: Godfrey Nicholson, a backbencher defeated at the last election; A. F. G. Renton, a colonel in the 11th Hussars; and Norman Bower, a barrister. They settled on Nicholson, whose chances were diminished somewhat by the emergence of an independent conservative, Mr. Linton T. Thorp. The fourth entry was named as Edward Miller, a King's and People's Champion.

Among the comments in the *Herald*—Linton Thorp and his two supporters, wearing monocles: 'Are you going to vote for Peter Pain?'; 'No, his party caused enough pain in 1931'. It was the first occasion in Farnham that candidates relayed their propaganda in the streets by means of a loud-speaker mounted on a car. Farnham, it was said in one of the daily papers, was one of the safest conservative seats in the country. Godfrey Nicholson polled 20,580 votes; Pain, 7,792; Thorp, 2,327; Miller, 154. Pain drew high praise from the editor of the *Herald* for the way in which he congratulated the winner and described him as 'a model candidate'.

Ursula, 13-year-old daughter of Otway McCannell, the Art School headmaster, won public acclaim on being elected to membership of the Women's International Art Club. When confronted by Ursula, the other members expressed surprise; they had expected an adult. Though still at Frensham Heights School, this remarkable artist was already exhibiting her works in London. She and her father appeared on television on 24 February.

Richard William Mason died on 20 February, aged seventy-nine. Born in West Street in 1858, son of Richard Mason, he went to Farnham Grammar School and read law in London before joining Hollest, Mason and Nash in 1900. This legal firm at 94 West Street could trace their history back to 1794, when Captain Jacob Hollest and his brother set up in partnership. R. W.'s son, R. C. R. Mason, as it so happened, was on the point of becoming a partner. John Robert Nash, senior partner, also died, on 28 April, aged ninety-one. Son of John Nash, auctioneer in Downing Street, he, too, was a product of the Grammar School.

At the Brewster Sessions that February, the *Holly Bush* at 37 West Street was referred for compensation; two others, the *Wheatsheaf* and the *Plough*, had their licences renewed. Later in the year, the *Plough* sprouted pseudo timbering.

Councillor Borelli and his sub-committee, exploring the possibilities of acquiring 'Vernon House' for the purposes of a library and museum, met with a setback. Duncan Bethune, the last scion of the Knight family, had sold the house to Mr. A. G. Mardon, who, without a word to anyone, was negotiating a re-sale to a Mr. E. J. Edward. This gentleman submitted an application, on the agenda of the April meeting, to convert the premises into a commercial garage. In the absence of evidence to the contrary, it must be assumed that Mr. Edward had not done his homework. Otherwise he would have known about Farnham's two most often narrated legends—repeated almost to the point of boredom—namely, Jonathan Swift's goings-on at 'Moor Park', and King Charles I's bed-and-breakfast at 'Vernon House'. It was a curious coincidence that, simultaneously, both these historic properties should be currently passing through a crisis. For 'Moor Park House' which, for a brief moment, had burgeoned as a residential club, was also on the market seeking a sympathetic buyer. Mr. Edward digested the outraged Council's refusal and submitted modified proposals, 'as evidence of his desire to satisfy local opinion', for a petrol-filling station in the courtyard of 'Vernon House'. When these, too, were rejected, Mr. Edward appealed to the Ministry of Health, whose inspector announced that he would come down to Farnham on 4 January 1938 and view the locus. The Council quickly passed a resolution under the Town Planning Acts and briefed a Town Planning Consultant to represent them, and the late King Charles, at the inquiry. This was an example of the fruits of the expensive Town Planning set-up; it protected places like the castle, for instance, from becoming bingo halls.

Government were exhorting fire brigades to put themselves on a war footing, undergo air-raid precautions practices, recruit additional manpower, and look to their hoses . . . Miss E. D. M. Winters, Head of the Girls' Grammar School, was off to a similar post at the City of London Girls' School. In her place came Miss F. W. King from Mitcham County Girls' School . . . A milk-bar came to one of the shops in the town hall arcade; this was Farnham's first adventure into the new craze for sitting on a stool at a bar, sucking iced milk-based drinks up a straw—it made a change from beer. Aylwards were allowed to attach a barrel-clock to the outside of their shop at 98/9 West Street . . . The *Regal* cinema again held a Good Friday service for a united congregation . . . An automatic telephone dialling system was introduced on 7 April.

In the local election on 3 April, Mr. King lost in the Waverley Ward to Herbert Rothwell of 'Glenhurst', Beaufort Road; in Wrecclesham, General Godby was knocked out by Frank Rawlinson of 'Leyland House'. Mr. Figg, now the Father of the Council, was chosen as Chairman, with Councillor Winter as Vice-Chairman.

Despite the growing possibility of war, the public's apathy towards A.R.P. showed no signs of lifting. All efforts by the dynamic Major Wade had failed to kindle a response and he now retreated from a lost cause. Finally, Colonel Underhill, who was technically in charge of local operations, admitted defeat—the job, it was said, was too big for him—and, in his report in May, he spoke of the difficulties arising from 'lack of enthusiasm' in certain quarters. He implored the Council's support—for A.R.P. must go on, the government had said so. In June, the colonel produced a person who, he said, was capable of forcing the doctrine on the unwilling public. This was Major H. J. Martin of 'The Mount', Boundstone, formerly of the Indian Ordnance Department, well versed in gas warfare. He was duly installed as Hon. Organizer and from that time onwards Farnham was at war with Hitler. Major Martin's performance over the next few months was impressive. He launched a campaign for the recruitment of volunteers, and set up training courses; he co-ordinated close relations with kindred bodies in the town such as the fire brigade, hospital and ambulance services; he requisitioned available buildings which could be adapted for wartime use, and he conferred with neighbouring authorities with a view to mutual exercises. His target was that one in 30 of Farnham's population should volunteer for involvement in some capacity.

On 5 July the electrification of the railway line was officially blessed. An immaculately appointed train, bearing high officials of the Southern Railway Company, made a special journey down the line, stopping at Aldershot to pick up Mayor W. J. North and his party of aldermen and senior officials, then at Farnham, where Chairman Figg, Councillor Baber and Mr. Minns stepped on board, and on to Alton for their distinguished company. Then the train returned to Aldershot, where the congregation adjourned to the *South-Western* hotel. After luncheon, Mr. E. J. Missenden, the Company's Traffic Manager, told his guests that the Southern Railway had spent a total of £16 million on the electrification of their system, and that it was the largest project of its kind in the world. Toasts were drunk, and the three Council Chairmen suitably replied. The new electric trains had more coaches than the old steamers and were too long for the platforms. It was a rigid rule that the forward end of a train should on no account project beyond the signal, so arriving down trains were brought to a halt with the rear carriages sticking out across the level-crossing (and passengers had to walk along the corridor to alight). During this period, the standard of invective passing between road-users and the signalman in the box reached a peak of perfection that has never been equalled.

Something for everybody had been arranged for Coronation Day, 12 May. The church bells would ring off and on; a united service in Gostrey and a meal in the Church House for the over-seventies. Bands would play in the park; there would be a funfair and a cricket match, and a free tea and mugs for the children. In the evening, a Grand Carnival Procession, with dancing and a torchlight display to follow; finally a bonfire and fireworks in the park, with floodlights on the castle. The Carnival Queen had been chosen at the *Regal* cinema on 28 April. She was Irene Gladys Haines of 13 Lower Church Lane, and her maids of honour were Josie Green and Joan Cockram. Sadly, a storm started at about 2.15 p.m. with thunder and lightning and buckets of rain. The cricketers fled to the pavilion after two wickets had fallen; the children missed out on their bun fight; the procession was a washout, and the firework display a damp squib.

In mid-July, the County Council published a compulsory purchase order detailing all properties in the way of the by-pass road. Mostly, the 63 acres of land required comprised parts of private gardens, allotments and yards. Thirty-one houses would have to go—they were 'Weydon House', Weydon Hill Road; 'Weydown', Firgrove Hill; 1–14 Castle View; 'Abbey House'; 'Kenmure Villa' and 'The Jungle', Abbey Street; 28, 29 and 30 Abbey Street; 1–8 Kelsey Villas; and the 'Laundry House', Darvills Lane. An Inquiry would be held later in the year to consider objections—there were twenty-five.

The town was not pleased with what County had done in Waverley Lane. The *Herald* mourned the loss of what 'was once one of the most beautiful lanes in Farnham'. Gone was the old wall at Broomleaf, also the ancient hedges. The footpaths were now so wide that a better name for the road would be Waverley Promenade.

W. F. Rankine's discovery of a Mesolithic Age pit dwellings site in the Tin Hut Field at the Sewage Farm attracted international attention. Dr. Grahame Clark of Cambridge University took charge. The pits, roughly oval in shape, were datable to *c.* 3000 B.C.; they measured about 12 feet by 18 feet, and were three feet to four feet deep. In one a hearth still blackened by fire was found. Nearly 300 pigmy implements were discovered, including a fine pointed butt-axe about five inches long. The site was fenced in and roofed; it drew many visitors.

Plans submitted for approval in July included one for showrooms and depot for Dibben, Ltd., at the end of East Street; and another for 143 houses in the angle formed by Weybourne Road and Lower Weybourne Lane. Twenty-seven houses on 6.8 acres of Three Stiles Road were also planned. Two London construction companies had submitted applications for blocks of flats in Hale Road and at Heath End. Permission for one multi-storeyed block would render subsequent refusals untenable, and the Council had to take immediate action to formulate a policy with flats. Tower blocks would prove disastrous to Farnham's townscape, and the threat must be stifled at all costs. Many towns in the country had not heeded the warning and would come in time to resemble miniature New Yorks. Wisely Farnham set a limit of not more than three storeys; blocks of this height had no harmful effect on the skyline.

Picking started at the end of August in Tice's hop garden at Badshot Lea. Old Mrs. Patrick of that village was now 80; she had first picked at Tice's 50 years earlier and never missed a year since . . . Hale councillor E. J. Varney was admonished for describing A.R.P. as 'tripe'.

'Moor Park House' had been withdrawn from the market. Rumours were circulating that the mansion had been bought by (a) an American millionaire, (b) a British lord, and (c) an Indian prince. No, said the *Herald,* it was reverting to a private residence for a Mr. W. J. Taylor, who was a director of the Onyx Investment Company, Limited, of London, a company which already had an interest in the property. He was thinking of changing the name to 'Compton House'—this, the *Herald* thought, would be a pity.

John Hawkes, 'Blenheim', Guildford Road, died on 26 September, aged eighty-one. He was a son of David Hawkes, pork butcher of 106 East Street. John had joined the fire brigade in 1881, was Chief Officer in 1908, and had retired after 56 years' service in 1924. He had been on duty on 3 November 1895 when Frensham vicarage burnt down; a nursemaid had died in the flames, and two maids were rescued unconscious. As a result of that fire, the brigade was given a new steamer. On the day of its inauguration, it was called out to a big fire at Waverley Mill, and returned to base with all its paintwork singed.

A case which attracted nationwide interest came before the Court during September and October. A Major Wilfred Foulston Vernon, who held an executive post in the Royal Aircraft Establishment at Farnborough, and who lived unconventionally in a wooden shack at Old Park, Farnham, was the victim of a break-in by four men who had driven down from London with that express intention. They had stolen documents and some cutlery; they were caught and committed to Quarter Sessions by the Farnham magistrates. At Kingston, the case became focussed, not on the four burglars, but on Major Vernon, who underwent a searching cross-examination as to his suspected communist leanings. The four intruders were bound over in the sum of 40s.; on leaving the dock, one gave a fascist salute. The newspapers made the most of it—who, they asked, had been in the dock, the four burglars or their innocent victim? Nevertheless, Vernon was suspended by the R.A.E.; on 21 October he appeared in Court charged with having in his possession certain top-secret documents to which he had no right of access. At a special Court in Farnham on 27 October, he pleaded guilty on two counts and was fined £50. He denied being a communist, but admitted socialist sympathies. In the final years of peace, the bogey of Soviet Russia was, if anything, more sensitive a subject than Hitler's Germany.

A bough fell off the King's oak at Tilford; it was some 70–80 feet in length and 10 feet in diameter. Tree surgeons moved in, cut out another five tons of dead wood and cemented together what was left. They then pronounced the tree cured forever.

The Inquiry held on 20 October to consider objections to the County Council's compulsory purchase order took the form of a wider argument about why the by-pass road was to come on the south side of the town, when local people wanted it through the park. It was the only chance the townspeople had of airing their views; previously negotiations had been behind shut doors in Council offices, County Hall and Transport House. L. A. Ellis, Chairman of the County Highways and Bridges Committee, stressed that the main reason was that the northern route would have meant a gradient of one in 20; that the southern road had been planned to interfere as little as possible with Farnham's amenities; that his Council were averse to a road being taken through the fine park. He said that money had been of no object in giving the town the best—the latest estimate was £337,230. The order affected several people. Robins in the Fairfield grumbled that they might have to close down; the laundry were annoyed about losing 3½ acres of their five-acre holding; Hickleys were anxious about finding themselves in the front line; the Council stood to lose land at the sewage farm, at the Bourne Mill estate and the Guildford Road pumping station.

The memorial tablet to George Sturt was unveiled on 3 November by Arundell Esdaile, M.A., F.S.A., Secretary of the British Museum and an admirer of Sturt. Of Hopton Wood stone, 2 feet by 1½ feet, and inscribed by Eric Gill, the tablet read, 'To the memory of George Sturt of this town. He wrote with understanding and distinction of the Wheelwright's craft and English peasant life. Born 1863–Died 1927'.

At the 147th Venison Dinner at the *Bush* hotel in November, the guest of honour, Sir Philip Henriques, Chairman of the Surrey County Council, spoke of the coming by-pass. He felt that the townspeople of Farnham would eventually come to the conclusion that the right action had been taken because the park would have been preserved intact and they would have a fine by-pass to the south to prevent people being killed more than necessary.

A warm feeling still existed between the town and their billetees in 1914—the 11th Battalion, King's Liverpool Regiment. Letters from the Battalion's Reunion Association appeared in the *Herald* from time to time . . . Public conveniences were built in Brightwells at a cost of £280, and a small pavilion on court No. 4 for the use of the Tennis Club . . . In *Further Stories from Lord Halifax's Ghost Book,* there was a reference to Waverley Abbey. During the war, 18 wounded men and their nurses repeatedly saw the ghost of a cardinal.

1938

Whilst Castle Street had not yet achieved the honour of being acclaimed the finest street in the south of England, it had started to attract a fashionable type of resident and its days of service as Farnham's Petticoat Lane and Tin Pan Alley were numbered. The removal of the Fairs, and of a Mr. Matthews in particular, would accelerate the process. Mr. Matthews was the proprietor of a steam roundabout equipped with a steam organ. This would have been the equivalent of the electric roundabout, with an electric organ, of our childhood days, with the added fascination—and noise—of belching forth steam.

Victorian Farnham: c. 1889

THE DAYS WHEN PUNCH-UPS in the town were not uncommon had passed. Now, deplored a correspondent in the *Herald,* Castle Street only had motor cars. But the dust of ages lingered; on heydays, a mock-up of the old fair might perhaps be nostalgically staged in Castle Street. On 10 May 1938, for instance, Trimmers Hospital augmented their funds with one. The ladies dressed up in period clothes, and everyone let off steam.

To say that Farnham had been moved to the depths by Mr. E. J. Edward's determination to convert the courtyard of 'Vernon House' into a petrol-filling station would be an understatement. As the time drew near for the appeal inquiry, the local media published overstatements. There was a learned plea from Father Robo, currently Farnham's historian, for the preservation of this ancient building. Said another, 'There are in Farnham many houses which are older and more beautiful than Vernon House but, apart from the Old Vicarage, it is doubtful whether any has a more interesting history'. The *Herald* had a photograph of tempera work discovered behind panelling in a bedroom in 1926 which displayed the arms of the Diocese of Winchester and of Bishop Horne, who was at the castle from 1561 to 1580. But mainly the outworn legend of Charles I tended to steal the thunder.

Duncan Bethune, a bachelor, had died back in 1926, leaving 'Vernon House' to a cousin, Mrs. Rose Emily Morrison, who put it on the market, where it had stood, neglected and deteriorating, ever since. Finally, in desperation, Mrs. Morrison had 'almost flung it' at Mr. Mardon in 1933. Mr. Mardon now found himself in a similar position of desperation, for nobody seemed to want the place. Though steeped in tradition, the house was nevertheless without any great visual merit. Mr. Edward must have seemed like the second coming—a few petrol pumps, indeed, might even brighten the place up. On 4 January, Mr. S. L. G. Beaufroy, A.R.I.B.A., of the Ministry of Health walked right into a barrage of 300 years of local history hurled by a strong opposition on behalf of King Charles I. He returned to London and, after a decent interval, dismissed Mr. Edward's appeal.

All this time, Mr. Borelli and his sub-committee had been hovering in the wings, wondering how they could persuade the ratepayers to spend a few paltry pounds on buying the place for a museum. In April, Mr. Mardon came out with a deadline of one month and an asking price of £3,500. The Council considered this; it was certainly worth a try. The library might also be moved there. The St John Ambulance Brigade and the V.A.D. were currently without homes; the back garden would make a nice public pleasure ground. The Surveyor reported favourably on adaptation prospects. But being a non-essential project, public subscriptions would be necessary, and £3,500, plus conversion costs, was a lot of money. Then Mr. Mardon's ultimatum expired and he withdrew his offer. During the deliberations, there was mild speculation on the present whereabouts of King Charles's nightcap. This was thought to be in the drawing-room of St John's College, Oxford; no, St. John's, Cambridge, thought another. Both were refuted by Mrs. Morrison, writing from 8 King's Bench Walk, Temple, who pointed out that the cap was in her possession. They were all wrong, the cap had remained in the scattered Vernon family.

A fair percentage of the townspeople were now taking a reluctant interest in their own preservation and collectively in that of people who weren't. Major Martin had been joined by an understudy, Mr. W. H. Ramsden, and together they set up office in 'Morley House', South Street. The Council said of them 'they are dealing with the problems with energy and resolution and they are to be congratulated upon the results which are now rewarding their efforts'. It was the dynamic major's policy to keep the public well informed; his sitrep in January was full of goodies. Forty volunteers had completed their training as instructors and wardens, and 24 others were going through the courses. Red Cross and St John Ambulance had also trained a number of persons. Of the 150 wardens required in Farnham, 68 had now been recruited, of whom 43 would soon be holding public meetings in their areas. His immediate programme included: the choice of a site for the storing and assembling of the town's 30,000 civilian respirators; a senior officers' course for heads and deputies of departments; an anti-gas course for fire brigade personnel; the formation of decontamination squads for buildings and vehicles; first-aid courses; public lighting restrictions; air-raid shelters; the formation of a committee of heads of local business firms; and the further recruitment of volunteers in all capacities.

Major Martin was also testing out types and sites of an air-raid warning siren, with an eye to making use of the fire alarm in the Council yard. He was not satisfied until a six h.p., electrically-driven siren was obtained for £112. He tried this out on 18 May; the mournful wail was heard clearly in Rowledge. It became known, in politer circles, as 'Wailing Willie'.

Post office engineers digging trenches in the road at the top of Downing Street re-exposed the foundations of the old Round House, which was, actually, rectangular in shape . . . Two dozen trees and 14 dozen shrubs were planted in the new Waverley Lane . . . The new mortuary in Victoria Road was receiving its first customers . . . Dr. Greig, the first Bishop of Guildford, died on 28 March. Of greater impact was the death on 1 April of Police Superintendent Runegar, at the early age of forty-six. His efficiency was outstanding and he was very popular in the town; he was given a civic funeral. His successor was Stanley D. Cox from Oxted.

The air-raid wardens began their house-to-house canvass in March in order to compile a detailed list of gas-mask requirements. There is no record of a follow-up by Patricks, listing burial requirements, though this aspect of the bizarre situation must have passed through householders' minds. It was a measure of Major Martin's able handling of the scheme that the Home Office chose Farnham as one of the three experimental areas on whose statistics would be based the size ratio for respirators throughout the country. Major Martin had had some 18 years' experience in defence against poison gas and explosives, and was quite obviously fitted for one of the top appointments now being advertised in the national press. These carried good salaries and the Council were acutely conscious that they were getting first-class service for nothing. So, indeed, was the major, though he confessed to a preference for staying in Farnham for personal reasons. In May, he was made a full-time officer of the Council at a salary of £300, plus a travelling allowance of £50.

The County Council yielded to pressure for improvements in the Farnham library facilities. Local criticism had included letters in the *Herald,* disparaging the absurd opening times—two hours one day a week. One from across the border in Hampshire caused the editor to enquire what the writer was doing, using a Surrey library, let alone complaining about it. The voluntary librarians had done a fine job of work, but borrowers, because of the poor opening hours, numbered only about 10 per cent. of the population, well below other Surrey towns, which averaged 20 to 30 per cent. These volunteers could not be expected to give up more time, so County agreed to a part-time paid librarian, costing up to one-eighth of a penny rate. There were 26 applications for the 25s. a week job; it went to Miss Audrey Manning of 'Ewtor House', Heath End, who was already well known as a star of the Brightwells tennis courts. Opening times were increased to 5.30 p.m. to 8 p.m. on Mondays and Fridays, and 2.30 p.m. to 5 p.m. on Wednesdays, plus children's hours, 4 p.m. to 5.30 p.m. on Thursdays. The membership increased to six hundred.

Mr. A. Taylor opened up a fish and chip shop at 32 East Street. A similar application by Lionel Stevens at 13 East Street met with a petition signed by 22 protesters . . . County submitted plans for a central school on six acres of land at Hale Reeds . . . Major Anderson congratulated all concerned on the improved Waverley Lane . . . No poll was necessary that April. Councillors Varney and Avery did not re-stand and their places were taken by James Chuter and Brigadier Godby. Mrs. Gertrude Stroud became Farnham's first lady Chairman.

Captain J. H. Hewes vacated the Rangers House in the park and returned to the *Coach and Horses.* The Park Golf Club looked wistfully at the place for a club-house, but this was rather ambitious in view of the fact that the Council were already underwriting the club's losses. Councillor Chuter suggested using the house for A.R.P. purposes, and that is what happened. The Golf Club had been waiting for Captain Hewes to vacate his grazing area in order that it might be used for extending their course to 18 holes. But there were snags to this. The public enjoyed full right of way in the park, and they had a way of pausing right in the line of fire to watch the uncertain strokes of some novice, perhaps, who had not the least idea which direction his ball would take. Extending the course would double the risk of having to pay compensation. On 13 July, A. G. Rose of *The Wheatsheaf* holed out in one on the 4th in a game with Jack Sims.

Council staff were encouraged to join Territorial Army units and promised every facility for training purposes. Some did so and were thus able to make sure of their commissions before the rush started. Others went to the drill halls, but did not like what they saw.

The hairdressers put their charges up from sixpence to eightpence; for school-boys from fourpence to sixpence. . . . The Chamber of Commerce brought out a third edition of their *Book of Farnham* . . . A census of cellars was undertaken, and first-aid posts were established at the brewery, East Street school, and in village institutes . . . Half a million sandbags were indented for . . . A Women's Voluntary Service unit was formed in London.

The Duke and Duchess of Gloucester were among the guests at a Red Cross Gala Performance at the *Regal* on 16 July. Walt Disney's 'Snow White and the Seven Dwarfs' was shown.

The Bowling Club's new green in Bear Lane was opened by Mr. A. G. Mardon on 27 July. It was, Mr. Mardon said, his third occasion of declaring a bowling green open, having presided in both Gostrey and Brightwells. The six-rink green had been constructed by his firm at a cost of between £1,800 and £1,900. The club—President, W. S. Hart; secretary, P. Ashbery—had moved from their old green in the *Bush* hotel garden, where Farnham men had played bowls for upwards of 100 years.

Ursula McCannell, now aged 15, had two canvases on exhibition at the Redfern Gallery in London, entitled 'Head of a Girl' and 'Girl with a Dog'. She told a *Daily Sketch* reporter she was very thrilled to be in company with painters like Augustus John, Sickert, Max Ernst, and Nevinson.

Horace Scott Evans, manager of Lloyds Bank, and personally named as the Council's Treasurer, retired in August. A public fund was raised towards a presentation. As from 1 September, the bank became the Council's Treasurer in their corporate capacity.

Work was now in full swing on the by-pass road. Two gargantuan earth-shifting machines, named 'Anne' and 'Elizabeth', worked late into the night. The scene, illuminated by powerful lights, drew many spectators. In a ceaseless stream, lorries carted away the excavated rubble. Later, a third shifter, by the name of 'Audrey', joined in.

In August, £500 was paid to Cordingley and McIntyre as architects of the new Council offices in Brightwells. A similar amount was paid to Archibald Pursglove, the quantity surveyor. To date, some £1,627 had been disbursed on this fool-hardly scheme and the Council were acutely embarrassed. Councillor Aldridge tabled a motion that 'in view of the contemplated expense in regard to the provision of new council offices at Brightwells, no further action be taken by the Council in pursuing the scheme, but that active steps be taken with a view to the enlargement of the existing office accommodation'. The feeling of the appalled ratepayers was why send good money, their good money, after bad? The Surveyor estimated an extension of the existing offices at about £17,100, a saving of something like £7,000 on the Brightwells project. This scheme provided for a three-storeyed extension south of the present building, which would double the length of its frontage to South Street, and a wing at right-angles at the back. Any further extension would be possible by returning from the end of this wing in a northerly direction, completing three sides of a quadrangle. The Council Chamber, committee rooms and offices would be in the extension, leaving the ground floor of the existing building for fire brigade purposes; the old offices on the first floor would revert to their original use, namely the caretaker's quarters, and the present Council Chamber would be available either as a small public hall or as a museum or library. The floor area of the extension would measure 12,695 square feet; the total area, including the present building, would be 15,507 square feet. The size of the Brightwells buildings was 812 square feet less than this. Mr. McIntyre agreed that the extension was feasible. He was invited to prepare the plans. Perhaps it was a case of sending bad money after bad, for neither project materialised.

When Hitler invaded Czechoslovakia in September, the country was put on the alert. A communication from the Home Office, dated 24 September, called for the immediate assembling and distribution of civilian respirators and the digging of trenches. Major Martin told a special meeting two days later that the masks were being given out. The Clerk authorised trench-digging at Timberclose, Gostrey, the park, and recreation grounds in the villages. An executive committee of the Council was formed to deal with emergencies, and all business of a non-essential nature was postponed indefinitely. A recruiting centre was opened at 'The Chestnuts', and Food Control centres were manned. Council staff who had joined the T.A. were called up. Then Neville Chamberlain grovelled to Hitler. A blanket of shame descended, but, on the other hand, war had been averted.

The crisis was effective, in that it made the public realise that Major Martin had not just been fooling around. Support for A.R.P. burgeoned. The town had an efficient team of lieutenants in the field, trained and ready. They were J. R. Heelis, Lieutenant-Colonel W. Anderson, H. Armstrong, Lieutenant-Colonel A. A. G. Duke, Lieutenant-Colonel A. E. Fennell, G. L. Fulford, H. J. Knight, W. H. Ramsden, and A. O. Snell. Over 2,000 volunteers would serve under them. There were still some things to be ironed out, like standard practice for blacking-out windows; but the biggest headache—public apathy—had been overcome. Instead of recovering the gas-masks after the crisis had passed, people were told to retain them and look after them carefully. The sick jokes proliferated—the masks were fine for straining the vegetables; the cardboard containers, hung by string from the shoulder, were ideal for carrying one's sandwiches in. Probably many people did.

The ordinary things of life filtered back. The close watch on building work on the Brambleton estate, the proposed development of the 14-acre Burr Ride estate at Wrecclesham. County were fidgeting over their proposed central school in The Hart, and homes for people evacuated from the by-pass road site. Interest was re-awakened in the Mesolithic finds at the sewage farm, and papers were read by Dr. Clark and Mr. Rankine before the Prehistoric Society at Burlington House on the subject. The artefacts went on show in December at the British Museum.

At a special meeting on 13 December, the Council considered a hint from Mr. Mardon that, if the Council would agree to pay him an annuity of £200 for the remainder of his lifetime and that of his wife, then he would be willing to convey 'Vernon House' to them. His offer was subject to the settlement of a claim made by him against the County Council in respect of alleged injurious affection to the property because of that Council's refusal to permit a petrol-filling station to come there. His offer was accepted.

Father Etienne Robo was presented with a cheque for £274 in commemoration of his 25 years in the local Catholic church. The story of this priest from Brittany is a truly remarkable one. Coming to Farnham via the Southwark diocese, he held services for the few local Catholics in small makeshift premises in Bear Lane; with great determination, he decided to build a church dedicated to Saint Joan of Arc. By selling land in France, he contributed largely to the building fund. When Bernard Shaw's play, 'Saint Joan', was showing in London, he went every evening to stand outside the theatre, shaking his collecting box.

That winter, there was a white Christmas—just like Switzerland, commented the *Herald*. The children tobogganed in Farnham Park.

1939

For several weeks relations had been strained between Pantamonia and Phosgenia. There was no doubt that Phosgenia had tried to pick a quarrel with Pantamonia. The last straw occurred on August 1st, when Phosgenia alleged that the Captain of a visiting Pantamonia cricket team deliberately turned his back on, and thereby insulted, the Phosgenia flag. Although Pantamonia, on the advice of England, immediately sent an apology, Phosgenia proceeded to despatch troops to the frontier dividing the two countries.

Farnham in a state of war: *Farnham Herald*, 13 August 1938

HOPE KINDLED BY THE MUNICH AGREEMENT had flickered briefly before expiring like a damp squib. It was soon realised that the object of the British prime minister's humiliating pilgrimage had been to gain at all costs—even the sacrifice of Czechoslovakia—a little extra time in which to rally his country's forces. Farnham had been designated by the government as a neutral zone—that is, neither as an area from which civilians would be evacuated, nor as a reception place for evacuees from high-risk centres. The reason, given in a Ministry circular, was that the town might be needed for the billeting of the expected overspill of troops from the nearby camps of Aldershot and Bordon. Then, in January 1939, a further communication from Whitehall announced that, after consultation with the War Office, the Minister had re-classified Farnham as a reception centre because it would be easily accessible from London, and the Council was asked to carry out a survey of all available spare accommodation in their district.

Translated into practical terms, this was no mean task. It fell naturally to Mr. Holloway's Rating Department because the staff knew their way around the town's front doors, having in their time probably knocked at every one of them. Behind these doors, however, lurked householders whose wish it was to protect their homes, not only from the ravages inflicted by the Luftwaffe, but also from ravages inflicted by Cockneys. The two questions—'How many bedrooms?' and 'Number and relationship of persons normally resident (husband and wife pairing)?'—produced many evasive answers. Personal memories hardened one's determination. World War One, and air-raids on London; of cowering in the basement with Mum and big sister; and Mum—'Enough is enough, tomorrow we leave'. There had been no government evacuation scheme then; no Register of Accommodation; no good Samaritan to meet the family at the station and show them to their safe lodgings. This time, thanks to Neville Chamberlain's scrap of paper, there would be.

Major Martin had perfected a proficient A.R.P. establishment from scrap material. Now undergoing intensive training were:

Air-raid wardens (182 male and 60 female) under Colonel A. A. G. Duke, 242
First-aid post staff, 48
Eight first-aid parties, 40
Personnel for two ambulances and seven sitting-case cars, under Dr. E. H.
   Hunt, 54
Rescue parties, 30
Two decontamination squads, 14
Two repair parties, 14
Report centre staff (Rangers House), under Colonel Underhill, 96

There were laughs to be had. In one 'all systems go' exercise, a rescue party, detailed off to go to the aid of 'casualties' trapped in a supposedly bombed house, broke into the wrong house and rudely disturbed the slumbers of the astonished occupants.

Major Rupert Anderson was not, technically, a native, for he had not arrived until the age of six. He was now approaching his eightieth birthday and, on 3 January 1939, he and Mrs. Anderson were celebrating their golden wedding. Among their many presents was an engraved silver-gilt coffee set, subscribed for by some six hundred townspeople. Side by side with a family group photograph in the *Herald* of 7 January, was another of old family servants, six of them with over fifty years' service; one, Moses Fry, had completed 60 years.

Richard Combe, lord of the manor of Frensham, died on 14 April. He, too, was 79 years old. He had come to Frensham in 1908, when head of Combe and Co.'s brewery, in the days before its amalgamation with two rivals, Watney and Co. and Reid's Brewery Co. A product of Eton and Oxford—though the *Herald* noted that, for a short period, he had attended Farnham Grammar School—Mr. Combe had mixed his beer with local activities. His house, one of Norman Shaw's finer works, became a school.

Colonel George Chrystie was 97 when he died on 14 June. He had come to Shortheath Lodge in 1894, after 36 years in the Indian Army. It has been said that his was the first army unit to wear khaki uniforms. He had been involved in the Indian Mutiny; an uncle had been with Lord Nelson on the *Victory*, and another had served at Trafalgar. An uncle on his mother's side had perished when the 42nd Regiment was annihilated in the Gandamak Pass in 1842 during the Afghan War. For over 40 years, Colonel Chrystie had contributed the weekly weather bulletin in the *Farnham Herald*.

The Ministry of Transport sanctioned traffic lights at the Ridgway crossroads, with improved sightlines from Old Farnham Lane . . . A bus shelter was erected in South Street to the design of the Stedmans . . . County were wondering whether to bear the enormous expense of re-positioning Hickleys further down the street—had they a guilty conscience? . . . C. B. Mitchell of Edgeborough, Guildford, was allowed to use Frensham Place as a prep school for boys . . . At an enthusiastic meeting at the Institute on 6 March, the Farnham and District Ratepayers' Association was formed, with Mr. J. O. J. Stevens as Hon. Secretary.

The Provost of Guildford Cathedral implored the Council to help in raising funds to complete the first part of the new cathedral, costing £84,000, so that it might be consecrated in 1941. The avowed aim of the Farnham Deanery, namely to finance the Chapel of Chivalry in the cathedral, did not look like materialising, and so the bishop recommended a 'Farnham Week' from 21 to 27 May, with, say, the preaching of the Byworth Sermon on the Sunday. This raised a total of £4,067.

They held the election as usual. Councillors Lathey and F. G. Stevens lost their seats to Lieutenant-Colonel John Gage Lecky, the Ratepayers' Association representative, and Lionel Williams Stevens, the fishmonger of 28 Downing Street. Councillor H. G. Hale became Chairman, with Mr. Aldridge as Vice-Chairman. Mr. Hale was managing director of the Surrey Iron Company; he could claim a family connection with the famous 18th-century Hambledon Cricket Club, one of his ancestors having played in the local team against the Rest of England.

People went on building; in April there were 32 planning applications. And the Ecclesiastical Commissioners were working on the idea of a new thoroughfare from Knowles Lane to The Hart. A plan was approved in principle for a new Masonic Hall and Temple on a site facing 'Nash's Road'. This road, leading from West Street to The Hart was constructed in the last century, but never officially named. The Council negotiated for 2¾ acres of land with a 272-ft. frontage on the east side of this road for the purposes of a car park. Wrecclesham went ahead with arrangements for a flower show on 12 August, and a football pitch was laid on the Hillside Recreation Ground. Large-scale improvements were made to the Bourne Recreation Ground, and the ground in Morley Road was considered as a possible cricket field.

Mr. R. W. Cass died on 22 April. He had come from Pudsey, Yorkshire, in 1897 as the Council's surveyor. His claim to have pioneered a patent tar process for the repair of road surfaces has never been challenged.

In May, the Museum Committee staged an exhibition at 'The Chestnuts' of the artefacts from the Mesolithic Pit Dwellings, together with other local finds. Presided over by Mr. Rankine, the exhibition was described as being uniquely representative of successive periods of pre-history 'over thousands of years, perhaps 20,000 years, 50,000 perhaps; they may reach back to the last Ice-age', to quote one source.

'Genuine talent; remarkably good sense of tone', wrote the art critic of *The Times* of Ursula McCannell, currently exhibiting 37 of her paintings at the Redfern Gallery, Cork Street. She had sold 17 of them.

In his claim against the County Council for injurious affection, Mr. Mardon was awarded compensation of £1,650—the local Council's share of this being

£600. This enabled him to reduce his offering price for 'Vernon House' to £1,500, plus legal expenses. The councillors still hummed and hawed but eventually bought the house, despite protests from the Ratepayers' Association.

Phillips Bros. (Aldershot), Ltd., of 50 The Borough, advertised television sets for 35 guineas . . . Demolition of the old Sampson's almshouses in Mead Lane, on grounds of safety, was deferred so that they might be used as a blockhouse against any enemy designs on the brewery . . . *Merrie England* was produced by Mrs. Paton Hood in the castle grounds from 13 to 15 July, in aid of the new cathedral . . . Residents in the exclusive Seale and Sands areas south of the Hog's Back asked to be taken into the Farnham Urban District, not because of a wish to be sewered but, as they rather charmingly put it, because they felt they had a community of interests with Farnham.

The new Girls' Grammar School was formally opened in July (*The Story of a School: Farnham Girls' Grammar School, 1901-1973* gives this date as 20 July). The architects, Jarvis and Richards, the firm who had designed the Boys' Grammar School, had provided for 330 pupils, with possible future extension. The girls then numbered between 180 and two hundred. It was a grand occasion, performed by the Duchess of Gloucester. The band of the 1st King's Dragoon Guards played. It had cost nearly £50,000. The old school in West Street was taken over by the School of Art.

The Red Cross Gala Performance at the *Regal*, with a showing of *The Mikado*, and a supporting feature by Donald Duck, was presided over by the Lord Lieutenant of Surrey, Sir Malcolm Fraser, Bt., and the Bishop of Guildford.

They found time, too, to indulge in something which interested them far more than the coming war. The *Herald* of 29 July reprinted an extract from *The Hampshire Chronicle* dated 20 July 1789: 'Last week, several workmen began pulling down the ancient market house at Farnham, Surrey. Several coins bearing dates so long ago as 1057 were found; therefore it must be supposed that it is the oldest market house in the kingdom. A new one on a plan similar to that at New Windsor is going to be erected, with a statue of His present Majesty in front in order to commemorate his happy recovery'. John Clarke's market house in Castle Street—life span 1566 to 1866—was not demolished until 77 years later. Therefore, if the building referred to in *The Hampshire Chronicle* was that little-known, so-called Round House which once stood at the top of Downing Street, then certain conjectural possibilities arise. Nigel Temple, tracing the history of this building in *Farnham Buildings and People,* records that Trimmers held it on lease as a public house called *The Star* for a period of 14 years as from 1775 and that in 1789 the land 'on which it had lately stood' was offered for sale. This seems to confirm that the building referred to and described as 'the market house' was indeed the Round House. It becomes feasible to date it from *c.* 1057 to 1789. It is also reasonable to assume that, between 1057 and 1566 (when Clarke built in Castle Street) the Round House just outside the town gate served as the market house, and that the market place might then have been adjacent—that is, in the wide western half of The Borough.

On 29 July, the *Herald* recorded the start on the bridge which was to carry Firgrove Hill over the by-pass. With a span of 160 feet and a width of 60 feet, this would take many months to complete; it would be the most up-do-date bridge in the country.

H. V. Morton, who lived at Binsted, wrote to the paper under the heading 'Farnham forgets' that he was surprised to find that Farnham had no museum. Farnham Dairy was sold by W. H. Beile in August to Major J. M. J. Evans, poultry farmer of Wishanger, Churt. Mr. K. F. R. Cable, who had been manager for six years, became a director.

*   *   *   *   *

But the spectre of war was never far away. A.R.P. became a way of life. It spread its gospel from 3 Belle Vue, Union Road, into every nook and cranny of the town, where it was taken up by lesser echelons and translated into dummy practices. The minutiæ were attended to in precise detail. Those actively engaged in it had to have uniforms. The auxiliary firemen were kitted out by Manclark and Sons of Edinburgh in a hundred tunics at £1 6s. 3d. each; trousers at 9s. 2d. a pair; with overalls at 6s. 7d.; caps at 4s. 3d.; and rubber boots at 7s. 9½d a pair. The fire-ladies had 10 tunics and skirts at £1 18s. 9d. a set, with caps at 4s. 9d., and special coats were ordered for women ambulance drivers, nursing auxiliaries and first-aid-post staff. Forty sets of underwear were bought for the rescue and demolition parties. The overalls were dark blue, with red badges. The bill for A.R.P. had already reached £3,412 by February, though there was hope of a government grant. There was nothing really that the Rate-payers' Society could do about it—this part of the Commonwealth was at risk. For the fire brigade, too, extravagances were no longer curbed. Their Merry-weather engine had seen 17 years' service, and advantage was taken of the prevailing mood to replace this in June with a 90/95 h.p., six-cylinder, 500/600 gallon turbine Dennis motor fire engine, fitted with a first-aid pump, a 35-ft. extension ladder, a searchlight, 100 feet of cable and all the other trimmings, at a cost of £1,225. Then there were smaller items that would be needed by the chaps generally—like whistles at 7s. 6d. a dozen, handbells at 3s. 3d. each, and torches for use in the blackout. Major Martin had exhausted his abundant energies: he went sick in March, and did not return to the fold until July. Then he informed the Council that, in the event of hostilities, it was likely that he would be recalled to India. A successful appeal was made to the War Office for a deferment of this catastrophe.

A Home Office circular dated 18 April urged local authorities to accelerate the processes of Civil Defence. The Lord Privy Seal expressed confidence that authorities would recognise the need for the greatest possible expedition, and the government stressed that priority during the next three months should be given to Civil Defence measures over all other business. The Council responded by suspending all meetings of standing committees and authorising the Finance and General Purposes Committee to deal with any matter of an urgent nature. County A.R.P. notified that Farnham, Frimley and Camberley had, for the duration of the emergency, been transferred as a sub-group of the Hants County Council to the control of the Aldershot Command. Hampshire rather rudely refused to accept them at first, but later changed their minds. Aldershot called for an all-out passive defence exercise, which involved the mobilisation of all A.R.P. services. The exercise proved a severe test, but Farnham did so well that Aldershot sent letters of appreciation to section heads.

At a parochial level, a dummy run was held on 31 May to test the resources of Farnham's Report Centre. The Rangers House in the park had been fitted up as the Report Centre. Steel girders were injected for strengthening the control room and messengers' quarters on the ground floor. The P.O. had connected the essential telephonic communication network. Rudimentary furnishings had been introduced for the spartan use of the staff, and, of course, brewing-up equipment was installed. The staff was established as: officers i/c, two; message supervisors, two; plotting officers, two; plotting clerks, two; record clerks, two; women telephonists, eight; despatch riders. As far as possible, these had been recruited from the permanent staff of the Council offices.

The stage is set; the cast assembled. In the control room, Colonel Underhill sits at the Chief Officer's desk; the message supervisors sit at their table; the plotting officer and his clerk stand by their map, little flags poised; in the outer office, the record clerk is at the ready; the switchboard girls sit, plugs in hand. During the ensuing hours of darkness, some two, maybe three, calls come through. At half-time, light refreshments are served.

The Germans invaded Poland on 1 September. The Polish Ambassador called on Lord Halifax and formally invoked the Anglo-Polish Treaty. Two days later, on Sunday, 3 September, Britain went to war. Then the sirens wailed; only this time it was for real. That evening R.A.F. planes dropped six million leaflets over Germany. 'Good gracious', exclaimed one writer to the papers, 'they might have killed someone'.

Issued by the Ministry of Information in co-operation with the War Office and the Ministry of Home Security.

If the
INVADER
comes

WHAT TO DO — AND HOW TO DO IT

POSTSCRIPT TO PEACE

1940 – 1945

THEIR FINEST HOUR

Of this I am quite sure, that if we open a quarrel between the past and the present, we shall find we lost the future.
Sir Winston Churchill: House of Commons, 18 June 1940

ALL WARS ARE FRIGHTFUL, the earlier ones no less so, but each threatens at the outset the use of more advanced and therefore deadlier weaponry. In 1939, this took the form of Hitler's air force, already amply demonstrated in Europe, much publicised and numbingly awe-inspiring. Now, in September 1939, we were, potentially, on the receiving end. A nervous tension was discernible in the eyes and in the gait of passersby, in the way people went about their daily affairs, as if afraid to remain for long away from the dug-outs in their back gardens. As the weeks passed and the expected *blitzkrieg* did not come, the Englishman's sense of the ridiculous re-asserted itself in a spate of sick humour which derided the enemy's war machine. The mindless promise, for instance, to use the Siegfried Line as a washing-line probably made the Germans laugh as well. The 'phoney war' during these opening months was a curious anti-climax. Someone had cried 'wolf', but the wolf, it turned out, was a sheep in wolf's clothing.

Farnham passed the time mainly in perfecting their defences, digging more air-raid shelters, checking equipment. From 12 to 14 September, Aldershot Command held a rehearsal—'bombs', blackouts, the lot—which called for the full participation of Farnham's A.R.P. When the results came through later, it was found that Farnham had let the party down. The Regional Civil Defence Commissioners deprecated Farnham's 'operational efficiency'. County's Sir Philip Henriques looked in to see for himself and went away profoundly shocked; if the dummy run had been a real invasion, then Hitler would have found this part of England a piece of cake.

Major Martin dismissed the criticisms as 'baseless allegations'. But, at the enquiry which followed, the town's poor showing was blamed squarely on the voluntary personnel. They were not to be relied on. Many had opted out—the original number of 900 was already down to six hundred. The employment of a high percentage of volunteers, on the other hand, was important to the Council's economy; already the cost of maintaining an A.R.P. presence was running into the £20,000 a year region. The advice which now came from above, namely to take on more professional staff, met with howls of anguish.

There was more success with 'Mr. Spincer's Private Army', or, as it was known at the War Office, the 137th Light Anti-Aircraft Battery, Royal Artillery.

221

Mr.—now Major—A. C. Spincer, one of the local bank managers, had started this territorial unit before the outbreak of war under the delusion that it would remain in Farnham for the purpose of shooting down any member of the Luftwaffe foolish enough to fly over the town. Recruits flocked to it by the score; it soon reached its allotment of 200 officers and men, and was, indeed, used to man strategic points in the district before, like any other unit in the fighting services, being posted to a theatre of war. Sir Malcolm Fraser, Lord Lieutenant of Surrey, wrote to Major Spincer a letter full of praise.

Recruitment generally was for Farnham's real army, 'C' Company, 5th Queen's Royal Regiment, T.A. Or one could—especially if, meanwhile, one was involved in Fred Karno's civilian army—wait to see what happened in the sure knowledge that, one day, the call would come. Those who, because of age, have had the misfortune never to have been on active service during a war may 'think themselves accursed they were not here'. For the quinquennium which began in 1939 proved to be, at least for one, a grand time for getting to know himself, his fellow countrymen, citizens from the Commonwealth, G.I.s from the U.S.A., and, in due course, sons of Araby in North Africa, allied forces in Europe, and, latterly, the defeated peoples of Italy and Austria. He would not have missed it for all the tea in China.

The war caught some people by surprise. Len Heath of Frensham, the local motor-cyclist of renown, was competing at a six-day International Trial at Salzburg. All British nationals were advised to get back home as quickly as they could. Len said that the German customs people were very helpful. A band of strolling players, led by one Laurence Ray, cut short their tour in France, landed at Southampton, and were guided by some unseen hand to Farnham, where they paused for breath with little money left and no plans for the future. Here they were found by Mr. Borelli who told them of an empty building at 67a Castle Street which might, he thought, be suitable as a makeshift theatre. This rambling, timber-framed building had been put to many uses—as quarters for workmen building the castle, as a warehouse, cloth factory, roller-skating rink, a soft-drink factory, and a school of music and drama. After three months of scrubbing and re-decorating, it was turned into a small theatre, with tip-up seats and a raked auditorium, to hold 167 people at 1s. 6d. and 3s. 6d., with a membership fee of 2s. 6d. a year. The *Playhouse* became one of the country's smallest reps. It opened for the first time on 5 December 1939 with Shaw's *You Never Can Tell*. Travel to London theatres was now difficult, and people were thirsty for entertainment. The little *Playhouse* struggled through and took roots; it was to grow into the *Redgrave* theatre.

News of the first war casualties was not long in coming. F. A. Elkins, one of the Council's employees, went down with the ill-fated H.M.S. *Exmouth*; F. E. Pierce of the Surveyor's office, now a gunner in the R.A., died in a motor-cycling accident; local men were drowned when the *Royal Oak* was sunk at Scapa Flow on 14 October; Pilot-Officer Lecky, G. T. Scott Huxley, E. F. Mileham, F. C. Stapley, and others—killed on active service.

Civilians died, too. Alec Marsh of 'The Jungle', Abbey Street; he had been a matinee idol at the age of 24 at the *Avenue* theatre, and was later with the Carl Rosa and the Moody-Manners Opera companies. He had hunted big game in India and was once mistaken for the Duke of Connaught. Dr. H. F. Ealand died on 4 December at the age of 71—he had come to Farnham from Bath 40 years earlier; and Sammy Bates, the Swimming Club leader, and manager of Silvers; and Councillor Figg, who had been on the Council since 1904.

Farnham was full of London schoolchildren. They had been evacuated at the beginning of war to coastal towns, but were found to be at risk from the hit-and-run raids by enemy aircraft. The Greycoat Hospital School came in its entirety from Westminster, via Brighton, to share the Farnham Girls' Grammar School. With the influx of adult refugees and a considerable number of additional nursing staff for the County Hospital, the available billets in the town soon became exhausted, as did the small staff manning the Billeting Office.

In December 1940, the County Council declared the east and west sections— about half the total length of the proposed by-pass—completed and ready for use, a fine achievement in view of current difficulties. Through the middle part, traffic still had to thread its way along Red Lion Lane, Bridge Square, and Abbey Street, but no longer would the streets in the town be choked.

The women were wonderful; new initials appeared overnight—W.V.S., C.A.B.— they ran canteens for the soldiers, land armies, and the jobs of men called up, and they staffed the British Restaurant. This arrived in 1941, in two Nissen huts erected in Gostrey Meadow. It cost £2,237 to set up; Major G. Lloyd George, Parliamentary Secretary to the Ministry of Food agreed to open it. The Art School students were let loose on the internal decor, and a Mrs. D. S. Morser was appointed as supervisor/senior cook with effect from 8 December. It was officially opened on 16 January 1942; by February, Mrs. Morser was pulling in over two hundred diners. Mrs. Boreham, the Divisional Catering Officer, came to inspect on 17 March and was impressed by the soup and fish dishes—she even asked for the recipes. Later, Mrs. Morser left, and Miss L. L. Rider of London came. On entering the restaurant, one chose one's meal from the list displayed on the *à la carte* ticket-vending machine; the menu varied but little:

Soup and bread	2d.
Meat and two veg.	8d.
Pudding	2d.
Pastry	3d.
Tea	1d.
Child's meal (complete)	6d.

The summer of 1941 was indeed a swinging time. With a swollen captive audience, Farnham held open-air dances twice a week in Brightwells; there were military band concerts and recitals on Councillor Chuter's electric organ, and aquatic sports (on 16 July, 1,000 spectators packed into the baths). The Canadian soldiers billeted in the town took an enthusiastic part in putting on treats for the children.

The euphoria had diminished a year later, when the threat of being invaded by the enemy became a real possibility. The Minute book of the Council reflects a despondency. At the May 1942 meeting, a Triumvirate was officially appointed for the outlying areas of the Urban District, with powers to administer affairs in the event of being cut off from the town by enemy action. The Civil Defence force now realised that their ability to defend Farnham was limited; that their role was merely that of clearing up the mess after an air attack, or seeing that the public took cover in the shelters. The government stepped in to boost morale with exhortations to replace defeatism with 'an offensive will to victory' and urged the people to recognise the fact that complete immunity from danger was virtually unobtainable. A partial lifting of the gloom was reflected by the National Civil Defence Day on Sunday, 15 November 1942, when there was thanksgiving for the defeat of the German Luftwaffe in 1940/1, and, so far, the absence of invasion. Gradually the mood of depression passed. In February 1943, the Estates and Town Planning Committee were giving thought to the establishment of an industrial trading estate in Farnham; they invited the Regional Planning Officer down to view one or two prospective sites east of the town. Aldershot, too, seemed to be doing some post-war planning. They invited Farnham to preliminary talks on the formation of a joint large 'military borough'. Farnham declined—chalk and cheese. They saw this threatened invasion as no less objectionable than Hitler's.

In the spring of 1943, the word 'Holidays' re-appeared on the posters, though the Ministry of Health was careful to add the words 'at home'. Lord George Sanger's circus booked Gostrey Meadow for 4 May, and Sir Robert Fossett's circus performed in Morley Road recreation ground on 26/27 May. A 'Wings for Victory' week was planned for 19–26 June. West Surrey local authorities met for joint talks on post-war town planning matters; Farnham looked at their housing programme; the cricket pitch in the park was refurbished (though the golf course had been ploughed up for allotments); stocks of flags and bunting were renewed—these might be needed soon for peace celebrations. At the end of the summer term, the Greycoat School pulled out, profuse in their gratitude to the people of Farnham—such were the ties formed that, in at least one instance, letters continue to pass between one pupil and the family who took her into their home in the early years of the war. The essentially pacific Trees Sub-Committee were becoming vocal, too. They advised the planting of trees along the new by-pass.

But the war was not over yet. Twenty-five of the 31 members of the Council staff were still scattered throughout the world, this being the pattern generally in most of the town's institutions. The friendly Canadians were still fussing the children. Audrey Foss and the ladies of the W.V.S. were busy sorting out some

52,866 books given by the people for sending out to local men in the forces (a thank-you letter came from L.A.C. G. Wickham, serving in Jiwani, India). People also contributed £1,025 to a local fund towards the building of a new hospital in Stalingrad.

Major Martin died in January 1944. He had lived long enough to witness the achievements, however bedraggled they might have been, of his A.R.P. cohorts. Mr. J. L. Lee Jones had taken over as chief. Others who had recently died included Farnham's grand old man, James Alfred Eggar, Arthur George Ransom, Major H. R. Robins, and James William Wright, once Clerk of the Council.

At the meeting on 6 June, the Chairman spoke of the recent invasion of Europe by the Allies. The flying bombs, or 'Doodle Bugs' as they were dubbed, brought a renewed influx of refugees from London, and problems for the Billeting Office. When the Luftwaffe had ceased mass bombing, many evacuees had returned home; now panic brought them back—in May 1944, 383 were registered in Farnham; in June, 571; July, 759; and in August, 1,052. But the scare was short-lived; the people were already planning a Pageant of Farnham for celebrating peace.

There was a run-down in local civil defence. Fire guard duties were suspended; the dwindling functions of the Report Centre were transferred to the Council offices; the use of warning sirens was curtailed; A.R.P. personnel were reduced in number, with all paid staff going. The two first-aid posts were closed, the number of ambulances reduced from four to three, and rescue services lopped; the 2nd Surrey Home Guard—'Dad's Army'—stood down after 4½ years.

Towns were working on Welcome Home celebrations for their returning heroes, and on providing suitable war memorials for those who did not return, but Farnham thought this a little premature. Mr. Minns mentioned two members of the F.U.D.C. staff who would not be returning—Major C. R. Harris, R.E., killed on active service, and Staff-Sergeant J. O. Levison, a glider-pilot who had died at Arnhem. The fortunes of the other officers of the Council had varied considerably. Not all of them had handled a gun; some did not get overseas. Of those who did, only a handful saw the white of the enemy's eyes. There were campaign medals, but none for personal gallantry. They drifted back—one at least with reluctance. The 'Welcome Home' was not apparent; neither was it looked for. What there was came, individually, from the charming smiles and hand-clasps of sensitive folk like Charles Borelli.

On 2 January 1945, the councillors paid tribute to the 50th anniversary of the formation of the Farnham Urban District Council. On the table were the town's ancient charters and records and the Byworth Cup. Mr. Borelli proposed, with Mr. Dymott seconding: 'That the Urban District of Farnham, in commemoration of this, the Second day of January, One thousand, Nine Hundred and Forty-Five, the Fiftieth Anniversary of the Constitution of the Urban District, are unanimously of the opinion that this historic occasion should not pass without placing on record their sincere appreciation of the manifold services rendered to the Town and District by former councillors and officials during the past fifty years'. Mr. A. J. Barnard, councillor from 1908 to 1921 and Chairman in 1918/9, suitably responded. The Clerk handed to the Chairman an onyx inkstand inscribed: '1895–1945. Presented to the Farnham Urban District Council by the members of the staff in commemoration of the 50 years of the formation of the Council. January 1945'. The meeting that evening opened with expressions of sympathy because of the recent deaths of Major R. D. Anderson of Waverley Abbey, W. F. Harris of Wrecclesham Potteries, and Colonel J. F. Tyrrell.

In reporting the meeting, the *Herald* referred to John Clarke, the town's Bailiff who had received the first charter from Bishop Horne in 1566. Clarke's daughter had married a Bishop of Salisbury and the present Councillor, H. M. Philipson-Stow was a direct descendant of that union.

A letter in March from the commander of H.M.S. *Farnham Castle* asked whether a liaison might be formed between the townspeople of Farnham and his ship's crew. Farnham, however, was already committed with the H.M.S. *Chidding-fold,* with which the town had had close contact throughout the war. The letter was passed on to the Boys' Grammar School.

The war in Europe ended officially at one minute past 12 on Wednesday, 9 May 1945. In his broadcast, Winston Churchill, said, 'We may allow ourselves a brief period of rejoicing, but let us not forget for a moment the toil and efforts that lie ahead'.

The Council had invited Bishop Macmillan and the local clergy to a special meeting at 5.30 p.m., whereat a solemn resolution was taken acknowledging a safe deliverance from the war before proceeding to a united service in Gostrey. Some 2,000 people attended; the streets were garlanded with flags and bunting; Brightwells was gay with summer activities; the public houses stayed open until 11 p.m. A week later, Japan capitulated. There were two days of music in Gostrey, with dancing in the evening to Jim Chuter's Hammond La Fleur theatre organ, a Punch and Judy show and conjuring by Flying-Officer Arthur Dobbs, and a great bonfire in the park.

*   *   *   *   *

There are strangers these days in the bar at the *Bush*. The men one used to drink with back in the '30s are now mostly dead. The generation which has taken their place, and the staff who serve them, may not, many of them, have been born before the war. All observe the niceties, for the *Bush* has always contrived with no apparent effort to maintain its distinctive code of behaviour. It is easy to turn the clock back 40 years or so, and, through half-closed eyes, see the old faces come alive again. Outside in the street, it is the same. The buildings west of Bear Lane may look the same, but with few exceptions the traders are different. Where are Spencers, the Wyles', the Stratfords? One's now slower pace is a nuisance in the bustling tide of shoppers. But there is the same feel about the place; the

the old streets dispense the same enchantment. Woolmead does not belong to Farnham and one escapes to the reassurance of Castle Street or the Church Lanes, that rich legacy which has passed intact to each succeeding generation. Here one can feel wholly back in time.

More dramatically, times have changed in the Council Chamber in South Street. The room where for 70 years councillors once sat around a table planning the town's well-being is now filled with silent emptiness, and the town is no longer locally governed. For the time being, Farnham remains on its toes; there are few overt signs of having been forsaken by its administrators—only the occasional grumble in the press. Farnham is brisk and alert; but then it was, too, in 1925, when George Sturt, writing a foreword to a guide-book, was moved to exclaim 'the town is alive, alive!'

INDEX